MANDARIN
PHRASEBOOK

Mandarin phrasebook
4th edition – April 2000
First published – 1985

Published by
Lonely Planet Publications, Pty Ltd   A.C.N. 005 607 983

Lonely Planet Offices
Australia PO Box 617, Hawthorn, Victoria 3122
USA 150 Linden St, Oakland CA 94607
UK 10a Spring Place, London NW5 3BH
France 1 rue du Dahomey, 75011 Paris

Cover illustration
Don't Fence Me In by Mic Looby

ISBN 0 86442 652 6

text and maps © Lonely Planet 2000
cover illustration © Mic Looby

Printed by The Bookmaker Pty Ltd
Printed in China

About the Authors

Justin Rudelson grew up in California. In his teens, he became part of an extended Chinese family, which led him to study Mandarin and eventually 20 other languages including Uyghur, Uzbek, Russian, Japanese and Hebrew.

In his Asian Studies work at Dartmouth College and while earning a doctorate at Harvard University in Social Anthropology, he studied over for four years in China and Central Asia, the majority in Xinjiang, China. His book on the Uyghurs is entitled *Oasis Identities: Uyghur Nationalism along China's Silk Road* (Columbia University Press, 1997).

Justin has interpreted for Chinese and Taiwan Olympic Track and Field Teams, worked as a photographer and journalist in Central Asia for *National Geographic* magazine, and helped introduce drip irrigation technologies from Israel into China's deserts. He's the author of Lonely Planet's *Central Asia phrasebook*, co-author of the *Hebrew phrasebook*, and an editor of both the *Moroccan Arabic* and *Turkish phrasebooks*.

Charles Qin grew up and completed his undergraduate degree in English in beautiful Kunming, China. While travelling in the province, he met his partner, Kate Ritchie, who was teaching English at a university in Kunming.

Upon arrival in Australia in 1992, Charles and Kate established Chin Communications, a company which provides Chinese language and culture training, including preparing Australians to live in China, as well as interpreting and translating services. Following completion of postgraduate study, Charles is now one of Australia's most prolific Chinese translators and interpreters.

From the Authors

The majority of the updates for this edition come from a trip to China that Justin and his bride Chelle took in 1998. Justin would like to thank all the teachers who have helped him learn Chinese languages. Most profoundly, his studies have been guided by Hua-yuan Li Mowry of Dartmouth College. His roommates at Taiwan's Tunghai University were fantastic teachers, particularly Chen Tianjing. His special thanks go to Kai-li's niece, Eva Yihua Chen.

Justin dedicates his contribution on this book to his adopted Chinese family headed by Kai-li Wang Quigley, May Hung Hoeland and Kathy Chimei Lai Gatto.

Charles Qin gives many thanks to all at Lonely Planet for the opportunity to be involved in the new *Mandarin phrasebook*, and to Justin Rudelson. He also thanks his partner in life and business, Kate Ritchie, who introduced him to the world of Lonely Planet while he was still living in China.

From the Publisher

This book was developed from the 3rd edition of the Lonely Planet *Mandarin phrasebook* by Chris Taylor. This edition was edited by Vicki Webb and proofread by Catherine McCredie and Karin Vidstrup Monk. Patrick Marris was responsible for layout, design and the illustrations of Chinese hand counting. Juliette Kent illustrated the book, Mic Looby drew the cover illustration and Natasha Velleley produced the map.

CONTENTS

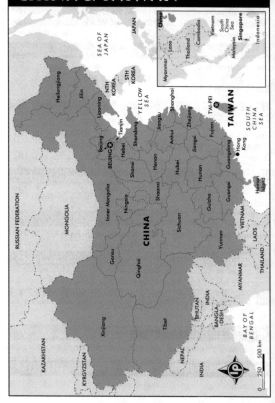

PEOPLE'S REPUBLIC OF CHINA & TAIWAN

The dialect spoken in Beijing, known in the west as Mandarin, is one of eight major Chinese dialects. It's the official language of the People's Republic of China, and one of the official languages of both Singapore and Taiwan, although the influence of local dialects has led to some marked differences in regional accents.

During the 20th century, the Beijing dialect was established as a national language. Mandarin is now taught in all Chinese schools, and Mandarin radio and television programs are broadcast throughout China. Although around 70 per cent of China's population speaks Mandarin, not all speak it as their first language. In the countryside, people are more likely to speak a local dialect as their first language.

CLASSICAL CHINESE

Throughout Chinese history and up to the present, the Chinese grew up speaking the dialect of the region where they were born. If they learned to read and write, they learned a classical form of the language that wasn't specific to any regional dialect.

The role of classical Chinese is comparable to that of Latin in medieval Europe. All communication and scholarly works written before the 20th century were written in classical Chinese. This language is written without obvious punctuation and with an economy of characters. In contrast, modern Chinese is written as it's spoken. Classical Chinese can be written horizontally from right to left or left to right, or vertically from top to bottom, left to right or right to left. Simplified Chinese, which is used in this book, is written horizontally from left to right.

SIMPLIFIED CHARACTERS

From the 1950s onward, the archaic written language was replaced with a more simplified, colloquial one that corresponded more or less to the Beijing dialect. Pen-strokes were diminished on many characters to the extent that some were radically altered. As a

INTRODUCTION

consequence, many standard Chinese classical characters became difficult to read in comparison to the new script. Some became totally unrecognisable, with meanings that differ widely from their corresponding classical ones.

The use of simplified characters has now become widespread in China, and these days only those with specialised training are able to read classical Chinese. While on one hand this has resulted in increased levels of literacy, it has also limited the population's access to ancient Chinese texts, philosophy and poetry. The introduction of simplified characters has also placed a literary divide between Chinese people living on the mainland and those living abroad who use the traditional non-simplified characters.

If you carry a phrasebook with you in China, you'll find plenty of opportunity to use it. Although in the big cities there are often a few students around who are keen to practise their English, you'll find yourself in plenty of situations where no one speaks English. If no one understands what you're reading from the book, simply point to the Chinese script on the right-hand side of the page.

DIALECTS

China's eight major dialects can be divided into many more sub-dialects, few of which are mutuall0y intelligible. 'Chinese', then, isn't a language, but a family of closely related languages. Mainland China has over one billion speakers of Chinese dialects, Taiwan has 22 million, and there are large Chinese-speaking communities living throughout the rest of the world.

The major Chinese dialects are largely unintelligible to each other. However, because they're based on the same grammar and written characters, once one dialect is learned, the others can be learned relatively quickly.

The eight major dialects are:

Mandarin(Putonghua)

Mandarin is spoken by around 900 million people in China. This dialect is quite nasal-sounding. Speakers tend to add an 'r' sound to many words, such as dianyingr 'movie', weir 'smell', neir 'there' and zher 'here'.

Cantonese (Yue; Guandong Hua)

Cantonese is spoken in Guangdong Province and Canton. With over 70 million speakers worldwide, it's the language most often spoken by Chinese people living abroad. Almost 50 million people speak this dialect in China, including the vast majority of of the six million inhabitants of Hong Kong. The language has seven tones, which accounts for its musical quality. It's also characterised by the presence of final consonants, as in the words pok, fut, wut, dut and luk.

Shanghainese (Wu)

This dialect is spoken by nearly 80 million people, or around eight per cent of the population of the People's Republic. It's spoken in Shanghai, Nanjing, Suzhou, Jiangsu south of the Yangzi River, Zhejiang, and east of Zhejiang. Many sounds are pronounced with rounded lips, giving this dialect a slightly French-sounding quality.

Minbei (Fuzhou)

Minbei is the most widely spoken of the five varieties of the Min dialect, which includes Minbei (north), Min'nan (south), Min Dong (east), Min Zhong (Central), and Puxian. Minbei is spoken in the Northern Fujian province, and by Chinese living in Singapore. It has over 11 million speakers, a little over one per cent of the population of the People's Republic.

INTRODUCTION

Fujian-Taiwanese (Minnan)

Fujian-Taiwanese is spoken by over 50 million people world-wide. Over 40 million speakers live in the People's Republic in Guangdong, Zhejiang, Jiangxi and Hainan Island. There are over 15 million speakers in Taiwan – the vast majority of Taiwan's population. It's also spoken in Malaysia and Singapore. This dialect is so unlike all the others that, to most Chinese, it can sound like a foreign language.

Xiang

Xiang is spoken by nearly 40 million people in China's Hunan Province, Sichuan, Guangxi and Guangdong. Linguistically, it falls somewhere between the Mandarin and Wu dialects, but is only marginally intelligible to these speakers.

Gan

Gan has almost 25 million speakers, mainly in Jiangxi, the south-east corner of Hubei, as well as in parts of Anhui, Hunan and Fujian. Gan is marginally intellible to speakers of the Mandarin and Shanghainese dialects.

Hakka (Kejia)

The dispersement of the Kejia population has given rise to their name, which means 'guest people'. Although the Kejia aren't classified as a distinct ethnic group by the Chinese government, they are recognised by the government of Taiwan. The Kejia dialect has over 35 million speakers worldwide, with 30 million in the People's Republic and Taiwan. It's also spoken in Malaysia, Indonesia, Singapore and Thailand.

ABBREVIATIONS USED IN THIS BOOK

adj	adjective
coll	colloquial
inf	informal
n	noun
neg	negative
pl	plural
pol	polite

INTRODUCTION

HOW TO USE THIS PHRASEBOOK
You Can Speak Another Language

It's true – anyone can speak another language. Don't worry if you haven't studied languages before, or that you studied a language at school for years and can't remember any of it. It doesn't even matter if you failed English grammar. After all, that's never affected your ability to speak English! This is the key to picking up a language in another country. You don't need to sit down and memorise endless grammatical details, and you don't need to memorise long lists of vocabulary. You just need to start speaking. Once you start, you'll be amazed how many prompts you'll get to help you build on those first words. You'll hear people speaking, pick up sounds from TV, catch a word or two that you think you know from the local radio, see something on a billboard – all these things help to build your understanding.

Plunge In

There's just one thing you need to start speaking another language – courage. Your biggest hurdle is overcoming the fear of saying aloud what may seem to you to be just a bunch of sounds. There are a number of ways to do this.

Once you're familiar with a few basics, and once you can get past the 'courage to speak' barrier, you can start making sentences. Don't worry that you're not getting a whole sentence right the first time. People will understand if you stick to the key word.

And you'll find that once you're in the country, it won't take long to remember the complete sentence.

The best way to start overcoming your fear is to memorise a few key words. These are the words you know you'll be saying again and again, like 'hello', 'thank you' and 'how much?'. Here's an important hint though – right from the beginning, learn at least one phrase that will be useful but not essential, such as a conversational piece like 'lovely day, isn't it' or 'it's cold today' (people everywhere love to talk about the weather). Having this extra phrase (just start with one, if you like, and learn to say it really well) will enable you to move away from the basics, and when you get a reply and a smile, it'll also boost your confidence. You'll find that people you speak to will like it too, as they'll understand that you've tried to learn more of the language than just the usual essential words.

Ways to Remember

There are several ways to learn a language. Most people find they learn from a variety of these, although people usually have a preferred way to remember. Some like to see the written word and remember the sound from what they see. Some like to just hear it spoken in context (if this is you, try talking to yourself in Mandarin). Others like to analyse the grammar of a language, and piece together words according to the rules of grammar. The very visually inclined like to associate the written word and even sounds with some visual stimulus, such as from illustrations, TV and general things they see in the street. As you learn, you'll discover what works best for you – be aware of what made you really remember a particular word, and keep using that method.

Kicking Off

Chances are you'll want to learn some of the language before you go, so you won't be hearing it around you. The first thing to do is to memorise those essential phrases and words. Check out the basics (page 37) ... and don't forget that extra phrase (see Plunge in). Try the sections on First Encounters or Greetings in Meeting

INTRODUCTION

People, pages 42 and 37, for a phrase you'd like to use. Write some of the words and phrases down on a piece of paper and stick them up around the place – on the fridge, by the bed, on your computer, as a bookmark – somewhere where you'll see them often. Try putting some words in context – the 'how much is it?' note, for instance, could go in your wallet.

Building the Picture

We include a chapter on grammar in our books for two main reasons. Firstly, some people have an aptitude for grammar and find understanding it a key tool in their learning. If you're such a person, then the grammar chapter will help you build a picture of the language, as it works through all the basics.

The second reason for the grammar chapter is that it gives answers to questions you might raise as you hear or memorise some key phrases. You may find a particular word is always used in a question – check out Questions in Grammar and it should explain why. This way you don't have to read the grammar chapter from start to finish, nor do you need to memorise a grammatical point. It will simply present itself to you in the course of your learning. Key grammatical points are repeated through the book.

Any Questions?

Try to learn the main question words (see page 31). As you read through different situations, you'll see these words used in the example sentences, and this will help you remember them. So if you want to hire a bicycle, turn to the Bicycles section in Getting Around (use the Contents or Index pages to find it quickly). You'll see the words for 'where' and 'bicycle' a number of times in this book. When you come across the sentence 'Where can I hire a bicycle?', you'll recognise the key words and this will help you remember the whole phrase. If there's no category for your need, try the dictionary (the question words are repeated there too, with examples), and memorise the phrases 'Could you write it down for me?' and 'What's this called?' (pages 89 and 54).

INTRODUCTION

Finally

Don't be concerned if you feel you can't memorise words. On the inside front and back covers are the most essential words and phrases you'll need. You could also try tagging a few pages for other key phrases, or write your own reminders.

PRONUNCIATION

People learning Mandarin encounter the same problem confronting those learning English – namely the enormous differences in pronunciation that occur from region to region. Consider the bewilderment of the Chinese student of English who travels from Glasgow to New York, or from Sydney to Manchester, and you'll have some idea of how students of Mandarin feel when they travel from Shanghai to Taipei or from Guangzhou to Beijing.

The best thing is to learn the standard form which is understood universally. That way you should have little trouble making yourself understood, even if you can't always make out the responses you get.

The pronunciation used in this phrasebook is based on Mandarin as it's spoken in Beijing. As this is a prestigious and national standard form of the language, your ability to master its sounds will be applauded.

PINYIN

In 1958, the Chinese officially adopted a system for writing their language using the Roman alphabet. This is known as 'Pinyin', meaning 'write sound'. Pinyin uses either one or two letters from the Roman alphabet to represent each sound in Mandarin.

In China, you'll see Pinyin next to the Chinese characters on signs, shopfronts and advertising billboards. Don't expect all Chinese people to be able to use Pinyin, however. In the countryside and in smaller towns you mightn't see a single Pinyin sign. This is where the script included in this book comes in handy.

PRONUNCIATION

TONES

For speakers of English, the sounds used in Mandarin are quite easy to reproduce. There are relatively few of them, and many have equivalents in English. However, the correct use of tone may be a little more difficult. In Mandarin, there are many words that are spelled and pronounced in the same way, but mean something quite different. These words are only distinguished by their tone. English speakers also frequently use tone to give emphasis or to convey emotion.

There are four basic tones in Mandarin Chinese, although it can be said that a fifth tone is one without tone at all. All four tones are indicated by a diacritic above a vowel.

The word **ma** can have five different meanings, depending on the tone, and whether a tone is used at all.

high	mā	mother
rising	má	hemp/numb
falling-rising	mǎ	horse
falling	mà	scold/swear
no tone	ma	marks a sentence as a question

high (ˉ)	high, flat, continuous tone
rising (ˊ)	rising tone similar to the intonation used in the question 'What?'
falling-rising (ˇ)	tone that falls then rises. You'll hear many Mandarin speakers 'swallow' the rising sound, only giving it a clear falling-rising pattern for emphasis.
falling (ˋ)	falling tone, similar to the one used when yelling 'Damn!'

VOWELS

a	as the 'a' in 'father'
e	as the 'u' in 'fur'
i	as the 'ee' in 'see'; after c, s or z, more like the 'e' in 'her'
o	as the 'o' in 'or'
u	as the 'u' in 'flute'; like ü when preceded by q, j or x
ü	as the French 'tu' or the German 'für'. Place your lips as if you were going to whistle and say 'ee'.

YOU ARE WHAT YOU WRITE

Calligraphy can vary as much as signatures, and it's believed to give an insight into a person's character. Thick, sturdy brush strokes, for example, are thought to indicate a firmness of purpose. The Chinese enjoy analysing one another's calligraphy, particularly that of their leaders – Mao's grass-style calligraphy apparently indicated a creative and poetic soul.

Diphthongs

ai	as the 'y' in 'fly'
ao	as the 'ow' in 'now'
ei	as the 'ay' in 'day'
ia	as the 'ya' in 'yard'
ie	as the 'ye' in 'yes'
iu	as the 'yo' in 'yolk'
ou	as the ow' in 'low'
ua	pronounced *wah*
üe	as the 'you a' in the words 'you ate'
ui	as the word 'way'
uo	as the word 'war'
iao	as the 'iao' in 'miaow'
uai	as the word 'why'

COMBINED LETTERS

an	as the 'on' in 'upon'
en	as the 'en' in 'broken'
eng	pronounced *ehng*
er	as the 'er' in 'her' (the 'r' is pronounced)
ian	as the word 'yen'
iang	pronounced *yahng*
in	as the word 'inn'
ing	pronounced *eeng*
iong	pronounced *yohng*
ong	pronounced *ohng*
uan	after j, q and x, pronounced *oowen*; elsewhere pronounced *oowan*
un	pronounced *ohng*
uang	pronounced *wong*
üan	as the words 'you an'
ün	pronounced *yuen*

PRONUNCIATION

BEIJING–PEKING

Outside mainland China, a number of systems are used to represent Chinese characters in romanised script. In Taiwan, the Wade-Giles system is used. In this system, an apostrophe is used to distinguish between aspirated consonants (pronounced with a puff of air) and unaspirated ones.

The 'k' sound is indicated by a 'k' followed by an apostrophe, as in the word 'k'ung'. Without the apostrophe, the 'k' actually indicates a sound closer to 'g'. The same holds for the letters 'b' and 'p' (represented as p and p') as well as 'd' and 't' (indicated by t and t'). Using the Wade-Giles system, 'Beijing' becomes 'Peking' and 'Nanjing' changes to 'Nanking'. Many Taiwanese not familiar with the Wade-Giles system eliminate the apostrophes, leaving pure chaos for anyone trying to learn the system.

CONSONANTS

You'll notice that several consonants in Mandarin have a similar pronunciation. The sound q, for example, sounds a little like ch. Similar pairs are x and sh, and j and zh. All consonants not listed here are pronounced as they would be in standard English.

c	as the 'ts' in 'cats'
g	as the 'g' in 'gone'; never as the 'g' in 'gentle'
h	as the 'ch' in Scottish 'loch' or German 'Bach'
j	as the 'j' in 'jeans'
q	as the 'ch' in 'cheese'
s	as the 's' in sir; never as the 's' in 'pleasure'
x	as the 'sh' in 'shock'
z	as the 'ds' in 'fads'

PRONUNCIATION

STICKS & TONES

Many words in Mandarin sound the same except for their tone, which leaves a lot of scope for creating puns – and making faux pas. Being 'pregnant' (huaí yùn) could easily be mistaken for 'bad luck' (huài yùn), while hitting the wrong tone can turn a 'poem' (yī shoú shī) into a 'handful of shit' (yī shoǔ shī).

Retroflex Sounds

Retroflex sounds are formed by curling the tongue over and pressing it onto the roof of the mouth. The following consonants are always pronounced in this way.

ch	as the 'ch' in 'cheese'
sh	as the 'sh' in 'shock'
zh	as the 'j' in 'jeans'
r	as the 'r' in 'radio'

When the vowel i appears after a retroflex consonant, it's always pronounced as 'r'.

chi	pronounced *chr*
shi	pronounced *shr*
zhi	pronounced *jr*
ri	a growling sound like 'rrrr'

PRONUNCIATION

GRAMMAR

Mandarin grammar is relatively straightforward. There are no verb conjugations, no plurals, no articles (a/the), and no gender or tenses. At an elementary level, sentence order is similar to English.

WORD ORDER
Like English, word order in Mandarin is subject-verb-object. For example, the sentence 'I study Chinese' follows exactly the same word order in Mandarin.

I study Chinese.   **wǒ xué hànyǔ**
(lit: I study Chinese)

NOUNS
Nouns are usually made up of two words (characters), called 'compounds'. There are no masculine, feminine or plural forms of nouns.

restaurant	**fàn guǎn**
	(lit: rice hall)
restaurants	**fàn guǎn**
	(lit: rice hall)
person	**rén**
people	**rén**

DEMONSTRATIVE PRONOUNS

this	zhèi
that	nèi
this one	zhèige
that one	nèige
these ones	zhèixiē
those ones	nèixiē

ADJECTIVES

As in English, adjectives precede the nouns they describe.

the big hotel   dà fàndiàn
                                 (lit: big hotel)

PRONOUNS

Both subject (I) and object (me) pronouns take the same form.
Plural pronouns are formed by adding the suffix -men to the
corresponding singular form.

PRONOUNS	
I/me	wǒ
you	nǐ
he/him	tā
she/her	tā
it	tā
we/us	wǒmen
you (pl)	nǐmen
they/them	tāmen

POSSESSION

To show ownership or possession, simply add de to a pronoun
and follow it with the thing that is possessed.

my backpack   wǒde bèibāo
                                 (lit: I's backpack)
their room   tāmende fángjiān
                                 (lit: they's room)

GRAMMAR

CLASSIFIERS

In Mandarin, when you talk about quantities of any noun, it's important to put a classifier or 'measure word' between the number and the noun. There are many such words in English, as in 'two **pairs** of pants', 'three **sheets** of paper', 'five **pieces** of candy', and 'one **cube** of sugar'. Some of the more common classifiers are:

thin, flat objects	zhāng
four tickets	sì zhāng piào
	(lit: four zhāng tickets)
animals	zhī
two dogs	liǎng zhī gǒu
	(lit: two zhī dogs)
businesses	jiā
five restaurants	wǔ jiā fànguǎnr
	(lit: five jiā restaurants)

While there are many different classifiers in Mandarin which categorise the kind of noun being counted, the good news is that there's an all-purpose classifier, ge, that can be used in all circumstances.

three cups	sān ge bēizi
	(lit: three ge cups)

It's worth remembering that classifiers are also required between demonstrative pronouns and nouns.

people	wèi
that man	nèi wèi xiānshēng
	(lit: that wèi man)
places	ge
this place	zhèi ge dìfang
	(lit: this ge place)

GRAMMAR

buildings	suǒ
this house	zhèi suǒ fángzi
	(lit: this suǒ house)
rivers and streams	tiáo
that river	nèi tiáo hé
	(lit: that tiáo river)

VERBS

In Mandarin, verbs don't change according to their subject.

to eat	chī
I eat	wǒ chī
you eat	nǐ chī
he/she/it eats	tā chī
we eat	wǒmen chī
you (pl) eat	nǐmen chī
they eat	tāmen chī

Tense

Verbs in Mandarin don't change according to tense. Instead, tense is indicated by expressions of time like 'yesterday', 'tomorrow', 'a while ago', and so on. However, the particle le is added to a verb to indicate whether or not an action has been completed. In many cases, this corresponds to the English past tense.

Yesterday I ate fish.	wǒ zuótiān chī yú
	(lit: I yesterday eat fish)
He is going to Shanghai.	tā qù Shànghǎi
	(lit: he go Shanghai)

GRAMMAR

KEY VERBS

able (can)	néng	love	ài
arrive	dào	make	zuò
be	shì	mail	jì
can	néng	move	dòng
come	lái	need	xūyào
do	zuò	pay	fùqián
drink	hē	queue (line up)	páiduì
drive	kāi	read	kàn
eat	chī	rent	zū
feel (perceive)	juéde	rest	xiūxi
forget	wàngjì	say	shuō
give	gěi	sit	zuò
go out	chūqù	speak	jiǎng
go	qù	stop	tíng
have (possess)	yǒu	study	xué
know (someone)	rènshì	tell	gàosu
know	zhīdào	thank	xiè
(something)		think	xiǎng
laugh	xiào	travel	lǚxíng
leave	zǒu	wait	děng
like	xǐhuān	walk	zǒu
listen	tīng	want	yào
located	zài	wash	xǐ
looking for	zhǎo	write	xiě

GRAMMAR

He has gone to Shanghai.   tā qùle Shànghǎi
(lit: he go- le Shanghai)

For things that have happened some time in the unspecified past, the particle guò is used.

I have been to Hong Kong.   wǒ qù guò Xiānggǎng
(lit: I go guò Hong Kong)

The verb yaò , 'to want', can be used to indicate the future. The future can also be expressed by using the words:

thinking about	xiǎng
plan to	dǎsuàn
I will go to the park.	wǒ xiǎng daò gōngyuan qù (lit: I thinking-about arrive park go)
They're planning to eat Japanese food.	tāmén dǎsuàn chī rìběn cài (lit: they plan-to eat Japanese food)

GRAMMAR

TO BE

Although Mandarin has an equivalent to the English verb 'to be', shì , it isn't used in quite the same way as in English. The verb shì is only ever used with a noun, as in the sentence:

I'm a student.	wǒ shì xuéshēng (lit: I am student)

The word shì is dropped altogether with adjectives – a Mandarin speaker would say 'I hungry', not 'I am hungry'. (The particle le indicates that it's a temporary condition, and not that I'm hungry all the time.)

I am hungry.	wǒ è le (lit: I hungry le)

TO HAVE

The verb 'to have' and its negation, 'no have', are expressed in Mandarin by the words **yǒu** and **méi yǒu** respectively.

I have a camera.	**wǒ yǒu zhàoxiàngjī** (lit: I have camera)
She doesn't have a passport.	**tā méi-yǒu hùzhào** (lit: she no-have passport)

MODALS
To Want

The verb 'to want' in Mandarin is expressed by the word **yao**.

I want to eat.	**wǒ yào chī** (lit: I want eat)
He doesn't want to leave.	**tā bú yào zǒu** (lit: he no want leave)

Need To

The verb 'to need' is expressed by the compound word **xūyào**, which includes the word **yào**, meaning 'to want'.

They need to go to the toilet.	**tāmén xūyào shàng cèsuǒ** (lit: they need go toilet)
You don't need anything.	**nǐ shénme dou bù xūyáo** (lit: you whatever all not need)

NEGATIVES

There are basically two particles that are used to form negative sentences in Mandarin. The one you're most likely to need is **bù**, 'no', which is placed before verbs or adjectives. (When **bù** appears before a word with the same tone, its tone is changed to a rising tone, **bú**).

GRAMMAR

I'm not going to Shanghai.   **wǒ bú qù Shànghǎi**
                               (lit: I no go Shanghai)

It's not good.   **bù hǎo**
                               (lit: no good)

The particle **méi** is used to indicate a negative in the past tense.

I didn't go to Shanghai.   **wǒ méi qù Shànghǎi**
                               (lit: I neg go Shanghai)

COMMANDS

Commands in Mandarin are basically formed by giving emphasis to a verb.

   Go away!   **zǒu!** (lit: leave!)

Negative commands are formed by using one of the following:

   not want   **búyào**
   do not   **bié**
   Don't go!   **búyào zǒu!**
                               (lit: not-want leave!)

   Don't be noisy!   **bié chǎo!**
                               (lit: do-not noisy!)

QUESTIONS

Questions in Mandarin are usually formed by adding the particle **ma** to the end of the sentence.

   He's going to Shanghai.   **tā qù Shànghǎi**
                               (lit: he go Shanghai)

   Is he going to Shanghai?   **tā qù Shànghǎi ma?**
                               (lit: he go Shanghai ma?)

GRAMMAR

QUESTION WORDS

Who?	**shéi?**
Who are you?	**nǐ shì shéi?**
	(lit: you are who?)
Which?	**něi ge?**
Which place?	**něi ge dìfang?**
	(lit: which ge place?)
What?	**shénme?**
What's this?	**zhèi ge shì shénme?**
	(lit: this ge is what?)
Where?	**nǎr?**
Where's he going?	**tā qù nǎr?**
	(lit: he go where?)
How?	**zěnme?**
How do I get there?	**zěnme zǒu?**
	(lit: how-go?)
When?	**shénme shíhou?**
When do you go?	**nǐ shénme shíhou qù?**
	(lit: you what time go?)

GRAMMAR

YES & NO

There are no words in Mandarin that specifically mean 'yes' and 'no' when used in isolation. When asked a question, repeat the verb used in the question to answer in the affirmative. To give a negative answer, use the word **bù**, meaning 'no', together with the verb. The word **bù** always comes before the verb. Remember that when **bù** appears before another word with a falling tone, it changes to **bú**.

Are you going to Shanghai?	**nǐ qù shànghǎi ma?**
	(lit: you go Shanghai ma?)

Yes.	**qù**	(lit: go)
No.	**bú qù**	(lit: no go)

Often you'll hear the word **duì** being used as an equivalent to 'yes' – it literally means 'correct'.

Are you going to Shanghai tomorrow?
    nǐ míngtiān qù Shànghǎi ma?
    (lit: you tomorrow go Shanghai ma?)

Yes. I go tomorrow.   **duì, míngtiān qù**
                       (lit: correct, tomorrow go)

When a question is in the past tense, you can also use the word **yǒu**, meaning 'have', to answer in the affirmative.

Have you studied Chinese?
    nǐ xúe le zhōngwén ma?
    (lit: you study le Chinese ma?)

Yes.   **xué le** (lit: study le)
No.   **méi yǒu** (lit: **neg** have)

COMPARISON

Comparisons in Mandarin are made using the word **bǐ**, 'compare'. The thing being compared comes before the object of comparison.

Beijing is bigger than Shanghai.
    běijīng bǐ shànghǎi dà
    (lit: Beijing compare Shanghai big)

This one's cheaper than that one.
    zhèi ge bǐ nèi ge piányi
    (lit: this **ge** compare that **ge** cheap)

PREPOSITIONS

Location is indicated by the word zài, which literally means 'is located'. Zài is used with almost all prepositions, and precedes them in a sentence.

Your book is next to the table.
nǐde shū zài zhuōzi pángbiān
(lit: your book is-located table next-to)

He is walking behind me.
tā zǒu zài wǒde hòubiānr
(lit: he walk is-located my behind)

behind	(zài) hòubiānr
between	(zài) zhōngjiànr
below	(zài) xiàbiànr
opposite	(zài) duìmiànr
in front of	(zài) qiánbiānr
on top of	(zài) shàngbiānr
next to	(zài) pángbiānr

However, not all prepositions appear with zài:

Before we ate, we saw a performance.
wǒmén chīfàn yǐqián, kàn-le biǎoyǎn
(lit: we eat-rice before, see-le performance)

about	chàbuduō
above	shàngbiār
after (time)	yǐhòu
at	zài
before (time)	yǐqián
from	cóng
for	wèi le
to	dào
towards	wǎng
with	gēn

CONJUNCTIONS

To connect two words or phrases, use a conjunction between the
two choices.

Are you going to
Shanghai or Beijing?
   **nǐ qù Shànghǎi
   háishi qù Běijīng?**
   (lit: you go Shanghai
   or go Beijing?)

CONJUNCTIONS	
and	hé
because	yīnwèi
if	yàoshi/rúguǒ
or	háishì/huòzhě

Do they like cake or ice cream?
   tāmén xǐhuān dàngāo háishi bīngqílín?
   (lit: they like cake or ice cream?)

FEATHERS FROM AN IRON ROOSTER

Chinese idioms and aphorisms, **chéng yǔ**, say a great deal about Chinese perceptions of society, social risk taking and the protection of social networks. The mark of a cultivated, educated Chinese person is that they can quote hundreds of idioms appropriate to every social situation.

tié gōng jī, yì máo bù bá   铁公鸡，一毛不拔

You can't get blood out of a stone.

(lit: like an iron rooster, you can't pull a single feather out)

In China, an 'iron rooster' is a slang term for a train. This expression refers to a stingy person – you can't get a cent out of a stingy person, just like you can't pull a feather from an iron rooster.

wèn gù zhī xīn   温故知新

Those who don't learn from the past are doomed to repeat it.

(lit: review the ancient, gain new insights)

A very Confucian saying.

yī kǒu chī bù chéng pàngzi   一口吃不成胖子

There's no such thing as a free lunch.

(lit: you can't get fat from a single bite)

To succeed, you have to make an effort over a very long time.

gǒu ná hǎozi   狗拿耗子

Don't stick your nose where it doesn't belong.

(lit: like a dog catching mice)

This is reminiscent of Deng Xiaoping's favourite saying, 'It doesn't matter if it's a white cat or a black cat, as long as it catches mice', meaning it doesn't matter if it's communist or capitalist – as long as it gets results.

kǔ kǒu pó xīn   苦口婆心

Coming on too strong.

(lit: bitter mouth, old woman's heart)

This describes someone who tries too hard to persuade people.

GRAMMAR

FEATHERS FROM AN IRON ROOSTER

xiǎo cōng bàn dòufu, yi qīng èr baí   小葱拌豆腐，一
清二白

It's as plain as the nose on your face.
(lit: like scallions on tofu, it's green and white)
    Scallions on tofu is a Chinese appetiser that's white with
    green sprinkled on top. The colours white and green also
    signify somethings that's 'clear and translucent'.

GRAMMAR

MEETING PEOPLE 与人见面

YOU SHOULD KNOW   须知

Hello.	nín hǎo	你好。 *nee how*
Goodbye.	zàijiàn	再见。 *dsyj yen*
Please.	qǐng	请。 *cheeng*
Thank you.	xièxie	谢谢。 *shye shye*
You're welcome.	bú xiè	不谢。
Excuse me.	láo jià	劳驾。 *low jya*
I'm sorry.	duìbuqǐ	对不起。 *dayboochi*

GREETINGS   问候与道别

The all-purpose greeting in China is:

Hello. (inf)	nǐ hǎo	你好。
Hello. (pol)	nín hǎo	您好。

The following greetings can be used to greet people you don't already know.

Good morning.	zǎo/zǎoān	早/早安。
(until around 10 am)		
Good afternoon.	xiàwǔ hǎo	下午好。
Good evening.	wǎnshàng hǎo	晚上好。

When the Chinese greet friends and acquaintances, they're much more likely to use informal greetings.

How's it going?	nǐ chī le ma?	你吃了吗？
(around meal times)	(lit: have you eaten?)	
Where are you off to?	nǐ qù nǎr?	你去哪儿？

Another common way of greeting friends is to call out their name

| Hey, young ...! | ài, xiǎo ...! | 哎，小 ...! |

Other greetings include:

young friend	xiǎo péngyou	小朋友
little younger brother	xiǎo dìdi	小弟弟
little older sister	xiǎojiě	小姐
(used for young women)		

GOODBYES   再见

Goodbye.	zàijiàn	再见。
Goodnight.	wǎn'ān	晚安。
See you tomorrow.	míngtiān jiàn	明天见。
Sleep well.	shuì de hǎo	睡得好。

If you're seeing someone off on a long trip, the Chinese have an equivalent to 'bon voyage' that literally means 'smooth winds all the way'.

| Bon voyage! | yílù shùnfēng! | 一路顺风! |

FORMS OF ADDRESS   称呼

When the Chinese address each other, they almost always use surname and some kind of title. In the case of good friends, or people who have a fairly informal relationship, this will probably take the form of a prefix such as:

| xiǎo (lit: young) | 小 |
| lǎo (lit: old) | 老 |

Thus the young university student sitting opposite you on the train might be known to most of her friends as:

| mǎo Zhāng | 小张 |
| (lit: young Zhang) | |

MEETING PEOPLE

...ile the middle-aged man in the corner might be:

lǎo Liú   老刘
(lit: old Liu)

NO THANKS, I'M GIVING UP

It's considered polite for men to offer other men a cigarette
when they meet. If you want to refuse such an offer, do so
politely with a smile and a wave of the hand.

...on the other hand, you're dealing with the Chinese on a less
...sonal basis, it's useful to remember the importance of giving
...m 'face' (see page 47) by addressing them with a polite title.
...like xiǎo and lǎo, all other titles are placed after the person's
...name.

Perhaps the most common and useful form of address is:

shīfu   师傅

...ically, shīfu is a polite way of addressing someone who has a
...l of some kind. Using it to address the person serving you in
...staurant or a department store, or the person selling tickets at
... bus station, is a mild form of flattery that gives the addressee
...e' and helps get things done.

Some of the more common forms of address used in China,
...t are always placed after a person's name, are:

	dàifu/yīshēng	大夫/医生
...ver	sījī	司机
...nd	péngyǒu	朋友
...e friend	xiǎo péngyǒu	小朋友
...nager	jīnglǐ	经理
...ster	shīfu	师傅
...(lit: skilled person)		

MEETING PEOPLE

Miss	xiǎojiě	小姐
Mr	xiānshēng	先生
Mrs	fūrén	夫人
Ms	nǚshì	女士
professor	jiàoshòu	教授
teacher	lǎoshī	老师

NAMES   姓名

The convention in China is to place surnames before given name
In general, the surname consists of only one syllable.

xìng míng   surname + given name   姓名

Some of the more common surnames include:

Lǐ	李	Wáng	王
Huáng	黄	Zhāng	张
Chén	陈	Liú	刘

Given names have one or often two characters, and are selecte
for both their meaning and their sound. A particular name migh
be chosen because it embodies some quality the parents woul
like to see in their child. Names are even chosen for patrioti
reasons. While certain names are considered feudal, and man
names dating from the Mao era have been abandoned, it's sti
not uncommon in China to bump into people with names like

| jiànguó (lit: founding of the country) | 建国 |
| wèijūn (lit: defend the army) | 卫军 |

CIVILITIES   寒暄

Generally, the terms 'please' and 'thank you' aren't as common i
China as in the west, and peppering your speech with these term
could make you sound overly formal. It's worth rememberin
that a compliment goes much further than a formal 'thank yo
in China.

Thank you.	xièxie	谢谢。
Not at all.	bú xiè	不谢。
It was nothing.	méi shénme	没什么。
It's nothing.	méi shì	没事。
No need to thank.	bú yòng/xiè	不用/谢。

If someone treats you to a meal, you might instead say:

| That was delicious. | hǎo chī jí le | 好吃极了。 |

If someone's done you a favour, a polite response is:

You've given you so much trouble.
máfan nǐ le   麻烦你了。

LOSING FACE

Perhaps the worst thing anyone can do in China is to get angry. Anger won't get you very far, and it is the severest way for you to 'lose face'. Seeing a foreigner get blue in the face and yelling is, for many Chinese, like watching a circus side-show, and the answer will still be **méi yǒu**, 'no'. The best thing to do is to take a deep breath and be patient.

If someone refuses you something essential, try staying put for a while and waiting to talk to someone who speaks English. Be pleasant, and the intransigent bear at the gate will melt. Another effective tactic is to cry – shed tears but do not sob. Some Chinese people can be rendered defenseless by the tears of a foreigner.

REQUESTS   请求

When asking a question, it's polite to start with the phrase:

| May I ask? | qǐng wèn | 请问。 |

This expression is only used at the beginning of a sentence, never at the end.

MEETING PEOPLE

Excuse me, where's the railway station?

qǐng wèn, huǒchēzhàn zài nǎr?	请问，火车站在哪儿？

If you want to squeeze past someone on a crowded bus, the following is more appropriate:

Excuse me.	**láo jià**	劳驾。
Excuse me for squeezing past.	**jièguāng** (lit: may I borrow some light)	借光。

A polite way to make a request is to begin with the word **qǐng** meaning 'please'.

Please give me a hand.

qǐng nǐ bāng wǒ ge máng	请你帮我个忙。

Finally, **qǐng** may be used on its own, with the meaning of 'after you'.

APOLOGIES   道歉

I'm sorry; Excuse me.	**duìbuqǐ**	对不起。
I'm so sorry.	**wǒ zhēn duìbuqǐ**	我真对不起。
It doesn't matter.	**méi guānxi**	没关系。

FIRST ENCOUNTERS   初次见面

You'll have no shortage of opportunities to chat while you're in China. Many Chinese are curious about foreigners – to the extent that in the more out-of-the-way spots you'll attract small crowds of onlookers wherever you go. Many call out in the only English they know as you walk past, and hearing 'hello' fifty times a day can try your patience.

The only thing that holds the Chinese back in most cases is the lack of a common language. Remember the cultural differences and try not to be offended if someone asks you personal questions such as how old you are or how much you earn.

When exchanging names with people you meet, it's best to use the polite expression:

May I ask your name?
  nín guì xìng?   您贵姓？

This literally asks the 'honourable surname' of the person you're talking to. The other person will respond simply by giving his or her surname:

My (sur)name is Chen.
  wǒ xìng chén   我姓陈。

You can follow this up with the question:

How should I address you?
  wǒ zěnme chēnghu nǐ?   我怎么称呼你？

Most Chinese will respond by giving you one of the following two prefixes (see Forms of Address, page 38):

young	xiǎo	小
old	lǎo	老

How are you?	nǐ hǎo ma?	你好吗？
Very well, and you?	hěn hǎo, nǐ ne?	很好，你呢？

I'd like to introduce you to ...
  wǒ xiǎng gěi nǐ jièshào ...   我想给你介绍 ...
I'm pleased to meet you.
  hěn gāoxìng rènshi nǐ   很高兴认识你。
Are you here on holiday?
  nǐ zài zhèr shì dùjià ma?   你在这儿是度假吗？

I'm here (on) ...   wǒ zài zhèr shì ...   我在这儿是 ...
  holiday   dùjià   度假
  business   chūchāi   出差
  to study   liúxué   留学

How long are you here for?
  nǐ zài zhèr zhù duō jiǔ?   你在这儿住多久？
I'm/We're here for ... weeks/days.
  wǒ/wǒmén zài zhèr   我/我们在这儿
  zhù ... xīngqī/tiān   住 ... 星期/天。

Do you like it here?
  nǐ xǐhuān zhèr ma?   你喜欢这儿吗？
I/We like it here very much.
  wǒ/wǒmén hěn xǐhuān zhèr   我/我们很喜欢这儿。
What are you doing?
  nǐ zài gàn shénme?   你在干什么？
What do you think about ...
  nǐ rènwéi ... zěnmeyàng?   你认为 ... 怎么样？
Can I take your photo?
  wǒ kěyi gěi nǐ zhào   我可以给你照
What's this called?
  zhè ge jiào shénme?   这个叫什么？
Are you waiting too?
  nǐ yě zài děng ma?   你也在等吗？
That's strange!
  zhēn guài!   真怪！
That's funny. (amusing)
  zhēn hǎoxiào   真好笑。
It was nice talking to you.
  hěn gāoxìng gēn nǐ tánhuà   很高兴跟你谈话。
I have to get going now.
  wǒ děi zōu le   我得走了。
Have a great day/evening.
  zhù nǐ báitiān/wǎnshàng   祝你白天/晚上
  wán de hǎo   玩得好。
See you soon.
  huí tóu jiàn   回头见。

NATIONALITIES   国籍

Unfortunately we can't list all countries here, however you'll find
that some country names in Mandarin sound similar to their
English equivalents. If this isn't the case for your country, you
might try pointing to the map.

Where are you from?
  nǐ shì něi guó rén?;   你是哪国人？
  nǐ cóng nǎr lái?   你从哪儿来？

I'm from ...	wǒ shì cóng ... lái de	我是从 ... 来的
Australia	àodàlìyà	澳大利亚
Canada	jiā' nádà	加拿大
China	zhōngguó	中国
Denmark	dānmài	丹麦
England	yīngguó	英国
Europe	ōuzhōu	欧洲
France	fǎguó	法国
Germany	déguó	德国
Holland	hélán	荷兰
Ireland	àiěrlán	爱尔兰
Italy	yìdàlì	意大利
Japan	rìběn	日本
Mongolia	měnggǔ	蒙古
New Zealand	xīnxīlán	新西兰
Norway	nuówēi	挪威
Scotland	sūgélán	苏格兰
Singapore	xīnjiāpō	新加坡
South Africa	nánfēi	南非
Sweden	ruìdiǎn	瑞典
Switzerland	ruìshì	瑞士
Taiwan	táiwān	台湾
the US	měiguó	美国
Wales	wēiěrshì	威尔士

I come from a/the ...
  wǒ shì cóng ... lái de   我是从 ... 来的

I live in/at the ...   **wǒ zhù zài ...**   我住在 ...
  city   **chéngshì**   城市
  countryside   **nóngcūn**   农村
  mountains   **shānqū**   山区
  seaside   **hǎibīn**   海滨
  suburbs of ...   **... qū**   ... 区
  village   **cūnzhuāng**   村庄

CULTURAL DIFFERENCES   文化差异

How do you do this in your country?
  zài guì guó, zhè ge   在贵国，这个
  zěnme zuò?   怎么做？
Is this a local or national custom?
  zhè shì běndì xísú háishì   这是本地习俗还是
  quánguó xísù?   全国习俗？
I don't want to offend you.
  wǒ bù xiǎng màofàn nǐ   我不想冒犯你。
I'm sorry, it's not the
custom in my country.
  duìbuqǐ, wǒmén guójiā   对不起，我们国家
  de xísú bú shì zhèyàng   的习俗不是这样。
I don't mind watching, but
I'd prefer not to participate.
  wǒ kěyǐ kàn, kěshì   我可以看，可是
  wǒ bù xiǎng cānjiā   我不想参加。

BODY LANGUAGE   身体语言

Westerners needn't worry too much about inadvertently upsetting anyone on this front while they're in China, however, there are a few differences to keep in mind. The Chinese, for example, gesture with their palm downwards rather than upwards when they want someone to come to them.

MEETING PEOPLE

While shaking hands is common, some Chinese may bow when being introduced. This isn't a deep Japanese-style bow, but one involving only a dip of the head and shoulders.

Physical contact between men and women in public was once considered indecent, but now it's not uncommon to see young men and women arm in arm. Hugging, and kissing friends on the cheek, can be beyond comprehension to many Chinese, unless they've spent time abroad.

In China, when someone's listening to you speak, they'll often shake their heads forward and back and let out a staccato hao, hao, hao, meaning 'good, good, good', that shows they're following what you're saying. When someone disagrees, or is about to refuse you permission to do something, they'll often smile broadly and let out a long, subdued laugh.

In indicating consent or approval, the Chinese use the thumbs up sign as well as the victory sign. Soldiers particularly like it when foreigners flash them the victory sign. In the south of China, the 'fuck you' gesture is made by placing the thumb between the index and middle fingers.

It's not uncommon for people to spit, yell, throw garbage in the streets and push and shove. Be prepared, and try not to take it personally – it's an opportunity to become one with the masses.

SAVING FACE

The concept of 'face' can loosely be defined as status, ego or self-respect. Essentially, it's about avoiding being made to look stupid or being forced to back down in front of others.

In situations where conflict arises, negotiating an outcome that benefits both parties is always preferable to direct confrontation. If one tack fails, try another.

MEETING PEOPLE

LANGUAGE DIFFICULTIES

语言困难

I don't speak Chinese.
wǒ bú huì jiǎng zhōngwén

我不会讲中文。

Do you speak English?
nǐ huì jiǎng yīngyǔ ma?

你会讲英语吗？

Would you say that again please?
qǐng nǐ zài shuō yībiàn

请你再说一遍。

Could you please speak more slowly?
qǐng nǐ shuō màn yīdiǎnr

请你说慢一点儿

Please point to the phrase in this book.
**qǐng nǐ zài zhèi běn
shūlǐ zhǐchū yào shuōde huà**

请你在这本
书里指出要说的话.

Let me see if I can find it in this book.
**wǒ chácha zhèi běn shū lǐ
yǒu méi yǒu**

我查查这本
书里有没有。

I understand.	**wǒ dǒng**	我懂。
I don't understand.	**wǒ bù dǒng**	我不懂。
What does this/ that mean?	**zhèi/nèi shì shénme yìsi?**	这/那是 什么意思？

AGE

年龄

How old are you?
nǐ jǐ suì? (for young children)
nǐ duō dà? (for everyone else)

你几岁？
你多大？

I'm ... years old.	**wǒ ... suì**	我 ... 岁。
18	**shíbā**	十八
25	**èrshíwǔ**	二十五

(See Numbers & Amounts, page 187 for your age.)

OCCUPATIONS   职业

What do you do?
   nǐ zuò shénme gōngzuò?   你做什么工作？

I'm (a/an) ...   wǒ shì ...   我是 ...
   actor   yǎnyuán   演员
   artist   yìshùjiā   艺术家
   businessperson   shāngren   商人
   doctor   yīshēng   医生
   engineer   gōngchéngshī   工程师
   farmer   nóngchǎngzhǔ   农场主
   journalist   jìzhě   记者
   lawyer   lùshī   律师
   manual worker   gōngrén   工人
   mechanic   jìgōng   技工
   nurse   hùshì   护士
   office worker   zhíyuán   职员
   scientist   kēxuéjiā   科学家
   teacher   jiàoshī   教师
   waiter; service worker fúwùyuán   服务员
   writer   zuòjiā   作家

I'm (a) ...   wǒ ...   我 ...
   retired   tuìxiū le   退休了
   unemployed   shīyè   失业
   student   xuéshēng   学生
   on holiday   dùjià   度假

Do you enjoy your work?
   nǐ xǐhuān zìjǐ de   你喜欢自己的
   gōngzuò ma?   工作吗？
How long have you been
in your job?
   nǐ gōngzuò duō jiǔ le?   你工作多久了？
What are you studying?
   nǐ zài xué shénme?   你在学什么？

MEETING PEOPLE

I'm studying ...	wǒ zài xué ...	我在学 ...
art	yìshù	艺术
arts	wénkē	文科
business	shāngyè	商业
teaching	jiàoyù	教育
engineering	gōngchéng	工程
humanities	rénwén xuékē	人文学科
languages	yǔyán	语言
law	fǎlǜ	法律
linguistics	yǔyánxué	语言学
medicine	yīxué	医学
science	kēxué	科学

RELIGION   宗教

What's your religion?
  nǐ xìn shénme jiào   你信什么教？
I'm not religious.
  wǒ bú xìnjiào   我不信教。

I'm ...	wǒ xìn ...	我信 ...
Baha'i	bāhāyī jiào	巴哈依教
	(shìjiè dàtóng jiào)	(世界大同教)
Buddhist	fójiào	佛教
Catholic	tiānzhǔjiào	天主教
Christian	jīdūjiào	基督教
Confucianist	rújiā sīxiǎng	儒家思想
Daoist	dàojiào	道教
Hindu	yìndùjiào	印度教
Jewish	yóutàijiào	犹太教
Muslim	yīsīlánjiào	伊斯兰教
Protestant	xīnjiào	新教
Chinese Folk Religion	mínjiān zōngjiào	民间宗教

FAMILY

家庭

Are you married?	nǐ jiéhūn le ma?	你结婚了吗？
No, I'm not.	hái méi ne	还没呢。
I'm single.	wǒ hái méi jiéhūn	我还没结婚。
Yes, I'm married.	wǒ jiéhūn le	我结婚了。

Is your husband/wife also here?

nǐde zhàngfu/qīzi
yě zài zhèr ma?

你的丈夫／妻子
也在这儿吗？

Do you have any children?
  nǐ yǒu háizi le ma?   你有孩子了吗？

No.	hái méi ne	还没呢。
Yes, one.	yǒu yí ge	有一个。
Yes, two.	yǒu liǎng ge	有两个。
Yes, three.	yǒu sān ge	有三个。
I have a daughter.	wǒ yǒu ge nǚér	我有个女儿。
I have a son.	wǒ yǒu ge érzi	我有个儿子。

How many brothers and
sisters do you have?
  nǐ yǒu jǐ ge xiōngdì jiěmèi?   你有几个
                                           兄弟姐妹？

I have ...
  wǒ yǒu ... ge   我有 ... 个。
I don't have any brothers or sisters.
  wǒ méi yǒu xiōngdì jiěmèi   我没有兄弟姐妹。
Do you have a boy/girlfriend?
  nǐ yǒu meiyǒu nán/nǚ péngyǒu? 你有没有男/女朋友？

HUSBAND OR LOVER?

Sometimes you'll come across the gender-neutral term **àiren**, (lit: loved one) for 'husband' or 'wife'. Be careful when using it, however. Outside China, the term means 'lover' and has an illicit connotation that doesn't always go down well.

For mainland Chinese, the term **tàitài**, for 'wife', has a feudal connotation.

Family Members

Chinese kin terms can get very complicated, as there are different titles according to whether (for brothers and sisters) they are older or younger than the speaker, or whether (for uncles and aunts) they are maternal or paternal relations. Only the words for immediate family members are included here.

AUNTIE NO MORE

China's efforts to limit its vast population through their 'one child' policy is rendering several kin terms obsolete. Most Chinese no longer have uncles or aunts in the People's Republic, so the array of words for 'uncle' and 'aunt' are on the endangered list.

However, children often address their parents' friends as shūshu, 'uncle', and āyi, 'aunt', as they do foreigners. But the array of kin terms for uncles and aunts – such as for one's father's younger brother as distinct from his older brother – are still used in Taiwan, Singapore and the rest of the Chinese world outside of the People's Republic.

brother (elder)	gēge	哥哥
brother (younger)	dìdi	弟弟
daughter	nǚér	女儿
father	fùqīn	父亲
husband	zhàngfu	丈夫
mother	mǔqīn	母亲
sister (elder)	jiějie	姐姐
sister (younger)	mèimei	妹妹
son	érzi	儿子
wife	qīzi	妻子

FEELINGS

感受

I'm (very) ...	wǒ (fēicháng) ...	我(非常) ...
angry	shēngqì	生气
happy	gāoxìng	高兴
hungry	è	饿
thirsty	kǒukě	渴
tired	lèi	累

MEETING PEOPLE

Are you ...?	nǐ ... ma?	你 ... 吗?
afraid	pà	怕
angry	shēngqìle	生气了
cold	juéde lěng	觉得冷
happy	gāoxìng	高兴
hot	juéde rè	觉得热
hungry	èle	饿了
in a hurry	yǒu jíshì	有急事
right	duì	对
sad	nánguò	难过
sleepy	juéde kùn	觉得困
sorry (condolence)	zhēn kěxǐ	真可惜
thirsty	kěle	渴了
tired	lèile	累了
well	hǎo	好
worried	dānxīn	担心

I'm sorry. (regret)	duìbuqǐ	对不起。
I'm grateful.	wǒ hěn gǎnxiè	我很感谢。
Are you keen to ...?	nǐ hěn xiǎng ma?	你很 想 ... 吗?

USEFUL PHRASES

常用短语

What's this/that called?
 zhèi/nèi jiào shénme míngzi? 这/那叫什么名字?
Can I take a photo?
 wǒ kěyǐ zhào ge xiàng ma? 我可以照个相吗?
Do you live here?
 nǐ zhù zài zhèr ma? 你住在这儿吗?
Yes, I live here.
 duì, wǒ zhù zài zhèr 对, 我住在这儿。
No, I don't live here.
 bù, wǒ bú zhù zài zhèr 不, 我不住在这儿。
It's beautiful, isn't it?
 hěn piàoliang, shìma?

Lovely day, isn't it?
tiānqì zhēn hǎo, shìma?　　天气真好，是吗？

That's interesting.
nà hěn yǒu yìsi　　那很有意思。

We love it here.
wǒmen hěn xǐhuān zhèr　　我们很喜欢这儿。

Really?	zhēn de ma?	真的吗？
Never mind.	méi guānxi méi shì	没关系/没事。
No problem.	méi wèntí	没问题。
Sure.	yídìng/kěyǐ	一定。/可以。
Maybe.	kěnéng	可能.

What a cute baby!
duōme kěài de háizi a!

GUANXI

Guānxi, meaning 'connections', is the practice of using social networks to obtain favours. In Mandarin it's also known as zǒu hòu mén or 'going through the back door'. The system is rife in China, and the phrase 'it's not what you know but who you know' holds reign in the Middle Kingdom.

Guānxi quite simply opens doors. Guānxi helps avoid hearing the words méi yǒu, 'there isn't/aren't any'. It gets you a job, a good apartment and admission to a good school. Foreigners too can cultivate guānxi by taking officials out to dinner, promising admission to universities abroad, or by just being friendly.

If someone does you a favour, more likely than not you'll eventually be expected to return it. Foreigners can always sweeten the guānxi with gifts – it's a game that takes patience, but it can smooth your path.

MEETING PEOPLE

I can't stand the smell/smoke in here.

wǒ tǎoyàn zhèr de
chòuwèr/yānwù

我讨厌这儿
的臭味儿/烟雾。

Just a minute.	**děng yī děng**	等一等。
It's OK.	**hǎo**	好。
It's important.	**hěn zhòngyào**	很重要。
It's not important.	**bú zhòngyào**	不重要。
It's possible.	**kěnéng**	可能。
It's not possible.	**bù kěnéng**	不可能。
Look!	**kàn**	看!
Listen!	**tīng**	听!
Listen to this!	**tīngting zhèi ge**	听听这个!
I'm ready.	**wǒ zhǔnbèi hǎo le**	我准备好了。

Are you ready?

nǐ zhǔnbèi hǎo le ma?

你准备好了吗?

You're so smart.

nǐ zhēn cōngming

你真聪明。

You've been too good to us.

nǐ duì wǒmén tài hǎo le

你对我们太好了。

Just a second!

děng yīhuìr!

等一会儿!

Awesome!

gàile màor! (lit: puts on the hat)

盖了帽儿。

GETTING AROUND 旅游

China has three main tourist offices that can help with travel bookings. The China International Travel Service may sell hard-to-get tickets but, according to many travellers, the service is poor and the prices high. The China Travel Service sells tickets and can also help with visas. The China Youth Travel Service offers the same services as the others and, as it must compete with these larger organisations, the service is often better although the prices aren't necessarily cheaper.

China International Travel Service (CITS)
zhōngguó guójì lǚxíngshè 中国国际旅行社
China Travel Service (CTS)
zhōngguó lǚxíngshè 中国旅行社
China Youth Travel Service (CYTS)
zhōngguó qīngnián lǚxíngshè 中国青年旅行社

FINDING YOUR WAY 寻踪找路

I'd like to go to ... **wǒ xiǎng qù ...** 我想去 ...
How can I get to ...? **zěnme qù ...?** 怎么去 ...?

How much is it to go to ...?
qù ... duōshǎo qián? 去 ... 多少钱?
Excuse me, what direction is ...?
qǐngwèn, ... něige fāngxiàng? 请问, ... 哪个 方向?

Excuse me, am I going in the right direction for ...?
qǐngwèn, qù ... zǒu zhèige fāngxiàng duì ma? 请问, 去 ... 走 这个方向对吗?

Is there another way to get there?
yǒu biéde bànfǎ qù ma? 有别的 办法去吗?

GETTING AROUND

Where's a/the ...?	... zài nǎr?	…在哪儿？
airport	jīchǎng	机场
bus station (central)	qìchē zǒngzhàn	汽车总站
bus stop	qìchē zhàn	汽车站
subway station	dìtiě zhàn	地铁站
train station	huǒchē zhàn	火车站
ticket office	shòupiào chù	售票处

Is it far?	yuǎn bù yuǎn?	远不远？
Yes, it's far.	hěn yuǎn	很远
No, it's not far.	bù yuǎn	不远。
Is it near here?	lí zhèr jìn ma?	离这儿近吗？
Can I walk there?	wǒ kěyi zǒulù ma?	我可以走路吗？
Is it difficult to find?	hǎo bù hǎo zhǎo?	好不好找？

What ... is this?	zhèi shì ...?	这是 …？
street	něitiáo jiē	哪条街？
suburb	něige qū	哪个区？

DIRECTIONS   方向

In China, the compass points are almost invariably used when giving directions.

north	běi	北
south	nán	南
east	dōng	东
west	xī	西

Turn ...	... zhuǎnwān	... 转弯
at the next corner	zài xià yíge guǎijiǎo	在下一个拐角
at the traffic lights	zài hónglù dēng	在红绿灯
right	yòubiānr	右边儿
left	zuǒbiānr	左边儿

straight ahead	yīzhí	一直
behind	hòubiānr	后边儿

in front of	qiánbiānr	前边儿
opposite	duìmiànr	对面儿
between	zhōngjiànr	中间儿
next to	pángbiānr	旁边儿
after	yǐhòu	以后
before	yǐqián	以前
upstairs	lóushàng	楼上
downstairs	lóuxià	楼下
far	yuǎn	远
near	jìn	近
here	zhèr	这儿
there	nèr	那儿
around here	zhè fùjìn	这附近
over there	zài nèibiānr	在那边儿
quare	jiē	街
street	guǎngchǎng	广场

ADDRESSES   地址

Postal addresses, or **dìzhǐ**, in China are written in the opposite order to those in the west. The first line gives the most general information, the country, while the last ends with the most specific, the individual.

> People's Republic of China
> Hunan Province (postcode)
> Changsha City
> Chairman Mao Steet, No. 137
> Mao Dehua Comrade

BUYING TICKETS   买票

Buying tickets in China for anything can be a nightmare. Lines in front of ticket windows are long and people push and cut in line.

When facing queues in China, one approach is to wait for someone who wants to practise English to offer to help you. They may charge a small fee, and you might cringe as your helper cuts in front of 50 other people, but otherwise you could find

GETTING AROUND

yourself trying to shove your way into a small ticket booth window while 50 to 100 others push from behind. You may have to
wait half an hour for your saviour to come, but bring a book, try
to relax and help should arrive.

Where's the ticket office?		
shòupiàochù zài nǎr?		售票处在哪儿？
Excuse me.	láojià	劳驾。
Are there any seats left?		
hái yǒu zuòwèi ma?		还有座位吗？
Can I reserve a place?		
wǒ néng dìng ge		我能定个
zuòwèi ma?		座位吗？
How much is it?		
yào duōshǎo qián?		要多少钱？
How much is a (hard-seat) fare to ...?		
qù ... de (yìngzuò) piào		去...的(硬座)票
duōshǎo qián?		多少钱？
I'd like to book a ticket to ...		
wǒ xiǎng dìng yìzhāng		我想订一张
qù ... de piào		去 ... 的票。

I'd like a ... ticket.	wǒ xiǎngmǎi	我想买
	yìzhāng ... piào	一张 ... 票。
one-way	dānchéng	单程
return	láihuí	来回
adult	chéngrén piào	成人票
child's	értóng piào	儿童票
1st class	tóuděng	头等
2nd class	èrděng	二等
economy	pǔtōng	普通

I'd like a (hard-seat) ticket to ...	
wǒ xiǎng mǎi yìzhāng qù ...	我想买一张去 ...
de (yìngzuò) piào	的(硬座)票。
How long does the trip take?	
lùshàng yào duōcháng shíjiān?	路上要多长时？

Is it a direct route?
  yīzhí zǒu ma? 一直走吗？

Is it an express train?
  shì tèkuài huǒchē ma? 是特快火车吗？

I'd like a(n) ... berth. **wǒ yào yīge ...pù** 我要一个 ... 铺。
  upper **shàng** 上
  middle **zhōng** 中
  bottom **xià** 下

I'd like to upgrade my ticket.
  wǒ xiǎng bǔpiào 我想补票。

I want to change to a ...
  wǒ xiǎng huàn ... 我想换 ...

fastest route **zuì kuàide lù** 最快的路
seat **zuòwèi** 座位
ticket **piào** 票

AT CUSTOMS 海关

I have nothing to declare.
  wǒ méiyǒu shénme 我没有什么
  yào bàoguān de 要报关的。

Do I have to declare this?
  zhèige wǒ xūyào 这个我要
  bàoguān ma? 报关吗？

I'd like to declare ...
  wǒ yào shēnbào ... 我要申报…

SIGNS		
海关	**hǎiguān**	CUSTOMS
免税	**miǎnshuì**	DUTY-FREE

GETTING AROUND

I didn't know I had to declare it.
    wǒ bù zhīdao
    xūyào shēnbào
我不知道
需要申报。

This is all my luggage.
    zhèi jiùshi wǒ de xínglǐ
这就是我的行李。

Can I call my embassy/consulate?
    wǒ kěyi dǎ diànhuà gěi
    wǒmén dàshǐguǎn
    /lǐngshìguǎn ma?
我可以打电话给
我们大使馆
/领事馆吗？

AIR   航空

The names of China's airlines are pretty straightforward – China Southern, China Northern and China Xinjiang, to name a few. The Civil Aviation Administration of China (CAAC) is the umbrella organisation of numerous airlines operating within China. Flights are available to all corners of China, although foreigners pay a special 'foreigners' fare' for tickets, which can be several times the standard price.

'CIVILISED' AIRPORTS

Airports in China often display signs with the expression wénmíng. Throughout China, this phrase is translated into English as 'civilisation', but the meaning's more in line with the idea of being polite, genteel, cultivated and courteous.

During your flight, flight attendants pass out fans, dried fruit and an assortment of cake-type foods, and the requisite cold chunk of chicken.

Is there a flight to ...?
    yǒu qù ... de fēijī ma?
有去...的飞机吗？

What time does the plane leave/arrive?
    fēijī jǐdiǎn kāi/dào?
飞机几点开/到？

When's the next flight to ...?
    qù ... de xiàbān fēijī
    shénme shíhou qǐfēi?
去 ... 的下班飞机
什么时候起飞？

How long does the flight take?
   yào zuò duōcháng
   shíjiān de fēijī?   要坐多长
                                              时间的飞机?
Please show your ...
   qǐng náchū nǐde ...   请拿出你的 ...
Is there a departure tax?
   yǒu méi yǒu líjìng shuì?   有没有离境税?
I'd like to check my luggage in.
   wǒ xiǎng tuōyùn xínglǐ   我想托运行李。
What's the charge for each excess kilo?
   chāoguò yī gōngjīn   超过一公斤
   shōu duōshǎo qián?   收多少钱?
My luggage hasn't arrived.
   wǒ de xínglǐ hái méi dào   我的行李还没到。

arrivals	dàodá	到达
baggage claim	xíngli lǐngqǔ	行李领取
boarding pass	dēngjī kǎ	登机卡
cancel	qǔxiāo	取消
confirm	quèrèn	确认
change	gēnggǎi	更改
check-in	yànpiào	验票
customs	hǎiguān	海关
customs declaration	hǎiguān	海关
	shēnbào dān	申报单
departures	líjìng	离境
domestic	guónèi	国内
duty-free	miǎnshuì	免税
flight	hángbān	航班
gate	mén	门
international	guójì	国际
passport	hùzhào	护照
plane	fēijī	飞机
transit lounge	huànjītīng	换机厅
smoking	xīyānqū	吸烟区
nonsmoking	fēixīyānqū	非吸烟区

GETTING AROUND

BUS
公共汽车

The best thing about long-distance bus travel in China is that during meal breaks, you get to stop in little towns and villages you wouldn't normally get the chance to see. On the other hand, buses are generally uncomfortable and crowded and breakdowns are frequent.

Long-distance bus trips can be gruelling, with a lot of noise and very little legroom. Buses aren't air-conditioned, and can be stifling in summer. Although 'No Smoking' signs are posted in buses, as well as other types of public transport, many passengers smoke voraciously, regardless of regulations. Frequently, even the driver will smoke.

In cities, maps of bus routes are available from hotels, local bookstores and travel agencies, although they're usually written in Chinese characters.

Before boarding a bus, it might be a good idea to have someone write down the name of the place you want to go to in Chinese characters, so you can show it to the driver or conductor.

Does this bus go to (the) ...?
  zhèiliàng qìchē qù ... ma?   这辆汽车去 ... 吗？
How frequently do the buses run?
  qìchē duōcháng   汽车多长
  shíjiān yībān?   时间一班？
What time does the bus leave/arrive?
  qìchē jǐdiǎn kāi/dào?   汽车几点开/到？
Could you let me know
when we get to ...?
  wǒmén dào ... de shíhòu,   我们到...的时候，
  nǐ néng bù néng gàosu   你能不能告诉
  wǒmén yíxià?   我们一下
Can you smoke on this bus?
  nǐ néng zài zhèi liàng   你能在这辆
  chēshàng xīyān ma?   车上吸烟吗？
Could you please speak more quietly?
  qǐng shuō xiǎo shēng yìdiǎnr,   请说小声一点儿，
  hǎo ma?   好吗？。

Please stop pushing.
qǐng bié tuī wǒ   请别推我。

Which bus goes to (the) ...?
něiliàng qìchē qù ...?   哪辆汽车去 ...？
city centre   **shì zhōngxīn**   市中心
train station   **huǒchē zhàn**   火车站

I want to get off!   **xià chē!**   下车！

When's the ... bus?   **... bānchē shénme**   ... 班车什么
                       shíhòu lái?   时候来？
next   **xià**   下
first   **tóu**   头
last   **mò**   末

bus route map   **shìqū/jiāotōng dìtú** 市区/交通地图
bus stop   **qìchē zhàn**   汽车站
intercity bus; coach   **chángtú qìchē**   长途汽车
local/city bus   **gōnggòng qìchē**   公共汽车

TRAIN   火车

Trains in China are reliable, fast and – with the exception of the
hard class where most Chinese sit – reasonably comfortable. There
are train services around every province in the country except Tibet.

Buying tickets from railway stations, although cheap, often
involves long queues. Hard-seat tickets are usually easy to get at
short notice, but if you're after a sleeper, it's best to book at tourist offices. Black market tickets are rife. Make sure you're buying
a genuine ticket and be aware that authorities in major cities will
fine you for using illegal tickets.

There are four classes of railway tickets:

hard-seat   **yìngzuò**   硬座
hard-sleeper   **yìngwò**   硬卧
soft-seat   **ruǎnzuò**   软座
soft-sleeper   **ruǎnwò**   软卧

Trains can be local, slow, fast and express varieties. The genera
terms are:

local train	pǔtōng chē	普通车
slow train	màn chē	慢车
fast train	kuài chē	快车

More specifically, they're called:

- **tèkuài**　　　特快
  special express. Fast with good facilities, and includes all classe
- **yóu**　　　游
  travel; similar to special express
- **kuàisù**　　　快速
  fast speed; similar to special express
- **zhǔn gāosù**　　　准高速
  standard high speed; especially fast
- **zhíkuài**　　　直快
  direct express. These make more stops than special expresses.
  but have fewer sleepers.
- **kuàikè**　　　快客
  fast passenger; these trains take short, suburban routes
- **zhíkè**　　　直客
  direct passenger. This service is slow, with frequent stops and
  no sleepers.
- **kè**　　　客
  passenger. Slow, but has some sleepers.

What time does the train leave/arrive?
　　huǒchē jǐdiǎn kāi/dào?　　　　　火车几点开/到？
Where are we now?
　　wǒmén xiànzài zài nǎr?　　　　　我们现在在哪儿？
Can you tell me when we get to ..?
　　dào ... de shíhòu,　　　　　　　到 ...
　　qǐng nǐ gàosù wǒ yíxià,　　　　请你告诉我一下,
　　hǎo ma?　　　　　　　　　　　好吗？

What station is this?
  zhèi shì něige zhàn?　　　　　这是哪个站？

What's the next station?
  xià yī zhàn shì nǎr?　　　　　下一站是哪儿？

The train is delayed/cancelled.
  huǒchē tuīchí le/　　　　　　火车推迟了／
  qǔxiāo le　　　　　　　　　　取消了。

How long will it be delayed?
  tuīchí duōcháng shíjiān?　　　推迟多长时间？

Is this seat taken?
  zhèr yǒu rén ma?　　　　　　这儿有人吗

Excuse me, this is my seat.
  duìbuqǐ, *jershee wordu(s)*　　对不起，
  zhè shi wǒde zuòwèi *tswarway*　这是我的座位。

I'm sorry, I really need to rest.
  duìbuqǐ, wǒ zhēnde　　　　　对不起，我真的
  xūyào xiūxi yíxià　　　　　　需要休息一下。

Let's find the attendant to
resolve this problem.
  wǒmen zhǎo lièchēyuán
  jiějué zhèige wèntí, ba　　　　解决这个问题，吧。

Where's the toilet?
  cèsuǒ zài nǎr?　　　　　　　厕所在哪儿？

dining car	cānchē	餐车
nonsmoking	jìnyān	禁烟
railway station	huǒchē zhàn	火车站
subway (station)	dìtiě (zhàn)	地铁(站)
train	huǒchē	火车
train station	huǒchēzhàn	火车站
train timetable	lièchē shíkèbiǎo	列车时刻表

TAXI　　　　　　　　　　　　　出租汽车

Long-distance taxis are usually booked through travel agencies
or hotels. The fees can be excessive, but are usually negotiable.
It's generally not difficult to find private taxi drivers who'll
charge much less.

GETTING AROUND

There are three types of taxis. Prices vary from city to city, and rates are posted on the side window. The cheapest is a yellow van that, because of its shape, is called a 'bread taxi'. These taxis carry up to six people, but they're so run down some seats may be missing. The next step up is a small red 'Jilin' taxi, while the most expensive taxis are foreign cars.

It's a good idea to get an estimate of the fare from someone before you take a taxi. If you feel

BREAD TAXIS

China's yellow, bread-shaped taxis are called:

miànbāo dīshì
面包的士

which is often shortened to:

miàndī
面的

you're being cheated, take down the driver's name, licence plate and identification numbers displayed in the taxi. The best way to gain the driver's cooperation is to threaten to report them.

I'd like to get a taxi.
   wǒ xiǎng jiào chūzūqìchē   我想叫出租汽车。

Is this taxi available?
   zhèi chē kěyǐ lā rén ma?   这车拉人吗？

Driver, could you take me to ...?
   shīfu, nǐ néng bǎ wǒ   师傅，你能把我
   sòngdào ... ma?   送到 ... 吗？

To ..., please!
   qǐng kāidào ...!   请开到 ...!

Can you wait for me?
   nǐ néng děng wǒ ma?   你能等我吗？

I'll be right back.
   wǒ mǎshàng jiù huílái   我马上就回来

I'll be back in ...
   wǒ ... jiù huílái   我 ... 就回来。

How much do I owe you?
   nà yào duōshǎo qián?   那要多少钱？

Please turn on your meter.
   qǐng nǐ dǎkāi biǎo　　　　　　请你打开表。

If you don't have a meter,
I'll get out of the taxi.
   méiyǒu biǎo, wǒ jiù xià chē　　没有表，我就下车

Something's wrong with your meter.
   nǐde biǎo yǒu wèntí　　　　　你的表有问题。

It seems to be going too fast.
   biǎo hǎoxiàng tiàode tàikuài　　表好象跳得太快。

Can you show me where we are
on this map?
   qǐng gàosù wǒ, wǒmen　　　　请告诉我，我们
   dìtúshàng zài shénme dìfang?　地图在上什么地方？

Where are we?
   wǒmén zài nǎr?　　　　　　　我们在哪儿？

Where are we going?
   wǒmen qù nǎr?　　　　　　　我们去哪儿？

I'll write down your licence number
and report you to the police.
   wǒ yào bǎ nǐde chēpái　　　　我要把你的车牌
   xiě xiàlái, ránhòu gǎo nǐ　　　　写下来，然后告你。

Instructions 指路

Turn to the left.	wàng zuǒ guǎi	往左拐。
Turn to the right.	wàng yòu guǎi	往右拐。
Go straight ahead.	yīzhí zǒu	一直走。
This is the wrong way.	zǒu cuò lù le	走错路了。

Stop at the next corner, please.
   qǐng tíng zài xiàge lù kǒu　　　请停在下个路口。

Stop at the next street on the left/right, please.
   qǐng tíng zài zuǒ/yòu　　　　　请停在左/右
   biānde xiàge lùkǒu　　　　　　边的下个路口。

Here's fine, thank you.
   zài zhèr tíng jiù xíng　　　　　在这儿停就行。

Careful!　　　　　xiǎoxīn!　　　　小心！

Please slow down.
   qǐng màn yīdiǎnr　　　　　　请慢一点儿。

Wait!	děng yīhuǐr!	等一会儿！
Stop!	tíng!	停！
OK.	hǎo	好。
Oh no!	ayā, bùxíng	啊呀，不行。

Please hurry.
qǐng kuài yīdiǎnr   请快一点儿。
Please wait here.
qǐng děng zài zhèr   请等在这儿。
How much (is it) to ...?
qù ... duōshǎo qián?   去 ... 多少钱
Does it cost extra for luggage?
xíngli lìngwài shōuqián ma?   行李另外收钱吗?
That's too expensive!
tài guì le!   太贵了！
Lower the price a little, OK?
shǎo yīdiǎnr ba   少一点儿吧。
So expensive!
némme guì!   那么贵！
How about (five) kuai?
(wǔ) kuài zěnmeyàng?   (五)块怎么样?
How about ...?
... hǎobùhǎo?   ... 好不?
That's not right, is it?
bú duì ba?   不对吧?

BOAT   船

With improved road and air transport, boats in China are
disappearing quickly. There are times, however, when boats are
the easiest way of getting around. Famous river journeys include the
Yangzi River trip from Chongqing to Wuhan, and the Li River
from Guilin to Yangshuo.

Although boat companies charge different rates for various
classes of room, often the only difference between rooms is that
those on an upper deck are more costly.

I'd like a ... ticket to (Wuhan).
  **wǒ xiǎng mǎi yīzhāng qù
  (wǔhàn) de ... piào**   我想买一张去
                                 (武汉)的 ... 票。

1st class	tóuděng	头等
2nd class	èrděng	二等
3rd class	sānděng	三等
4th class	sìděng	四等

Where does the boat leave from?
  chuán cóng nǎr líkāi?   船从哪儿离开？

What time does the boat leave?
  chuán jǐdiǎn kāi?   船几点开？

What time does the boat arrive?
  chuán shénme shíhou líkāi?   船什么时候离开？

How long will we stop here?
  wǒmén zài zhèr tíng duōjiǔ? 我们在这儿停多久？

What time should we be
back on board?
  wǒmen yīnggāi jǐdiǎn huílái? 我们应该几点回来？

Could you write it down
for me please?
  nǐ néngbunéng xiěxiàlái?   你能不能写下来？

I'm feeling a bit seasick.
  wǒ yǒudiǎnr yùnchuán   我有点儿晕船。

I'm feeling seasick.
  wǒ yùnchuán le   我晕船了。

I feel like vomiting.
  wǒ xiǎng tù   我想吐。

boat	chuán	船
cabin	kècāng	客舱
ferry	dùchuán	渡船
port	mǎtóu	码头

GETTING AROUND

BICYCLE   自行车

The best way to avoid overcrowded public transport in China is the bicycle. It's becoming easier for foreigners to rent bicycles though many require a passport as proof of your intention to bring the bike back.

If you're staying in one place in China, it makes sense to buy a new or used bike. In each town there are alleys or segments of streets where people sell their used bikes, which you can test-ride before buying. Make sure you obtain a bike licence and certificate of ownership, and remember that new bikes need to be registered with the Public Security Bureau. It may be better to buy a beaten up old bike than a new one, as there's less chance that it will be stolen.

Where can I hire a bicycle?
  wǒ zài nǎr néng zū zìxíngchē?   我在哪儿能租自行车？

I'd like to hire a bicycle.
  wǒ xiǎng zū yīliàng zìxíngchē   我想租一辆自行车。

How much is the rental?
  zūjīn yào duōshǎo?   租金要多少？

I'll return it tomorrow.
  wǒ míngtiān huán gěi nǐ   我明天还给你。

How much is it per ...?	**yī ... duōshǎo qián?**	一...多少钱？
hour	**xiǎoshí**	小时
morning	**shàngwǔ**	上午
afternoon	**xiàwǔ**	下午
day	**tiān**	天

How much is the deposit?
  yājīn yào duōshǎo?   押金要多少？

Where's the bicycle parking lot?
  zìxíngchē cúnfàngchù zài nǎr?   自行车存放处在哪儿？

Where can I find second-hand bikes for sale?
  zài nǎr néng mǎidào   在哪儿能买到
  jiù zìxíngchē?   旧自行车？

Is it safe to cycle on this road?
  zài zhèitiáo lùshàng qí   在这条路上骑
  zìxíngchē ānquán ma?   自行车安全吗？

Is there a place to fix my bike around here?
  zhèi fùjìn yǒu xiū zìxíngché   这附近有修自行车
  de dìfāng ma?   的地方吗？

I've got a flat tyre.
  wǒde lúntāi biě le   我的轮胎瘪了。

bicycle	**zìxíngchē**	自行车
brakes	**shāchē**	刹车
to cycle	**qíchē**	骑车

gear stick	biànsùqì	变速器
handlebars	bǎshǒu	把手
helmet	tóukuī	头盔
inner tube	chētāi	车胎
lights	chēdēng	车灯
lock	chēsuǒ	车锁
mountain bike	dēngshān chē	登山车
padlock	chēsuǒ	车锁
pump	qìtǒng	气筒
puncture	lúntāi dòng	轮胎洞
racing bike	sài chē	赛车
saddle	chē zuò	车座
tandem	shuāngrén zìxíngchē	双人自行车
wheel	chē lún	车轮

BIKE CRASH @#!!!

With Chinese earning power on the rise in urban areas, an increasingly large number of people are leaving their bikes at home and taking taxis. Bicycle accidents, too, have seen a rather dramatic change.

In the past, an accident between two cyclists would draw huge crowds, and it rarely mattered who was at fault. Instead, onlookers determined the matter by judging who was more polite or who had higher rank, and police would only step in as things were settling. In general, if you accidently hit an old woman, there was no way to win, and most people in this situation simply fled.

These days, people don't have time to stop and discuss losses or watch shouting matches, and you can go for days without seeing a bike accident spectacle.

CAR   车

Foreigners travelling on a tourist visa aren't able to hire a car or motorbike in China – only residents with a Chinese driver's licence can hire or buy a vehicle. If you're eligible to drive, there are restrictions on the distance you can drive from your place of residence.

Each province and special region, such as Beijing and Shanghai, has a distinct Chinese character for their licence plates. Most of these characters follow the ancient names of the regions. Beijing's symbol is simply the character jīng, meaning 'capital', while Guangdong uses yuè, the name of the local dialect. There are different colours for transport, military and government vehicles, and distinctive licence plates for resident foreigners.

Where's the nearest petrol station?
　　xià yīge jiāyóuzhàn　　　　下一个加油站
　　zài nǎr?　　　　　　　　　在哪儿？
I'd like ... litres.
　　wǒ yào ... gōngshēng　　　我要 ... 公升。
Can I park here?
　　zhèr kěyǐ tíngchē ma?　　 这儿可以停车吗？
Does this road lead to ...?
　　zhèi tiáo lù dào ...?　　　 这条路到 ...？

air	qìyā	气压
battery	diànpíng	电瓶
brakes	shāchē	刹车
car	qìchē	汽车
clutch	líhéqì	离合器
driver's licence	jiàshǐ zhízhào	驾驶执照
engine	yǐnqíng	引擎
garage	chēfáng	车房
leaded/regular	hán qiān/pǔtōng	含铅/普通
oil	jī yóu	机油
puncture	lúntāi dòng	轮胎洞
radiator	sànrèqì	散热器
roadmap	jiāotōng tú	交通图
seatbelt	ānquán dài	安全带
speed limit	xiànsù	限速
tyres	lúntāi	轮胎
unleaded	wúqiān	无铅
windscreen	dǎngfēng bōli	挡风玻璃

GETTING AROUND

RICKSHAWS

The rickshaw, or **yángchē** – a two-wheeled passenger cart pulled by someone on foot – are fairly rare in China nowadays. Some are kept on for the benefit of tourists, but generally they're considered a throwback to feudal society.

The rickshaw has largely been replaced by the pedicab, or **sānlúnchē**. These tricycles, which come in both leg-powered and motorised versions, have room for one or two passengers, and are cheaper than taxis. They usually don't have meters, so you'll have to negotiate the price.

Car Problems

We need a mechanic.
wǒmén xūyào jīxiūgōng   我们需要机修工。

The car broke down at ...
qìchē shì zài ... huài de   汽车是在 ... 坏的。

The battery is flat.
diànpíng méi diàn le   电瓶没电了。

I've got a flat tyre.
lúntāi biě le   轮胎瘪了。

It's overheating.
guò rè le   过热了。

I've lost my car keys.
wǒ de chē yàoshi diū le   我的车钥匙丢了。

I've run out of petrol.
méiyǒu qìyóu le   没有汽油了。

ACCOMMODATION 住宿

If you're staying in luxury hotels, it's unlikely that you'll need to use Mandarin very often. If, on the other hand, you're travelling around China on a budget, you'll need to know some phrases to negotiate cheaper rooms or a place in a dormitory.

You'll find three main types of accommodation in China – expensive hotels aimed at tourists and businesspeople, mid-priced places that cater to Chinese expatriates and high-ranking officials, and basic, often Chinese-only, accommodation with rock-bottom prices.

Most Chinese rooms for two will have two single beds, harking back to the days when travelling business comrades would share a room. Many of these beds can't be pushed together without leaving a dangerous gap in the middle, although single rooms sometimes have one bed large enough for two.

Top-range hotels and guesthouses in China cater mostly for foreigners and affluent locals.

| guesthouse | bīnguǎn | 饭店 |
| luxury hotel | fàndiàn | 宾馆 |

Some mid-range hotels are available to foreigners, but are often expensive.

| hotel | lǚguǎn | 旅馆 |

At the bottom of the range, and often inaccessible to foreigners, are hostels and dormitories.

| hostel | zhāodàisuǒ/lǚshè | 招待所/旅社 |
| dormitory | duōrénfáng | 多人房 |

ACCOMMODATION

FINDING ACCOMMODATION 寻找住处

Where's a ...?	... zài nǎr?	... 在哪儿？
hostel	zhāodàisuǒ/lǚshè	招待所/旅社
hotel	lǚguǎn	旅馆

I'm looking for a ... hotel.	wǒ zhǎo yījiā ... de lǚguǎn	我找一家...的旅馆。
cheap	piányi	便宜
good	hǎo	好
nearby	lí zhèr jìn	离这儿近

Could you write down the address
for me please?
 nǐ néng bù néng bǎ   你能不能把
 dìzhǐ xiěxiàlai gěi wǒ?   地址写下来给我？
Is it possible to walk from here?
 cóng zhèr zǒulù   从这儿走
 kěyǐ qù ma?   路可以去吗？
Yes, it's not far.
 kěyǐ, bù yuǎn   可以，不远。
No, it's a long way.
 bù kěyǐ, hěn yuǎn   不可以，很远。
How much is it to go there by taxi?
 zuò chūzū qìchē yào   坐出租汽车要
 duōshǎo qián?   多少钱？

BOOKING AHEAD 提前预订

I'd like to book a room, please.
 wǒ yào dìng yīge fángjiān   我要订一个房间。
Do you have any rooms available?
 nǐmén yǒu fángjiān ma?   你们有房间吗？
We'll be arriving at ...
 wǒmén ... dào   我们 ... 到。
My name is ...
 wǒ míngzi jiào ...   我名字叫 ...

CHECKING IN   住宿登记

I'd like a ...	wǒ xiǎng yào ...	我想要 ...
single room	yījiān dānrénfáng	一间单人房
double room	yījiān shuāngrénfáng	一间双人房
bed	yī ge chuángwèi	一个床位
bed for two	shuāngrén chuáng	双人床
dorm to share	zhù sùshè	住宿舍
room with a bathroom	yǒu yùshìde fángjiān	有浴室的房间

I want a room with a ...	wǒ yào yījiān yǒu ... de fángjiān	我要一间有...的房间。
bathroom	yùshì	浴室
shower	línyù	淋浴
telephone	diànhuà	电话
television	diànshì	电视
window	chuānghu	窗户

Is there ...?	yǒu méiyǒu ...?	有没有...?
air-conditioning	kōngtiáo	空调
heating	nuǎnqì	暖气

ACCOMMODATION

TYPES OF VISAS

When checking in to a hotel, there's usually a question on the registration form asking what type of visa you have. For most tourists, the answer is 'L', from the Mandarin word **lǚxíng**, meaning 'travel'. Other types of visas include:

Business	fǎngwèn	F
Resident	dìngjū	D
Stewardess	chèngwù	C
Student	liúxué	X
Transit	guòjìng	G
Working	rènzhí	Z

ACCOMMODATION

How much does it cost?
yào duōshǎo qián? 要多少钱？

Can I see the room?
wǒ néng kànkan 我能看看
fángjiān ma? 房间吗？

Are there any others?
háiyǒu biéde fángjiān ma? 还有别的房间吗？

Are there any cheaper ones?
yǒu méiyǒu piányi yīdiǎnr de? 有没有便宜一点儿的？

It's fine, I'll take it.
hǎo, wǒ jiù yào zhèijiān 好，我就要这间。

I'm going to stay for ... **wǒ dǎsuàn zhù ...** 我打算住 ...
  one night **yīge wǎnshàng** 一个晚上
  two nights **liǎngge wǎnshàng** 两个晚上
  three nights **sān'ge wǎnshàng** 三个晚上
  one week **yīge xīngqī** 一个星期

I'm not sure how long I'm staying.
wǒ bù zhīdào yào zhù 我不知道要住
duōcháng shíjiān 多长时间。

Is there a discount for
children/students?
háizi/xuéshēng yǒu 孩子/学生有
yōuhuì ma? 优惠吗？

I'm a student.
wǒ shì xuéshēng 我是学生。

Here's my student card.
zhè shì wǒde 这是我的
xuéshēngzhèng 学生证。

PAPERWORK

		书面资料
age	niánlíng	年龄
address	dìzhǐ	地址
date of birth	chūshēng rìqī	出生日期
driver's licence	jiàshǐ zhízhào	驾驶执照
name	xìngmíng	姓名
nationality	guójí	国籍
passport number	hùzhào hàomǎ	护照号码
place of birth	chūshēng dìdiǎn	出生地点
sex	xìngbié	性别
visa	qiānzhèng	签证

REQUESTS & QUERIES

要求与查询

Is there a lift?
  yǒu meiyǒu diàntī?
有没有电梯？

Where's the bathroom?
  yùshì zài nǎr?
浴室在哪儿？

Is there hot water all day?
  yītiān dōu yǒu rèshuǐ ma?
一天都有热水吗？

When does the hot water come on?
  jǐ diǎnzhōng kāi rèshuǐ?
几点钟开热水？

When's the heating turned on?
  shénme shíhòu kāi nuǎnqì?
什么时候开暖气？

Should I leave my key at reception
when I go out?
  wǒ chūqù de shíhòu, shì
  búshì yào bǎ yàoshi liúxià?
我出去的时候，是
不是要把钥匙留下？

Do you have a safe where I can
store my valuables?
  nǐmén yǒu méiyǒu cún
  guìzhòng wùpǐn de
  bǎoxiǎnxiāng?
你们有没有存
贵重物品的
保险箱？

Could I have a receipt for them?
  gěi wǒ yīzhāng
  shōujù, hǎo ma?
给我一张
收据，好吗？

ACCOMMODATION

Can you store this/these for me?
nǐmén néng bùnéng bāng
wǒ bǎ zhèi ge/xiē dōngxī
cún zài bǎoxiǎnxiānglǐ?

你们能不能帮
我把这个/些东西
存在保险箱里？

Do you have a laundry service?
yǒu méiyǒu xǐ
yīfu de fúwù

有没有洗
衣服的服务？

Is there somewhere to wash clothes?
yǒu méiyǒu xǐ
yīfude dìfang?

有没有洗
衣服的地方？

Is there a telephone I can use?
zhèr yǒu méiyǒu wǒ néng
yòng de diànhuà?

这儿有没有我
能用的电话？

How can I make an international call?
guójì chángtú zěnme dǎ?

国际长途怎么打？

To call (Canada) what
numbers do I dial?
(jiā ná dà) diànhuà yīnggāi
dǎ něixiē hàomǎ?

(加拿大)电话应该
打哪些号码？

Is there an extra charge for
making a local (international) call?
dǎ shìnèi (guójì) diànhuà,
yào búyào jiā fèi?

打市内(国际)电话，
要不要加费？

Is there a dining room?
zhèr yǒu méiyǒu shítáng?

这儿有没有食堂？

Please wake me up at
(6.30 am) tomorrow.
qǐng míngtiān zǎoshàng
(liùdiǎn bàn) jiàoxǐng wǒ

请明天早上
(六点半)叫醒我。

Can you clean my room?
néng bùnéng dǎsǎo yīxià
wǒde fángjiān

能不能打扫一下
我的房间。

Please change the sheets.
qǐng huàn chuángdān

请换床单。

I need a/some ...	wǒ xiǎngyào ...	我想要 ...
hangers	yījià	衣架
bar of soap	féizào	肥皂
towel	máojīn	毛巾

COMPLAINTS 抱怨

I don't like this room.
  wǒ bù xǐhuān zhèijiān fángjiān   我不喜欢这间房间。

There are cockroaches in my room.
  wǒde fángjiān yǒu zhāngláng   我的房间有蟑螂。

I saw a rat in my room.
  wǒ zài fángjiān lǐ   我在房间里
  kánjiàn le lǎoshǔ   看见了老鼠。

It's too ...	tài ... le	太 ... 了。
cramped	zhǎi	窄
damp	cháoshī	潮湿
dirty	zāng	脏
expensive	guì	贵
hot	rè	热
cold	lěng	冷
big	dà	大
small	xiǎo	小
smelly	chòu	臭
dark	àn	暗
noisy	chǎo	吵

Do you have	yǒu méiyǒu ...	有没有 ...
(a) ... room?	de fángjiān?	的房间？
another	qítā	其他
cheaper	gèng piányi	更便宜
better	gèng hǎo	更好

The ... doesn't work.	... huài le	... 坏了。
air-conditioner	kōngtiáo	空调
light	dēng	灯
shower	línyù	淋浴
tap (faucet)	shuǐ lóngtóu	水龙头
toilet	cèsuǒ	厕所

ACCOMMODATION

ACCOMMODATION

Can you get it repaired?
néng xiū ma? 能修吗？

I can't open/close the window.
chuānghu dǎbùkāi/ 窗户打不开/
guānbúshàng 关不上。

This ... isn't clean.	**zhège ... bù gānjìng**	这个 ... 不干净。
blanket	**tǎnzi/chuángdān**	毯子/床单
pillow	**zhěntóu**	枕头
pillowcase	**zhěntóu tào**	枕头套
sheet	**chuángdān**	床单

Please change them/it.
qǐng huàn yīxia. 请换一下。

My room number is ...
wǒ zhù ... hào fángjiān 我住 ... 号房间。

I'd like to change to another room.
wǒ yào huàn fángjiān 我要换房间。

CHECKING OUT   结帐

We'd like to check out ...	**wǒmen ... yào zǒu**	我们 ... 要走
now	**xiànzài**	现在
at noon today	**jīntiān zhōngwǔ**	今天中午
tomorrow	**míngtiān**	明天

I'm returning ...	**wǒ ... huílái**	我 ... 回来
tomorrow	**míngtiān**	明天
the day after tomorrow	**hòutiān**	后天
in a few days	**jǐtiān yǐhòu**	几天以后

Can I leave my bags here?
xínglǐ néng bùnéng 行李能不能
cún zài zhèr? 存在这儿？

Please prepare my bill.
qǐng jiézhàng 请结帐。

Can I pay by travellers cheque?
  kěyǐ fù lǚxíng zhīpiào ma?   可以付旅行支票吗？
There's a mistake in the bill.
  zhàngdān shàng yǒu cuòwù   帐单上有错误。

LAUNDRY   洗衣服务

Many Chinese hotels have a laundry service, and most of the larger, more expensive ones have a dry-cleaning service as well. However, the laundry service in Chinese hotels is often expensive. Laundries on the street usually charge by the kilo and charge prices comparable to western countries.

Is there somewhere to wash clothes?
  shénme dìfang xǐ yīfu?   什么地方洗衣服？

Could I have these clothes ..., please?	**qǐng bǎ zhèixiē yīfu ...**	请把 这些衣服 ...
dry-cleaned	**gānxǐ**	干洗
ironed	**yùn hǎo**	熨好
washed	**xǐ gānjìng**	洗干净

When will they be ready?
  shénme shíhòu néng xǐhǎo?   什么时候能洗好？

I need it ...	**wǒ ... xūyào**	我 ... 需要。
today	**jīntiān**	今天
tomorrow	**míngtiān**	明天
the day after tomorrow	**hòutiān**	后天

Is my laundry ready?
  wǒde yīfu xǐhǎo le ma?   我的衣服洗好了吗？
This isn't mine.
  zhè búshì wǒde   这不是我的。
There's a piece missing.
  shǎole yījiàn   少了一件。

ACCOMMODATION

air-conditioning	kōngtiáo	空调
bathroom	yùshì	浴室
bed	chuáng	床
bill	zhàngdān	帐单
blanket	tǎnzi	毯子
bucket	shuǐtǒng	水桶
candle	làzhú	蜡烛
chair	yǐzi	椅子
cot	értóngchuáng	儿童床
dining room	cāntīng	餐厅
double bed	shuāngrénchuáng	双人床
electricity	diàn	电
fan (electric)	diànshàn	电扇
key	yàoshí	钥匙
lamp	dēng	灯
lift (elevator)	diàntī	电梯
light bulb	dēngpào	灯泡
lock	suǒ	锁
mattress	chuángdiàn	床垫
mosquito coil	wénxiāng	蚊香
pillow	zhěntóu	枕头
quiet	ānjìng	安静
reception	fúwùtái	服务台
receipt	shōujù	收据
sheet	chuángdān	床单
shower	línyù	淋浴
soap	féizào	肥皂
suitcase	yīxiāng	衣箱
table	zhuōzi	桌子
toilet	cèsuǒ	厕所
toilet paper	wèishēngzhǐ	卫生纸
window	chuānghù	窗户

AROUND TOWN　市内

Most modern Chinese cities bear little resemblance to the China often depicted in the west – mazes of winding alleyways lined with picturesque wooden dwellings. Modern China is a world of boulevards and grey concrete, and most of the old buildings still standing are those built by westerners in cities like Shanghai, Wuhan and Tianjin.

Construction projects, fuelled by a booming market economy, are everywhere. Stretches of major boulevards and entire streets are being levelled to widen streets or put in elevated road systems, leaving traffic to jostle and bounce through the dust and dirt.

Unfortunately, urban development programs have advanced at the expense of the environment – Beijing's air is so bad that you can't see the sun for most of the year. The virtual reconstruction of China's cities that's taken place over the last 40 years has at least one advantage for the visitor, though. The grid-like street plan of many cities makes finding your way around a little simpler, even if there often isn't much to look at along the way.

LOOKING FOR ...　　　寻找 ...

I want to go to the ...
　　wǒ xiǎng qù ...　　　我想去 ...

Excuse me, where's the nearest ...?
　　qǐng wèn, zuìjìnde　　请问，最近的
　　... zài nǎr?　　　　　... 在哪儿？

I'm looking for the/a(n) ...	wǒ zhǎo ...	我找 ...
bank	yínháng	银行
cinema	diànyǐngyuàn	电影院
city centre	shì zhōngxīn	市中心
consulate	lǐngshìguǎn	领事馆
(Australian)	(àodàlìyà)	(澳大利亚)
embassy	dàshǐguǎn	大使馆
free market	zìyóu shìchǎng	自由市场
hotel	lǚguǎn	旅馆
library	túshūguǎn	图书馆
market	shìchǎng	市场
night market	yèshì	夜市
police	jǐngchá	警察
post office	yóujú	邮局
public telephone	gōngyòng diànhuà	公用电话
public toilet	gōnggòng cèsuǒ	公共厕所
university	dàxué	大学
zoo	dòngwùyuán	动物园
When does it open?	jǐdiǎn kāi mén?	几点开门？
When does it close?	jǐdiǎn guān mén?	几点关门？

AT THE BANK   在银行

As well as at banks and the foreign exchange counters of large hotels, you can exchange money at many Friendship Stores and some of the larger department stores. US dollars are still the easiest to exchange. The exchange rate for travellers cheques is often better than what you'll get for cash. Automatic teller machines in China can presently only be used by those with accounts at local banks.

It's possible to obtain money with a credit card at banks that cater to international clients. It makes banking somewhat of a pain, but it means you don't have to travel with travellers cheques. If you want to pay by personal cheque, you'll have to open a local account.

I'd like to change some money. *wor shyahng hoowan chyer*
wǒ xiǎng huàn qián 我想换钱。

I'd like to change some
travellers cheques.
wǒ xiǎng duìhuàn
lǚxíng zhīpiào *lncheeng* 我想兑换
旅行支票。*Jeep inow*

What's the exchange rate?
duìhuànlǜ shì duōshǎo? 兑换率是多少？

Can you cash a personal cheque?
kěyǐ duìhuàn sīrén 可以兑换私人
zhīpiào ma? 支票吗？

I'm expecting some money from ...
wǒ zhèngzài děng cóng ... 我正在等从 ...
huíláide yībǐ qián 汇来的一笔钱。

Could you write it down for me?
nǐ néng bùnéng 你能不能
xiěxiàlai gěi wǒ? 写下来给我？

MONEY TALKS

rénmínbì	民币	RMB Chinese currency (lit: people's money)
yuán	元	basic unit of RMB
kuài	块	colloquial word for yuán
jiǎo	角	unit of currency (10 jiǎo = 1 yuán)
máo	毛	colloquial word for jiǎo
fēn	分	cent (10 fēn = 1 jiǎo)

AROUND TOWN

I'd like to change | **wǒ xiǎng duìhuàn** | 我想兑换
some ... | **diǎnr ...** | 点儿 ...
US $ | **měiyuán** | 美元
UK £ | **yīngbàng** | 英镑
Hong Kong $ | **gǎngbì** | 港币

Canadian $	jiāyuán	加元
Australian $	àoyuán	澳元
Deutschmarks	mǎkè	马克
Japanese yen	rìyuán	日元
bankdraft	yínhánghuìpiào	银行汇票
banknote	chāopiào	钞票
cash	xiànjīn	现金
cashier	chū nà yuán	出纳员
credit card	xìnyòngkǎ	信用卡
exchange	duìhuàn	兑换
loose change	língqián	零钱
signature	qiānmíng	签名

AT THE POST OFFICE   在邮局

The postal service in China is reasonably efficient, but it's a good idea to send parcels from large cities, where post offices handle greater volumes of international mail. Theoretically, postal rates are uniform throughout China, but rates can differ between post offices. Don't expect postal workers to speak English.

AROUND TOWN

THEY MAY SAY ...

You might hear either of these responses when asking if something is available.

méi yǒu	There aren't any.
méi yǒu bànfǎ	There's no way.

In reply, you could try saying:

There is a way.	yǒu bànfǎ
There definitely is/are.	kěndìng yǒu
Truly, aren't there any?	zhēnde méiyǒu ma
It's impossible that there aren't any.	bù kěnéng méiyǒu

Post offices require international packages to be left unsealed, so it's a good idea to send any correspondence separately. Each worker has his or her own role, so don't be shocked if you're told the person who sells stamps didn't come to work and that you'll have to come back the next day. Boxes and wrapping materials are sold at some post offices.

All customs forms are written in Chinese and French. If you can't read French, there's sure to be someone nearby who can help fill out the form.

'd like to send a ...	wǒ xiǎng jì ...	我想寄 ...
letter	xìn	信
parcel	bāoguǒ	包裹

'd like to send a telegram.
wǒ xiǎng fā diànbào   我想发电报。

'd like to send this letter to ...
zhèifēng xìn wǒ xiǎng jìdào ...   这封信我想寄到 ...

How much is it
to send it to (Australia)?
jìdào (àodàlìyà) yào   寄到 (澳大利)
duōshǎo qián?   要多少钱?

(See page 45 for names of countries.)

'd like to buy a/an ...	wǒ xiǎng mǎi ...	我想买 ...
aerogram	hángkōng yóujiǎn	航空邮简
airmail envelope	hángkōngxìn	航空信
envelope	xìnfēng	信封
postcard	míngxìnpiàn	明信片
stamp	yóupiào	邮票

I'd like to send it by ...	**wǒ xiǎng jì ...**	我想寄 ...
airmail	**hángkōng**	航空
express mail	**tèkuài**	特快
registered mail	**guàhàoxìn**	挂号信
surface mail	**píngyóu**	平邮

mail box	**xìnxiāng**	信箱
postcode	**yóuzhèng biānmǎ**	邮政编码
poste restante	**cúnjú hòulǐng**	存局候领

TELECOMMUNICATIONS   电信

Most hotel rooms have phones from which you can make local calls free of charge. Domestic and international long-distance calls can be made from telecommunications offices. Reverse-charge calls are often cheaper than calls paid for in China.

International credit card calls with a specified number for separate carriers can be made in most major cities. Some smaller cities, towns, and even individual hotels and hostels can connect with an international phone line without going through an operator.

I'd like to make a long-distance
(international) call to ...
    wǒ xiǎng gěi ... dǎge   我想给 ... 打个
    (guójì) chángtú diànhuà   (国际)长途电话。
The number is ...
    diànhuà hàomǎ shì ...   电话号码是 ...
How much is it per minute?
    yìfēnzhōng duōshǎo qián?   一分钟多少钱？
What's the area code for ...?
    ... qū hào shì duōshǎo?   ... 区号是多少？

area code	**qūhào**	区号
answering machine	**lùyīn diànhuà jī**	录音电话机
dial tone	**bōhào yīn**	拨号音

AROUND TOWN

direct call	**jiàorén diànhuà**	叫人电话
engaged	**zhàn xiàn**	占线
operator	**zǒngjī**	总机
phonebook	**diànhuà bù**	电话簿
phonecard	**diànhuà kǎ**	电话卡
reverse-charge (collect) call	**duìfāng fùkuǎn diànhuà**	对方付款电话
(public) telephone	**(gōngyòng) diànhuà**	(公用)电话
urgent	**jǐnjí**	紧急

Making a Call 打电话

Hello.	**wéi**	喂。
Who's calling?	**nín shì shéi?**	您是谁？
It's ...	**wǒ shì ...**	我是 ...
He's/She's not here.	**tā bú zài**	他/她不在
I'll call back later.	**wǒ yǐhòu zài dǎ**	我以后再打。

Hello, do you speak English?
wéi, nǐ huì jiǎng yīngwén ma?
喂，你会讲英文吗？

Hello, is (Mr Li) there?
wéi, (lǐ xiānsheng) zài ma?
喂，(李先生)在吗？

Yes, hang on a minute.
tā zài, qǐng děng yīhuǐr
他在，请等一会儿。

Operator, I've been cut off.
zǒngjī, diànhuà duàn le
总机，电话断了。

AROUND TOWN

INTERNET   国际互联网

Internet cafes can be found throughout China, though mostly in large cities. Many only last for a year or two, so it's a good idea to ask around to find the nearest one. The quality of the cafes are as varied as their rates. Some are clean, well run, and even serve hot food and drinks. Others are dingy, dank, with cockroaches crawling out of the keyboards. Most expensive hotels have email facilities, but often at corporate prices.

Due to unreliable electricity supply and few external phone lines in outlying cities, some cafes lose email access for days on end. It's impossible to plug your hotel-room phone into your computer to send email, since rooms don't have dedicated lines and go through the switchboard for public security reasons. If you have access to a Chinese Internet service provider through a school or company, it's possible to send email by payphone or through a phone with a dedicated line. Access to some Internet sites is restricted.

AROUND TOWN

Do you have any computers available?

    yǒu méiyǒu diànnǎo
    kěyǐ yòng?
    有没有电脑
    可以用？

How much does it cost per hour to go online?

    kàn diànzǐ yóujiàn yī
    xiǎoshí duōshǎo qián?
    看电子邮件一
    小时多少钱？

Can I help me? My email has disconnected.

    kěyǐ bāng wǒ ma?
    wǒ diànzǐ yóujiàn
    hǎoxiàng duànxiàn le
    可以帮我吗？
    我的电子邮件
    好象断线了。

Can I check my own email account?

    wǒ chá yīxià zìjǐ de
    diànzǐ yóujiàn
    hǎoxiàng hù, hǎo ma?
    我查一下自己的
    email户，好吗？

Do you have access to ...?

    nǐmén yǒu ... ma?
    你们有 ... 吗？

Can you give me an email account?
**néng bùnéng gěi wǒ
yīge email hù?**
能不能给我
一个email户？

Is it possible to get an account with
a local Internet service provider?
**néng bùnéng nádào yíge
dāngdì yīntèwǎng
gōngsī de hù?**
能不能拿到一个
当地因特网
公司的户？

Do I have to pay if it doesn't
connect to the server I want?
**rúguǒ liánbúshàng wǒ
yào yòng de fúwùqì,
hái yào fùqián ma?**
如果联不上我
要用的服务器，
还要付钱吗？

Do you have a list of rates in English?
**yǒu méiyǒu yīngwén
jiàgédān?**
有没有英文
价格单？

This connection's really slow.
zhè fēicháng màn
这非常慢。

AROUND TOWN

SIGNS

入口	Rùkǒu	ENTRANCE
出口	Chūkǒu	EXIT
入场	Rùchǎng	ADMISSION
热/冷	Rè/Lěng	HOT/COLD
不得入内	Bù Dé Rùnèi	NO ENTRY
禁烟	Jìnyān	NO SMOKING
正在营业	Zhèngzài Yíngyè	OPEN
关门	Guānmén	CLOSED
禁止	Jìnzhǐ	PROHIBITED
已经预定	Yùdìng	RESERVED
公共厕所	Gōnggòng Cèsuǒ	PUBLIC TOILET

SIGHTSEEING   观光

Excuse me, what's that ...?	qǐngwèn, nèige ... shì shénme?	请问，那个 ... 是什么？
building	fángwū	房屋
monument	jìniànbēi	纪念碑
park	gōngyuán	公园

Do you have a local map?
    yǒu dāngdì dìtú ma?
有当地地图吗？

Can I take photographs?
    wǒ néng bùnéng
    zhàoxiàng?
我能不能
照相？

Can I take your photograph?
    wǒ kěyǐ gěi nǐ zhàoxiàng ma?
我可以给你照相吗？

Could you take my photograph?
    nǐ néng gěi wǒ
    zhàoxiàng ma?
你能给我
照相吗？

I'll send you the photos later.
    yǐhòu wǒ bǎ
    zhàopiàn jì gěi nǐ
以后我把
照片寄给你。

Please write down your name and address.
    qǐng xiěxià nǐde
    míngzi hé dìzhǐ
请写下你的
名字和地址。

What time does it open?		
jǐdiǎn kāi mén?		几点开门？
What time does it close?		
jǐdiǎn guān mén?		几点关门？

I'd like to see the/a(n) ...	**wǒ xiǎng kàn ...**	我想看 ...
ancient ...	**gǔlǎode ...**	古老的 ...
art gallery	**měishùguǎn**	美术馆
beach	**hǎitān**	海滩
church	**jiàotáng**	教堂
mosque	**qīngzhēnsì**	清真寺
museum	**bówùguǎn**	博物馆
palace	**gōngdiàn**	宫殿
statue	**diāoxiàng**	雕像
Taoist temple	**dàojiào guàn**	道教观
temple	**sìmiào**	寺庙

STREET SIGNS

Many street signs in China are written in both Pinyin and Chinese characters, which is a tremendous help to foreigners. However, the name of a single street in a major city often changes to indicate its location.

This is particularly the case in Beijing, where one major street begins at one end with the name **Fùxíng Lù**, then becomes **Fùxíngmén wài Dàjiē** (indicating that it's outside Fuxing Gate). It then becomes **Fùxíngmén Nèi Dàjiē** (indicating it is inside Fuxing Gate), and further on becomes **Chang an Jie**, Beijing's central boulevard which runs in front of Tiananmen. Later it's called **Jiàn guó mén Nèi Dàjiē** (indicating that it's inside Jianguo Gate), then **Jiàn guó mén Wài Dàjiē** (outside Jianguo Gate), and so on. And it's one very straight street.

wài	outside	外
nèi	inside	内
mén	gate	门
dàjiē	boulevard (lit: big street)	大街

AROUND TOWN

Ānhuī	安徽
Běijīng	北京
Fújiàn	福建
Gānsù	甘肃
Guǎngdōng	广东
Guǎngxī	广西
Guìzhōu	贵州
Hǎinán Dǎo (Hainan Island)	海南岛
Héběi	河北
Hēilóngjiāng	黑龙江
Hénán	河南
Húběi	湖北
Húnán	湖南
Nèi Měnggǔ (Inner Mongolia)	内蒙古
Jiāngsū	江苏
Jiāngxī	江西
Jílín	吉林
Liáoníng	辽宁
Shǎnxī	陕西
Shāndōng	山东
Shǎnxī (Shaanxi)	山西
Sìchuān	四川
Tiānjīn	天津
Xiāng Gǎng (Hong Kong)	香港
Xīzàng (Tibet)	西藏
Xīnjiāng	新疆
Yúnnán	云南
Zhèjiāng	浙江

INTERESTS

Don't expect people in China to be as forthright with their opinions as westerners. The years of upheaval that saw children turning in their parents, and friends turning in friends, has led many people to be wary of anything but superficial conversation with those they don't know well.

COMMON INTERESTS

共同兴趣

What do you do in your spare time?
nǐ yèyú shíjiān zuò shénme?   你业余时间做什么？

I like ...	**wǒ xǐhuān ...**	我喜欢 ...
I don't like ...	**wǒ bù xǐhuān ...**	我不喜欢 ...
Do you like ...?	**nǐ xǐhuān ... ma?**	你喜欢 ...

Can you show me how to play ...?
kě bù kěyǐ gàosù   可不可以告诉
wǒ zěnme wán ...?   我怎么玩 ...？

art	**yìshù**	艺术
billiards	**táiqiú**	台球
chess	**xiàngqí**	象棋
Chinese ...	**zhōng ...**	中 ...
cooking	**pēngtiáo**	烹调
cards	**pūkè pái**	扑克牌
dancing	**tiàowǔ**	跳舞
drawing	**huà huàr**	画画
gardening	**yuányì**	园艺
going out	**wàichū yúlè**	外出娱乐
mahjong	**májiàng**	麻将
movies	**diànyǐng**	电影
music	**yīnyuè**	音乐
painting	**huìhuà**	绘画
photography	**shèyǐng**	摄影
pool	**dànzǐqiú**	弹子球

reading	yuèdú	阅读
sculpture	diāokè	雕刻
sewing	féngrèn	缝纫
shopping	gòuwù	购物
theatre	jùyuàn	剧院
travelling	lǚyóu	旅游
TV	diànshì	电视
western ...	xī ...	西 ...

I'd like to see an/the art exhibition.
wǒ xiǎng kàn yìshù zhǎnlǎn　　我想看艺术展览。

Who are your favourite Chinese/
western authors?
nǐ zuì xǐhuān de zhōngguó/　　你最喜欢的中国/
xīfāng zuòjiā shì shéi?　　西方作家是谁？

Are you interested in fengshui?
nǐ duì fēngshuǐ gǎn　　你对风水感
xìngqù ma?　　兴趣吗？

Can you explain fengshui to me?
nǐ néng gěi wǒ jiěshì　　你能给我解释
yīxià fēngshuǐ ma?　　一下风水吗？

Very interesting!	hěn yǒu yìsi!	很有意思！
Really?	zhēnde?	真的？
Amazing!	zhēn liǎobùqǐ!	真了不起！
So-so.	mǎmǎhūhū	马马虎虎
Not possible.	bù kěnéng	不可能。

MUSIC　　　　　　　　　　　　　音乐

What music do you like?
nǐ xǐhuān shénme yīnyuè　　你喜欢什么音乐？

Which bands do you like?
nǐ xǐhuān nǎxiē yuèduì?　　你喜欢哪些乐队？

Do you play an instrument?
nǐ yǎnzòu yuèqì ma?　　你演奏乐器吗？

I'd like to see the Chinese
(Beijing) opera.
wǒ xiǎng kàn jīngjù　　我想看京剧。

INTERESTS

CHINESE ROCK

Chinese rock music developed under the lead of Cuī Jiàn and his band 'The Honking Donkeys'. One of the great supporters of Chinese rock was Dèng Xiaoping's son Dèng Pǔfāng, who's been confined to a wheelchair since being thrown out of his university dorm window during the Cultural Revolution.

China has been fairly successful in bringing Taiwanese pop singers to China. The patriotic song 'Descendants of the Dragon' was banned in Taiwan after its author moved to China, where his song became, and remains, a mega hit. And after the singer of the Taiwan nationalistic song Zhōnghúa Mín Gǔo, 'The Republic of China', sought Chinese citizenship, one crucial word of the song was changed to make it Zhōnghúa Mínzǔ, 'The Chinese Nationality. The song became a communist torchbearer.

Are there any performances
this time of year?

xiànzài yǒu yǎnchū méi yǒu?		现在有演出没有？

I'd like to reserve	**wǒ xiǎng**	我想
tickets for ... show.	**dìng ... piào**	订 ... 票。
this evening's	**jīntiān wǎnshàngde**	今天晚上的
tomorrow evening's	**míngtiān wǎnshàngde**	明天晚上的

band	**yuèduì**	乐队
classical music	**gǔdiǎn yīnyuè**	古典音乐
concert	**yīnyuè huì**	音乐会
gig	**tèyuē yǎnzòu**	特约演奏
jazz	**juéshì yuè**	爵士乐
karaoke bar	**kǎlā ok bā**	卡拉OK吧
local opera	**dìfāngxì**	地方戏
music	**yīnyuè**	音乐
musician	**yīnyuè jiā**	音乐家
opera	**xìjù**	戏剧
opera house	**jùyuàn**	剧院

INTERESTS

orchestra	guǎnxiányuè	管弦乐
Beijing (Peking) opera	jīngjù	京剧
popular music	liúxíng yīnyuè	流行音乐
singer	gēshǒu	歌手
stage	wǔtái	舞台
tickets	piào	票
venue	chángsuǒ	场所

NIGHTLIFE
夜生活

China's nightlife, or wǎnshàng yúlèjiémù, is improving rapidly. Bars, nightclubs and karaoke parlours are springing up in all major cities, and more cultural events are being held. The Chinese are also becoming avid bowlers, and many hotels now have bowling alleys. Although many restaurants close around 8 or 9 pm, a number of food stands offering snacks congregate in the night markets.

What's there to do in the evenings?
  wǎnshàng yǒu
  shénme yúlè jiémù?
  晚上有
  什么娱乐节目？

Is there a nightclub here?
  zhèr yǒu dísīkē ma?
  这儿有迪斯科吗？

Where are the best discos around here?
  zhèr zuìhǎode
  dísīkē zài nǎr?
  这儿最好
  的迪斯科在哪儿？

How much is it to get in?
  ménpiào duōshǎo qián?
  门票多少钱？

Shall we dance?
  wǒmén qù tiàowǔ, hǎoma?
  我们去跳舞，好吗？

Can I buy a tape of this music?
  wǒ néng mǎi zhèige
  yīnyuède lùyīndài ma?
  我能买这个
  音乐的录音带吗？

I like this place!
  wǒ xǐhuān zhèr!
  我喜欢这儿！

INTERESTS

I don't like the music here.

    wǒ bù xǐhuān zhèr de yīnyuè.   我不喜欢这儿的音乐。

Shall we go somewhere else?

    wǒmén qù biéde   我们去别的

    dìfāng, hǎo ma?   地方，好吗？

CINEMA & THEATRE   影院与剧场

I'd like to go to the ...	wǒ xiǎng qù ...	我想去 ...
cinema	diànyǐngyuàn	电影院
theatre	jùchǎng	剧场

I'd like to see a(n) ...	wǒ xiǎng kàn ...	我想看 ...
acrobatic troupe	zájìtuán	杂技团
movie	diànyǐng	电影
song and dance troupe	gēwǔtuán	歌舞团

Are there any foreign films showing?

    xiànzài yǒu méi yǒu   现在有没有

    wàiguó diànyǐng?   外国电影？

Are there any Chinese comedians
performing here?

    zhèr biǎoyǎn   这儿表演

    xiāngshēng ma?   相声吗？

SPORT   体育运动

The Chinese are great sports enthusiasts. All you have to do is switch on the television in China to see events as diverse as world championship ping pong, football, badminton, volleyball, gymnastics, billiards, swimming, chess, athletics, American football, ice skating, skiing, and more.

Chinese sports fans are prone to pandemonium (similar to the chaos caused by the first pandas exhibited in the London Zoo, which gave rise to the term). In China, football matches sometimes end in small riots, and when the Chinese women's volleyball team beat the US team in 1982, fans marched on the US embassy in Beijing.

INTERESTS

Do you like playing sport?
nǐ xǐhuān cānjiā 你喜欢参加
tǐyù yùndòng ma? 体育运动吗？

I like playing sport.
wǒ xǐhuān cānjiā 我喜欢参加
tǐyù yùndòng 体育运动。

I prefer to watch rather than play sport.
bǐqǐ cānjiā tǐyù yùndòng, 比起参加体育运动，
wǒ gèng xǐhuān kàn 我更喜欢看。

I'd like to see a martial arts competition.
wǒ xiǎngkàn gōngfū bǐsài 我想看功夫比赛。

Where I can study martial arts?
wǒ zài nǎr kěyí xuéxí gōngfū? 我在哪儿可以学习功夫？

Do you play ...?	**nǐ cānjiā ... ma?**	你参加 ... 吗？
Would you	**nǐ xiǎng**	你想参
like to play ...?	**cānjiā ... ma?**	加 ... 吗？
basketball	**lán qiú**	篮球
football	**zú qiú**	足球
golf	**gāoěrfū qiú**	高尔夫球
rock climbing	**pānyán**	攀岩
rugby	**gǎnlǎn qiú**	橄榄球
scuba diving	**sīkùbā qiánshuǐ**	斯库巴潜水
skiing	**huáxuě**	滑雪
soccer	**guójì zúqiú**	国际足球
surfing	**chōnglàng**	冲浪
swimming	**yóuyǒng**	游泳
table tennis	**pīngpāng qiú**	乒乓球
tennis	**wǎng qiú**	网球

See pages 152 to 154 in In the Country for hiking terms.

INTERESTS

POLITICS   政治

I'm (not) interested in politics.
  wǒ duì zhèngzhì
  (méi) yǒu xìngqù

我对政治
（没）有兴趣。

Who are the Chinese leaders
you respect most?
  nǐ zuì pèifú de zhōngzuó
  lǐngdǎo shì něi wèi?

你最佩服的中国
领导是哪位？

Are you a member of the
Communist party?
  nǐ shì dǎngyuán ma?

你是党员吗？

What happened to you during the
(Cultural Revolution)?
  (wén'gé) de shíhòu, nǐ
  fāshēng le shénme shìqíng?

（文革）的时候，你
发生了什么事情？

What do you think of the ...?	nǐ rènwéi ... zěnme yàng?	你认为 ... 怎么样？
Adolf Hitler		希特勒
Chiang Kai-shek; Jiǎng Jièshí		蒋介石
Confucius		孔子
Dèng Xiǎopíng		邓小平
Hú Yàobāng		胡耀邦
Henry Kissinger		基辛格
Jiāng Qīng (Madame Máo)		江青
Kim Ilsong (deceased long-time leader of North Korea)		金日成
Léi Fēng		雷锋
Lín Biāo (Máo's attempted assassin)		林彪
Máo Zédōng		毛泽东
Margaret Thatcher		撒切尔
Richard Nixon		尼克松
Ronald Reagan		里根

INTERESTS

What do you think of (the) ...?	nǐ rènwéi ... zěnmeyàng	你认为 ... 怎么样?
air/water pollution	kōngqì/shuǐ wūrǎn	空气/水污染
autonomous regions	zìzhìqū	自治区
Chinese Communist Party	zhōng guó gòng chǎn dǎng	中国共产党
Hong Kong	xiāng gǎng	香港
human rights	rén quán	人权
market reforms	shì chǎng gǎi gé	市场改革
one child policy	dúshēng zǐnǚ zhèngcè	独生子女政策
opening of China	zhōng guó kāi fàng	中国开放
Three Gorges Dam	sān xiá dà bà	三峡大坝
Tiananmen turmoil	Tiānānmén fēng bō	天安门风波

ASTROLOGY   占星

As with the western system of astrology, the Chinese zodiac has 12 signs. Signs are based on the year, rather than the month, in which you were born, and run on a 12-year cycle. Still, this is a simplification. The exact day and time of birth is also carefully considered in charting an astrological path.

Each sign is named after an animal which is supposed to represent the main characteristics of people born under its sign.

When's your birthday?
nǐde shēngrì shì něi tiān?   你的生日是哪天?
I don't believe in astrology.
wǒ bù xiāngxìn zhànxīngshù   我不相信占星术。
What zodiac sign are you?
nǐde xīngzuò shì nǎge?   你的星座是哪个?

WORKING OUT YOUR ZODIAC SIGN

If you want to know your Chinese zodiac sign, look up the year you were born in this chart.

Rat	1924	1936	1948	1960	1972	1984	1996
Ox/Cow	1925	1937	1949	1961	1973	1985	1997
Tiger	1926	1938	1950	1962	1974	1986	1998
Rabbit	1927	1939	1951	1963	1975	1987	1999
Dragon	1928	1940	1952	1964	1976	1988	2000
Snake	1929	1941	1953	1965	1977	1989	2001
Horse	1930	1942	1954	1966	1978	1990	2002
Goat	1931	1943	1955	1967	1979	1991	2003
Monkey	1932	1944	1956	1968	1980	1992	2004
Rooster	1933	1945	1957	1969	1981	1993	2005
Dog	1934	1946	1958	1970	1982	1994	2006
Pig	1935	1947	1959	1971	1983	1995	2007

I'm a ...	wǒ shǔ ...	我属 ...
Rat	shǔ	鼠
Ox/Cow	niú	牛
Tiger	hǔ	虎
Rabbit	tù	兔
Dragon	lóng	龙
Snake	shé	蛇
Horse	mǎ	马
Goat	yáng	羊
Monkey	hóu	猴
Rooster	jī	鸡
Dog	gǒu	狗
Pig	zhū	猪

INTERESTS

BAD MANDARIN

Don't expect to use any of this language without repercussions – if you want a smooth trip, keep quiet if you hear this type of language and be on your way.

Arsehole!	pì yǎn! (lit: butt eye!)	屁眼！
Bastard!	wángbā dàn! (lit: turtle egg!)	王八蛋！
Bullshit!	fèi huà! (lit: garbage talk!)	废话
Fuck you!	cào nǐ! (lit: fuck you!)	操你！
Go screw your mother!	cào nǐ mā! (lit: fuck your mother!)	操你妈！
Moron!	bèn dàn! (lit: stupid egg!)	笨蛋！
Piss off!	qù nǐ de! (lit: go to your place!)	去你的！
Rubbish!	gǒu pì! (lit: dog fart!)	狗屁！
Screw you!	rì nǐ! (lit: drill you!)	日你！

SHOPPING

Department stores now sell imported goods, which were once the domain of Friendship Stores. The large Friendship Stores in Beijing, Shanghai and Canton are in a class of their own for their extraordinary range of goods. Imported goods have quite a high mark-up, and if there's anything like coffee or film that you can't do without, it's a good idea to bring it with you. You'll also find plenty of markets.

SHOPPING

LOOKING FOR ...　　　　　　　　寻找 ..

Where can I buy ...?
wǒ zài nǎr néng mǎidào ...?　　我在哪儿能买到 ...?
Where is a(n) ...?
... zài nǎr?　　　　　　　　　... 在哪儿?

Where's the nearest ...?	zuìjìnde ... zài nǎr?	最近的 ... 在哪儿?
antique shop	gǔdǒngdiàn	古董店
bakery	miànbāodiàn	面包店
bank	yínháng	银行
bookshop	shūdiàn	书店
camera shop	zhàoxiàng qìcái shāngdiàn	照相器材商店
delicatessen	shúshídiàn	熟食店
department store	bǎihuò shāngdiàn	百货商店
fish shop	yúdiàn	鱼店
free market	zìyóu shìchǎng	自由市场
Friendship Store	yǒuyì shāngdiàn	友谊商店
general store	záhuòdiàn	杂货店
greengrocer	shūcàidiàn	蔬菜店
laundry	xǐyīdiàn	洗衣店
market	shìchǎng	市场
music store	yīnxiàngdiàn	音像店
newsagent	bàokāntíng	报刊亭
optician	yǎnjìngdiàn	眼镜店
pharmacy	yàodiàn	药店
shop	shāngdiàn	商店
shopping centre	gòuwù zhōngxīn	购物中心
shoe shop	xiédiàn	鞋店
souvenir shop	jìniànpǐn shāngdiàn	纪念品商店
supermarket	chāojí shìchǎng	超级市场
tailor	cáiféngdiàn	裁缝店
travel agency	lǚxíngshè	旅行社

MAKING A PURCHASE 购买

I'd like to buy ...	wǒ xiǎng mǎi ...	我想买 ...
I'm just looking.	wǒ xiān kànkan	我先看看。
Can I see it?	néng kànkan ma?	能看看吗？
Show it to me.	gěi wǒ kànkan	给我看看。
Do you have others?	nǐ yǒu biéde ma?	你有别的吗？
Sir!	shīfu!	师傅！
I don't like it.	wǒ bù xǐhuān	我不喜欢。
I'll take (buy) it.	wǒ jiù mǎi zhèige	我就买这个。
Can I have a receipt?	qǐng gěi wǒ fāpiào	请给我发票。
Does it have a guarantee?	yǒu bǎodān ma?	有保单吗？
I'd like to return this please.	wǒ yào tuìhuò	我要退货。

How much does this cost?
zhèige dūoshǎo qián?　　　　　　这个多少钱？

Can you help me?
nǐ néng bāngzhù wǒ ma?　　　　你能帮助我吗？

Can you write down the price?
nǐ néng bùnéng bǎ　　　　　　你能不能把
jiàqián xiěxiàlái?　　　　　　价钱写下来？

Miss! (used in Taiwan and increasingly in China)
fúwùyuán!/xiǎojiě!　　　　　　服务员！/小姐！

Excuse me, could you help me please?
duìbùqǐ, máfán　　　　　　　对不起，麻烦
nǐ bāngzhù　　　　　　　　你帮助我，
wǒ, hǎo ma?　　　　　　　好吗？

I'd prefer something of better quality.
wǒ gèng xǐhuān zhìliàng　　　我更喜欢质量
hǎo yìdiǎnr de　　　　　　好一点儿的

Do you accept credit cards?
xìnyòngkǎ shōu bùshōu?　　　信用卡收不收？

Please wrap it for me.
qǐng gěi wǒ bāo yīxià　　　　请给我包一下。

SHOPPING

It's faulty.	yǒu máobìng	有毛病。
It's broken.	huài le	坏了。
I'd like my money back.	wǒ yào tuìkuǎn	我要退款。

BARGAINING   讲价

Government-run stores are almost always subjected to fixed prices, and bargaining is unlikely to get you anywhere. On the streets, however, bargaining skills can come in handy.

Bargaining is a game. Some people like it, some people hate it. The best thing to do is to shop around. Find the lowest price then try to get merchants to bid against each other. Underbid someone by half and see their reaction. When counter-bids are made, exaggerate your expression of outrage. Try to get merchants to smile. You can always bring down a price by buying several pieces. Walk away from a purchase and see how the merchant responds.

Remember the important concept of 'face' (see page 47) when you're bargaining for anything in China. Any direct challenge (such as 'don't try to cheat me', or words to that effect) is going to result in a situation where somebody has to lose face. This is sure to raise the odds and increase the excitement, but it could also lead to some unpleasantness. Keep smiling and try to keep your cool.

Can you reduce the price?
   néng piányi yīdiǎnr ma?   能便宜一点儿吗？
Do you give discounts?
   néng dǎzhé ma?   能打折吗？

SHOPPING

It's too expensive.
tài guì le

我给你 ... 快。

I'll give you ... yuan.
wǒ gěi nǐ ... kuài

太贵了。

You're kidding!
kāi wánxiào!

开玩笑！

discount
zhékòu

折扣

HAND SYMBOLS

Finger counting is widely used in China, in conjunction with the spoken number when shopping or bargaining. However, there's some regional variation. The number one is indicated by holding up the index finger, two by raising the index and third finger, and so on up to five. The sign for six is made by extending the thumb and pinky.

The sign for seven is made by extending the first two fingers and placing them on the tip of your thumb of the same hand. A variation for seven is to use the thumb and index finger to make the number seven with the forefinger pointing down. The sign for eight uses the same fingers, but with the hand rotated so that the fingers form a moustache shape. This is the shape of the character for number eight.

The number nine is indicated by making a fist then raising the index finger and crooking it.

The most common symbol for the number 10 is to make a cross using both your index fingers. However, in many parts of China, the sign for the number '10' is made with a clenched fist, symbolising a rock. The word for rock is **shí**, the same sound that's used for 10.

Other common hand signals, which are used to indicate excellence, are the 'thumbs-up' sign, and the signal made by gently pulling the earlobe between the thumb and index finger.

SHOPPING

COUNTING SYMBOLS

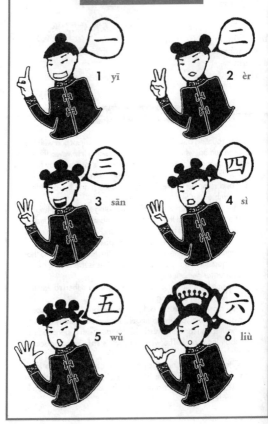

SHOPPING

COUNTING SYMBOLS

7 qī

8 bā

9 jiǔ

10 shí

ALTERNATIVES

7 qī

8 bā

10 shí

SHOPPING

ESSENTIAL GROCERIES   必备杂货

Where can I find the ...?	nǎr yǒu ...?	哪儿有 ...?
I'd like some ...	wǒ yào ...	我要 ...
batteries	diànchí	电池
bread	miànbāo	面包
butter	huángyóu	黄油
candles	làzhú	蜡烛
cheese	nǎilào	奶酪
eggs	jīdàn	鸡蛋
flour	miànfěn	面粉
matches	huǒchái	火柴
milk	niúnǎi	牛奶
olive oil	gǎnlǎn yóu	橄榄油
pepper	hújiāo	胡椒
salt	yán	盐
washing powder	xǐyīfěn	洗衣粉

SOUVENIRS   纪念品

Please show me some ...	qǐng gěi wǒ kànkan ...	请给 我看看 ...
calligraphy	shūfǎ	书法
carpets	dìtǎn	地毯
chinaware	cíqì	瓷器
chopsticks	kuàizi	筷子
earrings	ěrhuán	耳环
embroidery	xiùhuā zhìpǐn	绣花制品
fabrics	bùliào	布料
fans	shànzi	扇子
furniture	jiājù	家具
jade products	yùshí zhìpǐn	玉石制品
jewellery	zhūbǎo shǒushì	珠宝首饰
lacquerware	qīqì	漆器
musical instruments	yuèqì	乐器

paintings	huà	画
paper cuts	jiǎnzhǐ	剪纸
porcelain	cíqì	瓷器
pottery	táoqì	陶器
scrolls	juánzhóu	嫣卷轴
silk products	sīzhīpǐn	丝织品

SHOPPING

CLOTHING

衣服

backpack	bèibāo	背包
bathing suit	yóuyǒngyī	游泳衣
blouse	nǚchènshān	女衬衫
bra	rǔzhào	乳罩
button	niǔkòu	钮扣
cap	màozi	帽子
clothing	yīfu	衣服
coat	dàyī	大衣
dress	liányīqún	连衣裙
dressing gown	chényī	晨衣
gloves	shǒutào	手套
handbag	shǒutíbāo	手提包
hat	lǐmào	礼帽
jacket	shàngyī	上衣
jeans	niúzǎikù	牛仔裤
jumper	máoyī	毛衣
pyjamas	shuìyī	睡衣
raincoat	yǔyī	雨衣
sandals	liángxié	凉鞋
scarf	wéijīn	围巾
shirt	chènshān	衬衫
shoes	xié	鞋
shorts	duǎnkù	短裤
silk stockings	sīwà	丝袜
skirt	qúnzi	裙子
socks	wàzi	袜子
stockings	chángwà	长袜

SHOPPING

suit	xīfú	西服
swimming suit	yóuyǒngyī	游泳衣
trousers	chángkù	长裤
T-shirt	tīxùshān	体恤衫
underpants	nèikù	内裤

I'd like something like this.
  wǒ yào zhèige yàngzi de   我要这个样子的。

Can you show me another one?
  zài gěi wǒ kàn yījiàn, hǎo ma?   再给我看一件，好吗？

Can I try it on?
  wǒ kěyǐ shìshi ma?   我可以试试吗？

Is there a mirror?
  yǒu jìngzi ma?   有镜子吗？

It fits well.
  hěn héshì   很合适。

It doesn't fit.
  bù héshì   不合适。

It's too ...	tài ... le	太 ... 了。
big	dà	大
small	xiǎo	小
long	cháng	长
short	duǎn	短
loose	sōng	松
tight	jǐn	紧

Can it be altered?
  néng bùnéng gǎi yīxià?   能不能改一下？

MATERIALS

材料

brass	**huángtóng**	黄铜
ceramic	**táocí**	陶瓷
cotton	**miánbù**	棉布
handmade	**shǒugōngzhìde**	手工制的
glass	**bōli**	玻璃
gold	**jīn**	金
leather	**pígé**	皮革
linen	**yàmábù**	亚麻布
metal	**jīnshǔ**	金属
plastic	**sùliào**	塑料
satin	**duànzi**	缎子
silk	**sīchóu**	丝绸
silver	**yín**	银
synthetic	**héchéng**	合成
wood	**mùtou**	木头
wool	**chúnmáo**	纯毛

SHOPPING

THE GREAT MALL OF CHINA

Most tourist attractions have spawned a massive souvenir industry also known to some as the 'great mall of China'. When you arrive anywhere, say the Great Wall, you'll be besieged by people selling T-shirts, soft drinks, hats – the works.

If you climb the Great Wall for an hour, there'll be someone selling souvenirs. Go two hours, and there'll be another. If you want to be left alone, try placing your hands together as in Buddhist or Hindu prayer and saying the mantra of the Buddha of benevolence:

āmī tuófó　　　　　　　　阿弥陀佛

SHOPPING

COLOURS   颜色

black	hēisè	黑色
blue	lánsè	蓝色
brown	hèsè	褐色
dark	shēn	深
golden	jīnhuángsè	金黄色
green	lǜsè	绿色
grey	huīsè	灰色
light	qiǎn	浅
orange	júhóngsè	橘红色
pink	fěnhóngsè	粉红色
purple	zǐsè	紫色
red	hóngsè	红色
white	báisè	白色
yellow	huángsè	黄色

TOILETRIES   化妆品

aftershave	rùnfū xiāngshuǐ	润肤香水
comb	shūzi	梳子
dental floss	jiéyáxiàn	洁牙线
deodorant	chúchòujì	除臭剂
hairbrush	fàshuā	发刷
moisturiser	shīrùnjì	湿润剂
razor	tìxūdāo	剃须刀
razor blades	dāopiàn	刀片
shampoo	xiāngbō	香波
shaving cream	tìxūgāo	剃须膏
soap	xiāngzào	香皂
sunscreen	fángshàishuāng	防晒霜
tampons	yuèjīng miánsāi	月经棉塞
tissues	shǒujīnzhǐ	手巾纸
toilet paper	shǒuzhǐ	手纸
toothbrush	yáshuā	牙刷
toothpaste	yágāo	牙膏

FOR THE BABY

嬰儿用品

baby food	yīng ér shípǐn	嬰儿食品
baby powder	yīng ér shuǎngshēnfěn	嬰儿爽身粉
bib	wéixián	围涎
disposable nappies	yīcìxìng niàopiàn	一次性尿片
dummy (pacifier)	xiàngpí/sùliào nǎizuǐ	橡皮/塑料 奶嘴
formula	dàirǔpǐn	代乳品
nappy (diaper)	niàopiàn	尿片
nappy rash cream	niàobùzhěn rǔgāo	尿布疹乳膏
teat	nǎizuǐ	奶嘴

SHOPPING

ABACUS

The **suànpán**, or 'abacus', means literally a 'calculating plate' in Mandarin. It can be used to add, subtract, multiply and divide. Shopkeepers and street vendors use the **suànpán** to calculate sales, as they're faster than modern calculators. In fact, the **suànpán** served as a mathematic model for early electronic computers.

The standard **suànpán** is made of a wooden frame and beads, with a horizontal centre bar with two rows of beads above and five rows below. Each vertical row represents a multiple of ten. The beads in the rightmost column represent one unit. The beads in the subsequent columns to the left of the first column represent 10 units each, then 100 units, 1000 units, and finally 10,000 units. The beads in each row below the centre bar represent five units of that row.

The beads must be pushed against the centre bar to be counted. The bottom beads are pushed upwards to add value. The top beads are pushed downwards to add value. To subtract values, the beads are pushed away from the centre bar. The total is read using the centre bar, from left to right.

SHOPPING

STATIONERY & PUBLICATIONS   文具与出版物

Is there an English-language
bookshop nearby?
    fùjìn yǒu yīngwén shūdiàn ma?   附近有英文书店吗？
Do you have a copy of ...?
    nǐmen yǒu ... shū ma?   你们有 ... 书吗？
Do you know if this author is
translated into English?
    nǐ zhīdào zhège zuòjiā de   你知道这个作家的作
    zuòpǐn yìchéng yīngwén le ma?   品翻译成英文了吗？

address book	dìzhǐ bù	地址簿
adhesive tape	sùliào jiāodài	塑料胶带
calendar	rìlì	日历
colour marker	cǎibǐ	彩笔
dictionary	zìdiǎn	字典
drawing paper	túhuà zhǐ	图画纸
exercise book	liànxíběn	练习本
envelope	xìnfēng	信封
eraser	xiàngpí	橡皮
magazine	zázhì	杂志
... map	... dìtú	... 地图
city	chéngshì	城市
regional	dìqū	地区
newspaper	bàozhǐ	报纸
newspaper	(yīngwén) bàozhǐ	(英文)报纸
(English language)		
notebook	běnzi	本子
(English language)	(yīngwén)	(英文)
novel	xiǎoshuō	小说
pen (ballpoint)	yuánzhūbǐ	圆珠笔
pencil	qiānbǐ	铅笔
scissors	jiǎndāo	剪刀
wrapping paper	bāozhuāngzhǐ	包装纸
writing paper	xìnzhǐ	信纸

MUSIC 音乐

I'm looking for a ... CD.
wǒ yào zhǎo ... CD 我要找 ... CD。

What's the latest record by ...?
... zuìxīnde chàngpiàn
shì shénme? ... 最新的唱片是什么?

What music can you
recommend to take back to ...?
nǐ jiànyì yīng gāi dài
shénme yīnyuè huí ...? 你建议带什么音乐回 ...?

Can I listen to this CD here?
zhèipán CD néng
zài zhèr tīng ma? 这盘CD能在这儿听吗?

Do you	... shàng yǒu	... 上有这个吗?
have this on ...?	zhèige ma?	
cassette	cídài	磁带
CD	CD	CD
record	chàngpiàn	唱片

need (a) ...	wǒ yào ...	我要 ...
batteries	diànchí	电池
blank tape	kòngbái cídài	空白磁带
headphones	ěrjī	耳机

PHOTOGRAPHY 摄影

Although the Chinese are enthusiastic photographers, there's little in the way of photographic equipment for sale in China, although 'sure shot' cameras are fairly easy to come by. Film, especially slide film, is reasonably expensive to buy and process, and it can be difficult to find a place that processes or sells B&W film.

If your camera uses batteries, be sure to take spares, although AA and lithium batteries are readily available in major cities.

I'd like film for this camera.

SHOPPING

I'd like film for this camera.
**wǒ yào yījuǎn yòngzài
zhèizhǒng zhàoxiàngjīlǐ
de jiāojuǎr**

我要买一卷用在
这种照相机里
的胶卷。

How much do you charge
for processing?
**chōngxǐ zhèijuǎn
jiāojuǎn dūoshǎo qián?**

冲洗这卷
胶卷多少钱？

When will the pictures be ready?
**shénme shíhòu néng
chōngxǐ hǎo?**

什么时候能
冲洗好？

Can you fix cameras?
nǐmén xiū zhàoxiàngjī ma?

你们修照相机吗？

ASA	**měiguó biāozhǔn xiéhuì**	美国标准协会
B&W	**hēibáide**	黑白的
camera	**zhàoxiàngjī**	照相机
colour	**cǎisède**	彩色的
colour slide	**cǎisè huàndēngpiàn**	彩色幻灯片
film	**jiāojuǎr**	胶卷
flash	**shǎn guāng dēng**	闪光灯
lens	**jìngtóu**	镜头
lens cap	**jìngtóugài**	镜头盖
light metre	**cèguāngbiǎo**	测光表
shutter speed	**kuàimén sùdù**	快门速度

SMOKING   吸火

Smoking is still a popular pastime in China. Although there
are anti-smoking campaigns and 'no smoking' signs in most
public places, they're often unheeded.

SHOPPING

carton	yītiáo	一条
cigarettes	xiāngyān	香烟
cigarette papers	juǎnyānzhǐ	卷烟纸
filtered	guòlǜ	过滤
lighter	dǎhuǒjī	打火机
matches	huǒchái	火柴
menthol	bòhé xiāngyān	薄荷香烟
pipe	yāndǒu	烟斗
tobacco (rolling)	yāncǎo (juǎnyān)	烟草(卷烟)

No smoking.	bùzhǔn xīyān	不准吸烟。
I don't smoke.	wǒ búhuì xīyān	我不会吸烟。
Please don't smoke.	qǐngbié xīyān	请别吸烟。
Do you have a light?	yǒu huǒchái ma?	有火柴吗？

A packet of cigarettes, please.
qǐng gěi wǒ yībāo xiāngyān 请给我一包香烟。

Are these cigarettes strong/mild?
zhèixiē xiāngyān 这些香烟
jìng dà/xiǎo? 劲大/小？

Do you mind if I smoke?
wǒ xīyān nǐ jièyì ma? 我吸烟你介意吗？

I'm trying to give up.
wǒ zhèngzài jièyān 我正在戒烟。

WEIGHTS & MEASURES 重量与长度

milligram	háokè	毫克
gram	kè	克
kilogram	gōngjīn	公斤
millimetre	háomǐ	毫米
centimetre	límǐ	厘米
metre	mǐ	米
mile	yīnglǐ	英里
kilometre	gōnglǐ	公里
litre	shēng	升

SHOPPING

SIZES & COMPARISONS

大小比较

small	xiǎo	小
smaller	gèng xiǎo	更小
smallest	zuì xiǎo	最小
big	dà	大
bigger	gèng dà	更大
biggest	zuì dà	最大
heavy	zhòng	重
light	qīng	轻
more	duō	多
less	shǎo	少
enough	gòu	够
little/few	shǎo	少
a little bit	yìdiǎr	一点儿
many	hěn duō	很多
too much/many	tài duō	太多

When it's served in banquets or in high-class restaurants, Chinese cuisine is without doubt among the finest in the world. The long tradition of elevating cookery to an art form means that the modern Chinese are heirs to an astoundingly extensive range of cooking styles.

If you're watching every cent, it's likely that your diet will consist mainly of soup, noodles, rice and stirfried vegetables. However, it's worth checking the menus of some hotels and privately run restaurants, which are increasing in number as well as improving in quality.

breakfast	zǎo fàn	早饭
lunch	wǔ fàn	午饭
dinner	wǎn fàn	晚饭

VEGETARIAN MEALS

素食者

Even though the Chinese have a term for vegetarians, it's almost unheard of for a Chinese person to adopt a vegetarian diet by choice. Some travellers claim that the only way to make the Chinese understand that you're a strict vegetarian (and not keen on eating 'vegetable dishes' that have had most of the meat picked out of them) is to say you're Buddhist.

I'm vegetarian.	wǒ shì chīsù de	我是吃素的。
I don't eat meat.	wǒ bù chī ròu	我不吃肉。
I don't eat fish.	wǒ bù chī yú	我不吃鱼。
I'm a Buddhist.	wǒ shí fójiào tú	我是佛教徒。

BREAKFAST

早饭

A light breakfast isn't part of Chinese culture, and westerners often have a difficult time getting used to Chinese breakfast foods.

baozi

包子

steamed buns with various fillings

FOOD

cōngyóubǐng   葱油饼
   a small spring onion-flavoured chepati fried in oil

dòujiāng   豆浆
   sweet soy milk

dòushābāo   豆沙包
   sweet, steamed bean-paste bun

huāshēngmǐ   花生米
   peanuts

niú ròu gān   牛肉松
   dried, stringed beef

pàocài   泡菜
   pickled vegetables eaten with **xīfàn**

rè chá   热茶
   hot tea

shāobing   烧饼
   sesame seed pancake

tāngmiàn   汤面
   noodle soup

xīfàn/zhōu   稀饭/粥
   rice porridge

yóutiáo   油条
   fried bread sticks dripping in oil, which resemble doughnu
   but aren't sweet. They can be dipped in hot soy milk, and a
   delicious.

zhū ròusōng   猪肉松
   dried stringed pork

LUNCH & SNACKS   午饭与小吃

In general, most of the foods available for dinner can also b
eaten for lunch, but the latter tends to be a more restrained affa
than the all-out assault on the digestive tract that takes place i
the evening.

   Many Chinese have lunch at a snack shop, where the food
usually cheap, tasty and comes in small servings.

ái mǐfàn   白米饭
  steamed rice

háo fàn   炒饭
  fried rice

chāshāobāo   叉烧包
  steamed rolls filled with barbecued pork; eaten in southern
  China

guōtiē   锅贴
  fried dumplings

huājuǎn   花卷
  steamed roll, similar to **mántou**

húntun   馄饨
  small meat dumplings served in a soup, known in the west as
  'wonton'

mántóu   馒头
  plain steamed bun, a common staple in northern China

niúròu chǎomiàn   牛肉炒面
  beef stirfried noodles

shuǐjiǎo   水饺
  boiled dumplings usually filled with pork and/or vegetables

xiǎolóngbāo   小笼包
  small steamed dumplings usually filled with pork

zhēngjiǎo   蒸饺
  dumplings, like **shuǐjiǎo**, only steamed

FOOD

ARE YOU GAME?

A popular Chinese drinking game is called **huá quán**, meaning 'guess fingers'. It's something like the game 'rock, scissors, paper' but more difficult. The two opponents thrust their hand forward holding out a number of fingers. Contestants try to guess the combined number of fingers extended, and shout their guess in a high-pitched scream. A round of guessing lasts from five seconds to a minute, and the loser has to drink – and drink a lot.

AT THE RESTAURANT

在餐饣

In the days before economic reforms, it was very hard to fin
even one restaurant closeby. However, after Deng Xiaopir
shortened the working lunch break in 1985 from two or thre
hours to just one hour, most urban workers could no longer g
home to eat lunch, and restuarants opened everywhere.

A table for ... please.	... wèi	... 位。
Waiter!	fúwùyuán!	服务员!
I'd like ...	wǒ yào ...	我要 ...
I'm hungry.	wǒ è le	我饿了。
I'm thirsty.	wǒ kě le	我渴了。

Can I see the menu, please?
qǐng gěi wǒ kànkan càidān 请给我看看菜单。

Do you have a menu in English?
nǐmén yǒu yīngwén càidān ma? 你们有英文菜单吗?

What is this/that?
zhèi/nèi shì shénme? 这/那是什么?

Can you recommend a few dishes?
nǐ néng jièshào jǐge cài ma? 你能介绍几个菜吗?

Can I go to the kitchen to see what
vegetables you have?
wǒ kě bùkěyǐ dào chúfáng 我可不可以到厨房
kànkan nǐmén yǒu 看看你们有
shénme qīngcài? 什么青菜?

Another one, please!
qǐng zài lái yīge! 请再来一个!

Not too spicy, please.
qǐng búyào tài là 请不要太辣。

No monosodium glutimate
(MSG), please.
qǐng búyào fàng wèijīng 请不要放味精。

Please give me a knife and fork.
qǐng gěi wǒ chāzi hé dāozi 请给我叉子和刀子。

This isn't what I ordered.
zhè bú shì wǒ diǎn de cài 这不是我点的菜。

FOOD

The smell of this mutton is really strong.

zhèi yángròu de	这羊肉的
wèr hěn qiàng	味很呛。

The meal was delicious.

hǎochī jí le	好吃极了。

I'm full.

wǒ chībǎo le	我吃饱了。

The bill please.

qǐng jiézhàng	请结帐。

COMPLIMENTS TO THE CHEF

Your cooking is great!
nǐ zuò de cài zhēn hǎo chī!   你做的菜真好吃！
So delicious!
hǎo chī de hěn!   好吃的很！

FOOD

TYPICAL DISHES   典型菜肴

Poultry 禽类

běijīng kǎoyā   北京烤鸭
  Peking duck (difficult to get outside Beijing)

chénpí jī   陈皮鸡
  chicken cooked with dried tangerine peel

gōngbǎo jīdīng   宫保鸡丁
  a popular Sichuan dish consisting of chicken stirfried with
  peanuts and chillis

guàiwèi jī   怪味鸡
  (lit: strange-tasting chicken). In actual fact there's nothing
  strange about this chicken. It's prepared with a delicious
  pepper- and sesame-paste sauce.

húnán jī   湖南鸡
  chicken cooked Hunan-style

jiàngbào jīdīng   酱爆鸡丁
  marinated chicken breast stirfried in a special sauce

jiàohuā jī   叫化鸡
    known as 'beggar's chicken'. Marinated chicken wrapped i
    bamboo leaves and then roasted.

làzi jī   辣子鸡
    chilli chicken

qīngjiāo jīsī   青椒鸡丝
    chicken slices cooked with green pepper

xiāngsū yā/jī   香酥鸭/鸡
    crispy fried duck/chicken

FOOD

Pork 猪肉类

Pork is the meat most commonly eaten in China. If the meat i
a dish isn't specified, it's usually pork. In fact, the character fo
meat by itself means 'pork'.

báiqiē ròu   白切肉
    boiled pork eaten cold with various dips

dōngpō mēnròu   东坡闷肉
    pork fillet that's been marinated, boiled and steamed until it'
    as tender as bean curd. Dish created by the poet Dong Po.

gōngbǎo ròudīng   宫保肉丁
    shredded pork stirfried with chillis and peanuts

gǔlǎo ròu   古老肉
    sweet-and-sour pork

hóngshāo ròu   红烧肉
    (lit: red-cooked meat) a kind of stew made with a lightl
    sweetened dark soy sauce stock

huíguō ròu   回锅肉
    (lit: return-to-the-pot meat) a spicy pork dish for which the
    meat is first boiled and then stirfried

jiàngbào ròusī   酱爆肉丝
    marinated pork cooked in a special sauce

làzi ròudīng　　　　　　　　　　辣子肉丁
diced pork with chillis

mùěr ròu　　　　　　　　　　　　木耳肉
pork stirfried with wood ears (a kind of mushroom)

mùxū ròu　　　　　　　　　　　　木须肉
shredded pork and eggs with dried mushrooms

shīzi tóu　　　　　　　　　　　　狮子头
(lit: lion's head) meatballs served with cabbage

tángcù páigǔ　　　　　　　　　　糖醋排骨
sweet-and-sour spare ribs

yúxiāng ròusī　　　　　　　　　　鱼香肉丝
(lit: fish-flavoured meat) the rich flavour is produced by
stirfrying shredded pork with a liberal dollop of garlic, ginger
and chillis

FOOD

DON'T RACE YOUR RICE

In China, rice is a filler that's commonly eaten near the end
of a meal. At a banquet-style meal, the main dishes are the
important food – you could insult your host by asking for
rice first.

At a restaurant, you'll probably have to ask for rice if you
want it with your main dishes. Rice is placed in a small rice
bowl. When other food put on top, the rice absorbs the
juices. If you can't use chopsticks, use a soup spoon, as many
Chinese diners do.

Seafood　海鲜类

The word for fish, **yú**, also means 'plenty' or 'surplus', and is
traditionally given pride of place in celebratory banquets and in
feasts laid out for guests. If you're lucky enough to be invited
into a Chinese home for a meal, it's likely your hosts will pick
sparingly at the seafood while dolloping great spoonfuls into your
bowl. One way to make sure they eat some too is to reciprocate
by loading up their bowl.

gānshāo yú   干烧鱼
   fish braised with chillis and bean sauce
hóngshāo yú   红烧鱼
   red-cooked fish; the fish is braised in a soy sauce stock
qīngzhēng yú   清蒸鱼
   steamed fish; the fish is usually steamed in a marinade of soy
   sauce, garlic and spring onions
tángcù yú   糖醋鱼
   sweet-and-sour fish

Vegetables 蔬菜类

Simple vegetable dishes, like Chinese cabbage stirfried with garlic and soy sauce, are very popular with the Chinese and are considered a good accompaniment to meat dishes. Vegetarians travelling around China should always be able to find a restaurant that's able to prepare one of the following dishes.

báicài   白菜
   Chinese cabbage
chǎo gānlán   炒甘蓝
   stirfried broccoli
chǎo shíjǐn shūcài   炒什锦蔬菜
   stirfried mixed vegetables

FOOD

BOIL & BUBBLE

barbecued	tànhuǒkǎo	炭火烤
braised	gānshāo	干烧
deepfried	jiāozhà	焦炸
fried	zhà;	炸
roasted	kǎo	烤
stirfried	chǎo	炒
steamed	qīngzhēng	清蒸

hóngshāo dòufu	红烧豆腐
red-cooked bean curd	
xīhóngshì chǎo jīdàn/dòufu	西红柿炒鸡蛋/豆腐
stirfried tomatoes with scrambled eggs or tofu	
shāo èr dōng	烧二冬
stirfried vegetables with mushooms	
shāo qiézi	烧茄子
braised eggplant	
shūcài	蔬菜
vegetables	
suàntóu chǎo bōcài	蒜头炒菠菜
spinach stirfried with garlic	
xiānmǐ càihuā	鲜米菜花
stirfried mushrooms and cauliflower	

FOOD

Soup 汤

In China, soup is generally served at the end of a meal. With Peking duck, for example, it's customary for the meal to close with soup made from the bones of the duck. Chinese soups are often made of nothing more than a lightly seasoned stock, which is intended to aid digestion at the end of a meal and to make sure you leave feeling full.

dàn huā tāng	蛋花汤
egg flower soup	
jīdàn tāng	鸡蛋汤
egg-drop soup	
hōngzhà dōngjīng	轰炸东京
sizzling rice soup (lit: bombs over Tokyo)	
miàntāng	面汤
noodle soup	

suānlà tāng   酸辣汤
  hot-and-sour soup

jītāng   鸡汤
  chicken soup

xīhóngshì jīdàn tāng   西红柿鸡蛋汤
  egg and tomato soup

zhàcài tāng   榨菜汤
  pickled vegetable soup

FOOD

RESTAURANT WARS

A favourite Chinese sport is fighting over the bill in restaurants. You'll see people trying to pull the bill away from someone else at their table and shouting red-faced at one another. It's considered polite in China to offer to pay the bill once or even twice, even if you're clearly the guest. Protests may be made loudly to show sincerity, even when it's a bluff.

Even if you've been invited to eat, this doesn't settle who's going to pay the bill. If someone has invited you but you'd like to pay, you can jokingly say:

You invited, but I pay.   **nǐ qǐngkè, wǒ fùqián**

If you'd like to pay without having an all-out fight at the table, pay the bill the day before or sneak off to the 'toilet' and pay without your guests knowing. Although your companions might show displeasure at your sneak attack, it will often be welcomed. The secret is learning when it's appropriate to pay and when to be treated – use your best judgement.

Dessert   甜点

bābǎo fàn   八宝饭
  eight-treasure rice. A sweet rice eaten as a dessert, containing various colourful, sugary items resembling jewels that provide its white, green and red colour.

básī píngguǒ　　　　　　　　拔丝苹果
apple dipped first into hot caramel and then into iced water

dòufǔ huā　　　　　　　　　　豆腐花
soft bean curd with ginger-flavoured sweetened water

xìngrén dòufu　　　　　　　　杏仁豆腐
almond jelly (jello)

xìngrénsū　　　　　　　　　　杏仁酥
almond biscuit

yuè bǐng　　　　　　　　　　　月饼
lotus-paste cakes eaten at the mid-Autumn festival, **zhōngqiūjié**
(see page 184)

zǎoní bǐng　　　　　　　　　　枣泥饼
date-filled biscuits

FOOD

CHINESE REGIONAL CUISINES　　中国菜系

There are many regional differences in Chinese cuisine, but it
can broadly be divided into four major categories which follow a
north, south, east or west orientation. However, the Chinese don't
always agree about just what makes each regional cuisine unique.

Northern Cuisine　北方菜

Beijing (sometimes called Mandarin) and Shandong cuisines come
from one of the coldest parts of China, where foods made from
wheat like steamed bread and noodles, rather than rice, are the
staples. Basically, northern cuisine combines very simple
cooking techniques, such as steaming and stirfrying, with the
sophistication of imperial dishes.

běijīng kǎoyā　　　　　　　　北京烤鸭
Peking (Beijing) duck is China's most famous northern
speciality, and can be difficult to get outside Beijing. It's served
with small pancakes and plum sauce.

jiàohuā jī   叫化鸡
(lit: beggar's chicken) another northern specialty, supposedly created by a beggar who stole a chicken earmarked for the emperor and secretly cooked it buried underground. The dish is wrapped in lotus leaves and baked all day in hot ashes.

ménggǔ huǒguō   蒙古火锅
a winter dish, Mongolian hotpot is a combination of meat and vegetables cooked in a simmering broth over a burner placed on the dining table

ménggǔ kǎoròu   蒙古烤肉
Mongolian barbeque, a variation of Mongolian hotpot, features a slowly roasted goat or lamb along with a hotpot full of spicy vegetables

FOOD

RESTAURANT ETIQUETTE

The Chinese have a word for the atmosphere of their restaurants:

rènào   热闹

Literally, it means 'hot and noisy', and that's the way they like it. When the Chinese eat out they like to have fun – the western style of whispering couples sipping expensive wine by candle-light is definitely not for them.

There are a few do's and don'ts, particularly when you're dining with Chinese companions. Perhaps the most important thing to remember is to let others pour your drinks, and to keep an eye on theirs to make sure they stay topped up. Helping yourself is a sign that your hosts or companions aren't looking after you properly.

Bones from fish or chicken can usually be spat onto the tablecloth in front of you or on the floor.

Northern Cuisine	Běifāngcài	北方菜
Beijing cuisine	Běijīngcài	北京菜
Shandong cuisine	Shāndōngcài	山东菜

Cantonese & Chaozhou Cuisine 广东菜与潮州菜

In the south, Cantonese cuisine is the style of Chinese cooking that most westerners will already have come across, with its famous exports like sweet and sour and yum cha. Southern cooking entails lots of steaming, boiling and stirfrying. It uses the least amount of oil, is lightly cooked and not as highly spiced as dishes from other areas.

Common ingredients are seafood, vegetables, roast pork, chicken, steamed fish and fried rice. Specialities include abalone, dried squid, 1000-year eggs (traditionally made by soaking eggs in horse's urine), shark's fin soup, snake soup and dog stew. Other culinary exotica include pangolins (scaly anteaters), cats, rats, owls, monkeys, turtles and frogs. As the saying goes, Cantonese eat everything that flies except aeroplanes, and everything that moves on the ground except cars.

| Cantonese cuisine | Guǎngdōngcài/Yuècài | 广东菜/粤菜 |
| Chaozhou cuisine | Cháozhōucài | 潮州菜 |

diǎn xīn (dim sum) 点心
a variety of delicacies served from pushcarts wheeled around the restaurant floor, served either for breakfast or lunch

Eastern Cuisine 淮扬菜

The cuisine of eastern China encompasses Shanghai, Zhejiang, Fujian and the region of Jiangsu, and is the most diverse of China's regional cuisines. Using rice as a staple, dishes feature the eastern technique of 'red cooking' in a stock of soy sauce and rice wine to produce a tasty stew. Soups are a celebrated aspect of eastern cuisine, and there are hundreds of varieties. In the coastal regions, seafood is an important ingredient and is generally cooked simply, to enhance the natural taste.

Eastern Cuisine	**Huáiyángcài**	淮扬菜
Shanghai cuisine	**Shànghǎicài**	上海菜
Zhejiang-Jiangsu cuisine	**Jiāngzhè cài**	江浙菜

Sichuan Cuisine 川菜

This is the spiciest of the regional cuisines. Specialties include frogs' legs and smoked duck marinated in wine for 24 hours, covered in tea leaves and cooked again over a charcoal fire. Other dishes to try are shrimps with salt and garlic, dried chilli beef, bean curd with chilli, fish in spicy bean sauce and eggplant in garlic.

gōngbǎo jīdīng   宫保鸡丁

the most famous Sichuan dish, consisting of chicken stirfried with peanuts and chilli pepper. It's become a standard Chinese dish, found in restaurants all over China.

Other Chinese Regional Cuisines   中国他菜系
Chinese food	**zhōngcān**	中餐
Hunan food	**xiāngcài**	湘菜
Hakka food	**dōngjiāngcài/kèjiācài**	东江菜/客家菜
Muslim (halal) food	**qīngzhēn cài**	清真菜
Taiwanese food	**táiwāncài**	台湾菜
Xinjiang Uyghur (Turkic) food	**xīnjiāngcài**	新疆菜

FOOD

FAR FLUNG FOOD

French food	**făguócài**	法国菜
Indian food	**yìndùcài**	印度菜
Japanese food	**rìběnliàolĭ**	日本料理
Japanese teppanyaki	**rìběn tiěbǎnshāo**	日本铁板烧
Korean food	**cháoxiǎncài**	朝鲜菜
Thai food	**tàiguócài**	泰国菜
South-East Asian food	**nányángcài**	南洋菜
Vietnamese food	**yuènáncài**	越南菜
Western food	**xīcān**	西餐

FOOD

SELF-CATERING   自烹自调

Meat 肉类

beef	**niúròu**	牛肉
chicken	**jī**	鸡
dog meat	**gŏu ròu**	狗肉
duck	**yā**	鸭
eel	**shànyú**	鳝鱼
frog	**qīngwā**	青蛙
goat	**shānyáng**	山羊
ham	**huŏtuĭ**	火腿
liver	**gān**	肝
mutton	**yángròu**	羊肉
pangolin (scaly anteater)	**chuānshānjiă**	穿山甲
pork	**zhūròu**	猪肉
ratmeat	**lǎoshŭ ròu**	老鼠肉
sausage	**xiāngcháng**	香肠
tripe	**niúdù**	牛肚
turtle	**jiǎyú**	甲鱼
venison	**lùròu**	鹿肉

FOOD

Seafood 海鲜

abalone	bàoyú	鲍鱼
bream	biānyú	鳊鱼
carp	lǐyú	鲤鱼
crab	pángxiè	螃蟹
eel	shànyú	鳝鱼
fish	yú	鱼
lobster	lóngxiā	龙虾
mandarin fish	guìyú	鳜鱼
perch	lúyú	鲈鱼
prawns	duìxiā	对虾
seafood	hǎixiān	海鲜
shark's fin	yúchì	鱼翅
shrimp	xiāmǐ	虾米
squid	yóuyú	鱿鱼
sturgeon	huángyú	鳇鱼
yellow croaker	dà huángyú	大黄鱼

Vegetables 蔬菜

bamboo shoots	zhúsǔn	竹笋
beans	dòu	豆
chilli	làjiāo	辣椒
Chinese cabbage	báicài	白菜
cucumber	huángguā	黄瓜
eggplant	qiézi	茄子
garlic	dàsuàn/suàntóu	大蒜/蒜头
ginger	jiāng	姜
mushroom	mógū	蘑菇
potato	tǔdòu	土豆
rape	yóucài	油菜
spring onion	cōng	葱
tomato	xīhóngshì/fānqié	西红柿/番茄
vegetable	shūcài	蔬菜

Fruit 水果

apple	píngguǒ	苹果
apricot	xìng	杏
banana	xiāngjiāo	香蕉
cherries	yīngtáo	樱桃
Chinese dates	zǎo	枣
coconut	yēzi	椰子
grapes	pútao	葡萄
lemon	níngméng	柠檬
loquat	pípa	枇杷
lychees	lìzhī	荔枝
mango	mángguǒ	芒果
muskmelon	hāmíguā	哈密瓜
orange	júzi	橘子
peach	táozi	桃子
pear	lí	梨
plum	lǐzi	李子
sweet melon	tiánguā	甜瓜
tangerine	gānjú	柑橘
watermelon	xīguā	西瓜

FOOD

Dairy Products 乳品

Chinese for the most part are lactose intolerant, not possessing the enzyme lactase to break down milk. With the exception of yogurt, which is eaten in northern and western China, dairy products are a rarity. The Chinese don't use them at all in their cooking, and associate the drinking of milk and milk product with the diet of babies, not of adults.

Much of the milk-drinking culture in China is found in the north, which was influenced by nomadic cultures such as the Mongols and Manchus, who ruled China for centuries. Yogurt is sold in Beijing and most of the north-east of the country. In the far west, the Uyghurs, Kazakhs and Kyrgyz drink fermented mare's milk, an intoxicating bubbly beverage with a taste somewhere between yogurt and champagne.

butter	huángyóu	黄油
cheese	nǎilào	奶酪
cream	nǎiyóu	奶油
ice cream	bīngqílín	冰淇淋
milk	niúnǎi	牛奶
yogurt	suānnǎi	酸奶

Condiments 辛辣佐料

black pepper	hújiāo	胡椒
chilli	làjiāo	辣椒
chilli sauce	làjiàng	辣酱
cinnamon	guìpí	桂皮
cloves	dīngxiāng	丁香
garlic	suàn	蒜
ginger	jiāng	姜
honey	fēngmì	蜂蜜
monosodium glutimate (MSG)	wèijīng	味精
salt	yán	盐
sesame seed oil	zhīma yóu	芝麻油

soy sauce	jiàngyóu	酱油
star aniseed	dàliào	大料
sugar	táng	糖
tomato sauce	fānqié jiàng	番茄酱
vinegar	cù	醋

Other Food 其他食品

bean curd	dòu fu	豆腐
biscuits	bǐnggān	饼干
bread	miànbāo	面包
buns (steamed)	bāozi	包子
cake	dàn'gāo	蛋糕
congee (rice porridge)	xīfàn/zhōu	稀饭/粥
dessert	tiánpǐn	甜品
dumplings	jiǎozi	饺子
egg	jīdàn	鸡蛋
hors d'oeuvre (cold)	lěng pár	冷盘儿
kebab	kǎo ròuchuàn	烤肉串
noodles	miàntiáo	面条
rice noodles	mǐxiàn/mǐfěn	米线/米粉
noodles in soup	tāngmiàn	汤面
noodles (fried)	chǎomiàn	炒面
pastry	gāodiǎn	糕点
peanuts	huāshēng/ nánjīngdòu	花生/南京豆
rice	dàmǐ/mǐfàn	大米/米饭
plain rice	báimǐfàn	白米饭
fried rice	chǎofàn	炒饭
soup	tāng	汤
toast	kǎo miànbāo	烤面包

FOOD

DRINKS
饮料

During meals, the most popular drink in China is Chinese tea. Beer is also available in most restaurants.

If you're lucky enough to be invited to a banquet, you'll be expected to join in the toasts with **máotái**, a powerful spirit that makes an excellent substitute for metholated spirits. Many Chinese like to drink their guests under the table, and it can be a mistake to try matching anyone glass for glass. When former US President Richard Nixon first went to China, he practised toasting the 'white lightning' sorghum drink **máotái** so he'd be able to keep up with Chairman Máo. If you want to pace yourself and not down your drink in one swig, say:

IN YOUR EYE

When toasting somebody, remember to look them in the eye as you lift your glass.

FOOD

| At your pleasure. | suíbiàn | 随便 |

Alcoholic Drinks 酒类

beer	píjiǔ	啤酒
local spirit	máotái	茅台
spirits	báijiǔ	白酒
vodka	fútèjiā	伏特加
white/red wine	hóng/bái pútao jiǔ	红/白葡萄酒
rice wine	mǐ jiǔ	米酒
whisky	wēishìjì	威士忌
wine	pútaojiǔ	葡萄酒

THEY MAY SAY ...

When you're drinking with the Chinese, the usual toast literally means 'dry glass'. It's generally only used when you intend to finish the glass in one gulp.

| Cheers! | gānbēi! | 干杯 |

Non-Alcoholic Drinks 非酒类饮料

apple juice	**píngguǒzhī**	苹果汁
boiled water	**kāishuǐ**	开水
fizzy drink	**qìshuǐ**	汽水
fruit juice	**guǒzhī**	果汁
lemonade	**níngméng zhī**	柠檬汁
milk	**niúnǎi**	牛奶
mineral water	**kuàngquánshuǐ**	矿泉水
orange juice	**júzizhī**	桔子汁
soy milk	**dòu nǎi**	豆奶
water	**shuǐ**	水

FOOD

Hot Drinks 热饮

Generally speaking, the Chinese are tea rather than coffee drinkers, and outside the main cities you might have a hard time coming across anywhere that serves coffee.

coffee	**kāfēi**	咖啡
black	**qīngkā**	清咖
with milk	**jiā niúnǎi**	加牛奶

The good news is that China has many delicious teas, enjoyed not only for their taste but also for their medicinal qualities. Chinese tea is brewed by placing the leaves, flowers and/or herbs directly into the cup without a tea bag or a strainer. Let the tea brew for several minutes or you'll get a bit of tea leaf in your mouth with every sip.

green tea	**lùchá**	绿茶
jasmine tea	**mòlìhuāchá**	茉莉花茶
oolong tea	**wūlóngchá**	乌龙茶

TEA HOUSES

The traditional Chinese teahouse, or chádiàn, was once the equivalent in China of the French café or the British pub. Teahouse activities ranged from haggling over a bride's dowry to fierce political debate (and sometimes drinking tea). Other entertainments included storytelling, chess, cards, mahjong, smoking, and musical performances.

During the Cultural Revolution, China's teahouses were considered suspect meeting places for 'counter-revolutionaries' and closed down – but now are making a comeback.

FOOD

USEFUL WORDS 常用词语

ashtray	yānhuīgāng	烟灰缸
bowl	wǎn	碗
chopsticks	kuàizi	筷子
cold	lěng	冷
cup	bēizi	杯子
to drink	hē	喝
to eat	chī	吃
fast food	kuàicān	快餐
fork	chāzi	叉子
hot	rè	热
ice cubes	bīngkuànr	冰块儿
knife	dāozi	刀子
plate	pánzi	盘子
restaurant	cāntīng/fànguǎnr	餐厅/饭馆儿
snack	xiǎochī/diǎnxīn	小吃/点心
snack shop	xiǎochīdiàn	小吃店
soup spoon	tāng sháo	汤勺
spoon	sháozi	勺子
table	zhuōzi	桌子
toothpick	yáqiān	牙签

IN THE COUNTRY　　　郊游

China has opened up tremendously since the early 1980s, but some places in the countryside remain off limits, mainly because they lack accommodation for foreigners.

In spite of this, you'll still have plenty of opportunities to get a taste of Chinese country life while travelling in China. Bus journeys often break their trip in small country villages, and some of China's most interesting destinations are surrounded by countryside and villages that can be explored by bicycle.

WEATHER　　　天气

What's the weather like?
tiānqì zěnmeyàng?　　　天气怎么样？
The weather's nice today.
jīntiān tiānqi hěn hǎo　　　今天天气很好。
Will it rain tomorrow?
míngtiān huì xià yǔ ma?　　　明天会下雨吗？
Will it be very cold?
huì búhuì hěn lěng?　　　会不会很冷？

It's ...	hěn ...	很 ...
cold	lěng	冷
dry	gānzào	干燥
hot	rè	热
humid	mènrè	闷热

It's raining.	xià yǔ le	下雨了。
It's windy.	guā fēng le	刮风了。
It's snowing.	xià xuě le	下雪了。

cloud	yún	云
earth	tǔdì	土地
ice	bīng	冰
mud	níbā	泥巴

rain	yǔ	雨
rainy season	yǔjì	雨季
snow	xuě	雪
sun	tàiyáng	太阳
weather	tiānqì	天气
wind	fēng	风

SEASONS

spring	chūntiān	春天
summer	xiàtiān	夏天
autumn	qiūtiān	秋天
winter	dōngtiān	冬天

GEOGRAPHICAL TERMS   地理用语

beach	hǎitān	海滩
cave	shāndòng	山洞
city	chéngshì	城市
cliff	xuányá	悬崖
commune	gōngshè	公社
country bumpkin (hillbilly)	tǔ bāozi (lit: dirt dumpling)	土包子
farmer	nóngmín (lit: peasant)	农民
country person	xiāngxià rén	乡下人
desert	shāmò	沙漠
earthquake	dìzhèn	地震
farm	nóngchǎng	农场
footpath	rénxíng xiǎodào	人行小道
forest	sēnlín	森林
grassy plains	cǎoyuán	草原
harbour	gǎngkǒu	港口
hill	xiǎoshān	小山
hot spring	wēnquán	温泉

IN THE COUNTRY

island	dǎo	岛
jungle	cónglín	丛林
lake	hú	湖
landslide	shānbēng	山崩
mountain	shān	山
mountain range	shānmài	山脉
national park	guójiā gōngyuán	国家公园
nomadic people	yóumù mínzǔ	游牧民族
ocean	hǎiyáng	海洋
peak	shānfēng	山峰
river	hé	河
sea	dàhǎi	大海
slope	shānpō	山坡
valley	xiágǔ	峡谷
village	cūnzhuāng	村庄
waterfall	pùbù	瀑布

HIKING

徒步旅行

Hiking and camping are becoming increasingly popular, especiall along the Great Wall and in the five sacred mountains of China Along the Great Wall, camping is a wilderness type of enterprise The locals will think you're crazy, but what else is new? Yo probably won't find many, if any, supplies on the way, so stock up

Is it safe to climb/walk here?
    zhèr páshān/zǒulù
    ānquán ma?

这儿爬山／走路
安全吗？

Is it safe to climb this mountain?
    pá zhè zuò shān ānquán ma?

爬这座山安全吗？

Is there a hut up there?
    shàngmiàn yǒu xiǎo wū ma?

上面有小屋吗？

Do we need a guide?
    wǒme n xūyào xiàngdǎo ma?

我们需要向导吗？

Where can I find out about hiking
trails in the region?
    zhèi dìqū túbù lǚxíng
    lùjìng de cáiliào,
    cóng nǎr kěyǐ dédào?

这地区徒步旅行
路径的资料，
从哪儿可以得到？

Are there guided treks?
    yǒu méiyǒu lǐnglù yuǎnzú?

有没有领路远足？

I'd like to talk to someone who
knows this area.
    wǒ xiǎng gēn liǎojiě zhèige
    dìfāng de rén tántan

我想跟了解这个
地方的人谈谈。

How long is the trail?
    lùjìng yǒu duōcháng?

路径有多长？

Is the track well marked?
    lùjìng shàng biāozhì
    qīngchu ma?

路径上标志
清楚吗？

How high is the climb?
    zhèizuò shān yǒu duō gāo?

这座山有多高？

Which is the easiest route?
    zuì róngyi de lùxiàn
    shì něi tiáo?

最容易的路线
是哪条？

When does it get dark?
 tiān shénme shíhòu hēi? 天什么时候黑？

Where can I hire mountain gear?
 zài nǎr kěyǐ zūdào
 dēngshān gōngjù? 在哪儿可以租到
登山工具？

Where can we buy supplies?
 zài nǎr kěyi mǎidào
 rìyòngpǐn? 在哪儿可以
买到日用品？

Can I leave some things here
for a while?
 wǒde dōngxī kěyǐ zài
 zhèr liú yīhuìr ma ? 我的东西可以在
这儿留一会儿吗？

On the Path 在路径上

What a beautiful view.
 fēngjǐng zhēn měi 风景真美。

Where have you come from?
 nǐ cóng nǎr lái? 你从哪儿来？

How long did it take you?
 nǐ yòngle duōcháng shíjiān? 你用了多长时间？

Does this path go to ...?
 zhè tiáo lù dào ... ma? 这条路到 ... 吗？

How long is this path/road?
 zhèi tiáo lù yǒu duō cháng? 这条路有多长？

How far until we reach the top?
 dào dǐngbù hái yǒu duō yuǎn? 到顶部还有多远？

How many more steps are there?
 hái yǒu duōshǎo ge táijiē? 还有多少个台阶？

Where's the nearest village?
 zuìjìn de cūnzhuāng zài nǎr? 最近的村庄在哪儿？

Is there a store nearby?
 fùjìn yǒu xiǎomàibù ma? 附近有小卖部吗？

I'm lost.
 wǒ mílù le 我迷路了。

IN THE COUNTRY

CAMPING

野营

Where can we spend the night?
wǒmén jīntiān wǎnshàng zài nǎr zhù?
我们今天晚上在哪儿住？

Can we camp here?
wǒmén néng zài zhèr yěyíng ma?
我们能在这儿野营吗？

Can we light a fire here?
kěyǐ zài zhèr diǎn huǒ ma?
可以在这儿点火吗？

Is it safe to sleep in this place?
zài zhèr shuìjiào ānquán ma?
在这儿睡觉安全吗？

altitude	hǎibá	海拔
backpack	bèibāo	背包
binoculars	wàngyuǎnjìng	望远镜
candles	làzhú	蜡烛
to climb	pá	爬
compass	zhǐnánzhēn	指南针
dangerous	wēixiǎn	危险
downhill	xiàshān	下山
first-aid kit	jíjiù yàoxiāng	急救药箱
gloves	shǒutào	手套
guide	dǎoyóu	导游
guided trek	lǐnglù yuǎnzú	领路远足
hiking	túbù lǚxíng	徒步旅行
hiking boots	yuǎnzúxuē	远足靴
ledge	yánjí	岩脊
lookout	liàowàng tái	了望台
map	dìtú	地图
mountain climbing	dēngshān	登山
pick	gǎotóu	镐头
provisions	gōngyìngpǐn	供应品
rock climbing	pānyán	攀岩
rope	shéngzi	绳子

IN THE COUNTRY

signpost	zhǐshì pái	指示牌
sleeping bag	shuìdài	睡袋
steep	dǒu	陡
tent	zhàngpéng	帐篷
trek	yuǎnzú	远足
uphill	shàngshān	上山
to walk	xíngzǒu	行走

ANIMALS, BIRDS & INSECTS　　　　　动物虫鸟

bird	niǎo	鸟
bear	xióng	熊
butterfly	húdié	蝴蝶
camel	luòtuó	骆驼
cat	māo	猫
chicken	jī	鸡
cockroach	zhānglláng	蟑螂
cow	niú	牛
crocodile	èyú	鳄鱼
dog	gǒu	狗
donkey	lú	驴
fish	yú	鱼
fly	cāngyíng	苍蝇
frog	qīngwā	青蛙
goat	shānyáng	山羊
horse	mǎ	马
lizard	xīyì	蜥蜴
monkey	hóuzi	猴子
mosquito	wénzi	蚊子

IN THE COUNTRY

ox	**gōngniú**	公牛
panda	**xióngmāo**	熊猫
pig	**zhū**	猪
rooster	**gōngjī**	公鸡
sheep	**yáng**	羊
snake	**shé**	蛇
spider	**zhīzhū**	蜘蛛
turtle	**wūguī**	乌龟
water buffalo	**shuǐniú**	水牛
wild animal	**yěshòu**	野兽
yak	**máoniú**	牦牛

4-LEGGED HITLER

In general, the Chinese view dogs not so much as pets, but as as a means of guarding their homes. In Taiwan, people give their dogs murderous names like Hitler and Stalin. The Taiwanese also name them after hated politicians like former US President Jimmy Carter, who broke relations with Taiwan in the 1979.

FLORA & AGRICULTURE

植物与农业

agriculture	**nóngyè**	农业
to harvest	**shōuhuò**	收获
irrigation	**guàn gài**	灌溉
leaf	**yèzi**	叶子
planting/sowing	**zhòngzhí/bōzhòng**	种植／播种
rice field	**dàotián**	稻田
terraced land	**tītián**	梯田
tree	**shù**	树

HEALTH

健康

Doctors in China are just as likely to draw on Chinese traditional medicine as on western medicine, and in large hospitals treatment will probably combine both of these approaches.

In big cities with sizeable expatriate populations, like Beijing and Shanghai, there are international clinics with English-speaking doctors. Elsewhere, the chances of finding an English-speaking doctor are more remote. Medical services are generally relatively inexpensive, although foreigner surcharges may apply.

AT THE DOCTOR

看病

I'm sick.
> wǒ bìng le · · · · · 我病了。

My friend is sick.
> wǒde péngyǒu bìng le · · · · · 我的朋友病了。

I need a doctor.
> wǒ děi jiàn dàifu · · · · · 我得见大夫。

Is there a doctor who speaks English here?
> zhèr yǒu huì jiǎng
> yīngyǔ de dàifu ma? · · · · · 这儿有会讲
> 英语的大夫吗?

Can you get me a doctor?
> qǐng bāng wǒ zhǎo yīwèi dàifu? · · · · · 请帮我找一位大夫?

Where's a/the ...?   ... zài nǎr?   ... 在哪儿?
   doctor   dàifu   大夫
   chemist   yàodiàn   药店
   hospital   yīyuàn   医院

AILMENTS 病状

PASS THE PEPPER

A seemingly improbable Chinese cure for diarrhoea that actually works is to eat black charred meat covered in spicy red capsicum.

I feel dizzy.
  wǒ tóuyūn
  我头晕。

I feel weak.
  wǒ gǎndào sìzhīwúlì
  我感到四肢无力。

I feel tired all over.
  wǒ húnshēn méijìnr
  我浑身没劲儿。

I've been bitten by an insect.
  wǒ bèi chóngzi yǎo le   我被虫子咬了。

I have trouble breathing.
  wǒ hūxī kùnnán   我呼吸困难。

I've been vomiting.
  wǒ yīzhí zài tù   我一直在吐。

I can't sleep.
  wǒ shuìbùzháo   我睡不着。

I can't move my ...
  wǒde ... dòngbùliǎo   我的 ... 动不了。

It hurts here.   zhèr téng   这儿疼。

Can you get me a female doctor?
  qǐng gěi wǒ zhǎoge   请给我找个
  nǚ dàifu, hǎo ma?   女大夫，好吗？

I have (a/an) ...	wǒ ...	我 ...
altitude sickness	yǒu gāoshān fǎnyìng	有高山反应
anaemia	pínxuè zhèng	贫血症
asthma	xiàochuǎn	哮喘
burn	shāoshāng le	烧伤了
constipation	biànmì	便秘
cold	shāngfēng/ gǎnmào le	伤风/ 感冒了
cough	késòu	咳嗽

cramp	chōujīn le	抽筋了
diabetes	yǒu tángniào bìng	有糖尿病
diarrhoea	xièdùzi	泻肚子
dysentery	yǒu lìji	有痢疾
epilepsy	diānxián	癫痫
fever	fāshāo le	发烧了
food poisoning	shíwù zhōngdúle	食物中毒了
headache	tóuténg	头疼
heart condition	yǒu xīnzàngbìng	有心脏病
hepatitis	gānyán	肝炎
indigestion	xiāohuà bùliáng	消化不良
infection	fāyán le	发炎了
influenza	yǒu liúgǎn	有流感
itch	yǎng	痒
Japanese	liúxíngxìng	流行性
encephalitis B	yǐxíng nǎoyán	乙型脑炎
lice	yǒu shīzi	有虱子
low/high	xuèyā guòdī/	血压过低/
blood pressure	guògāo	过高
malaria	nüèji	疟疾
migraine	piāntóutòng	偏头痛
pneumonia	fèiyán	肺炎
rheumatism	fēngshī	风湿
skin rash	pífū zhěn	皮肤疹
sore throat	hóulong téng	喉咙疼
stomachache	dùzi téng	肚子疼
sunburn	shàishāng	晒伤
sunstroke	zhòngshǔ	中暑
toothache	yá téng	牙疼
travel sickness	lǚxíng xuányùn	旅行眩晕
typhoid	shānghán	伤寒
venereal disease	xìngbìng	性病

It's ...	zhèr ...	这儿 ...
broken	duàn le	断了
dislocated	tuōjiùle	脱臼了
sprained	niǔshāngle	扭伤了

HEALTH

HEALTH

I've been vaccinated.
  wǒ zhòngguò yìmiáo

I feel better/worse.
  wǒ hǎo duō le/gèng nánshòu le

This is my usual medication.
  zhèi shi wǒ píngcháng chī de yào

I'm on medication.
  wǒ zhèngzài chī yào

I have a skin allergy.
  wǒ pífū guòmǐn

我种过疫苗。

我好多了
/更难受了。

这是我平常
吃的药。

我正在吃药。

我皮肤过敏。

don't want a blood transfusion.
  wǒ bú yào shūxuè
我不要输血。

don't want an operation.
  wǒ bú yào zuò shǒushù
我不要做手术。

need a new pair of glasses.
  wǒ xūyào yī fù xīn yǎnjìng
我需要一副新眼镜。

have my own syringe.
  wǒ zìjǐ yǒu zhùshèqì
我自己有注射器。

Can I have a receipt for my
ealth insurance?
  wǒ yào shēnbào jiànkāng
  bǎoxiǎn, qǐng gěi wǒ
  fāpiào, hǎo ma?
我要申报健康
保险，请给我
发票，好吗？

WOMEN'S HEALTH

妇女健康

Could I see a female doctor?
  qǐng gě wǒ zhǎo yīwèi
  nǚ dàifu, hǎo ma?
请给我找一位
女大夫，好吗。

'm on the Pill.
  wǒ fú bìyùnyào
我服避孕药。

'm pregnant.
  wǒ huáiyùn le
我怀孕了。

think I'm pregnant.
  wǒ xiǎng wǒ huáiyùn le
我想我怀孕了。

haven't had my period for ... months.
  wǒ tíngjīng yǒu ... ge yuè le
我停经有 ... 个月了。

'd like to use contraception.
  wǒ xiǎng shǐyòng bìyùn fāngfǎ
我想使用避孕方法。

abortion	liúchǎn	流产
bleeding	liúxuè	流血
contraception	bìyùn	避孕
cramps	jìngluán	痉挛
cystitis	pángguāngyán	膀胱炎
diaphragm	zǐgōng mào	子宫帽

HEALTH

IUD	gōngnèi bìyùnqì	宫内避孕器
mammogram	rǔfáng āikèsīguāng zhàopiàn	乳房光照片
menstruation	yuèjīng	月经
miscarriage	xiǎochǎn	小产
pap smear	bāshì shìyàn	巴氏试验
period pain	yuèjīng tòng	月经痛
the Pill	bìyùn yào	避孕药
premenstrual tension	jīngqián jǐnzhāng	经前紧张
thrush	ékǒuchuāng	鹅口疮
ultrasound	chāoshēngbō	超声波
yeast infection	jiàomǔ gǎnrǎn	酵母感染

ALLERGIES 过敏

I'm allergic to ...	wǒ duì ... guòmǐn	我对 ... 过敏。
antibiotics	kàngjūnsù	抗菌素
aspirin	āsīpīlín	阿斯匹林
bee stings	mìfēng zhēcì	蜜蜂蜇刺
dairy products	rǔzhìpǐn	乳制品
penicillin	qīngméisù	青霉素
pollen	huāfěn	花粉

ALTERNATIVE TREATMENTS 其他治疗方法

I've tried western medicine, without any relief.
wǒ chī le xīyào, dànshì wúxiào 我吃了西药，但是无效。

I'd like to try Chinese medicine.
wǒ xiǎng shìshi zhōngyào 我想试试中药。

What kind of Chinese medicine is effective for my ...?
yào zhì wǒ de ..., shénme zhōngyào yǒuxiào? 要治我的 ..., 什么中药有效？

Does acupuncture hurt?
zhēnjiū téng buténg? 针灸疼不疼？

HEALTH

How many minutes is each
acupuncture treatment?
>   **měi cì zhēnjiǔ yào**   每次针灸要
>   **duōcháng shíjiān?**   多长时间？

What are the side effects of
this treatment?
>   **zhèi zhǒng zhìliáo yǒu**   这种治疗有
>   **shénme fùzuòyòng?**   什么副作用？

Should I have food with this?
>   **yīnggāi gēn fàn yìqǐ chī ma?**   应该跟饭一起吃吗？

How long will it take
to have an effect?
>   **duōcháng shíjiān**   多长时间
>   **cái yǒu xiàoguǒ?**   才有效果？

These pills are enormous!
>   **zhèi xiē yàowán zhème dà!**   这些药丸这么大！

How many pills do I take?
>   **měi cì chī jǐ lì?**   每次吃几粒？

How many times should I take
them per day?
>   **měi tiān chī jǐ cì?**   每天吃几次？

This medicine is very bitter.
>   **zhèi zhǒng yào hěn kǔ.**   这种药很苦。

How do I prepare this medicine?
>   **zhěi zhǒng yào zěnme zhǔnbèi?** 这种药怎么准备？

acupuncture	zhēnjiǔ	针灸
aromatherapy	fāngxiāng liáofǎ	芳香疗法
faith healer	xìnyǎng liáofǎ	信仰疗法
herbalist	cǎoyào yīshēng	草药医生
homeopathy	shùnshì liáofǎ	顺势疗法
massage	ànmó	按摩
meditation	mòniàn	默念
naturopath	zìrán liáofǎ yīshī	自然疗法医师
reflexology	fǎnshè liáofǎ	反射疗法
yoga	yújiā	瑜伽

HEALTH

PARTS OF THE BODY

身体部位

My ... hurts.	wǒde ... téng	我的 ... 疼。
ankle	jiǎohuái	脚踝
appendix	lánwěi	阑尾
arm	gēbo	胳膊
back	bèi	背
bladder	pángguāng	膀胱
blood	xuè	血
bone	gútóu	骨头
brain	nǎozi	脑子
breast	rǔfáng	乳房
buttocks	pìgǔ	屁股
chest	xiōngbù	胸部
ear	ěrduǒ	耳朵
elbow	zhǒu	肘
eye	yǎnjīng	眼睛
face	liǎn	脸
finger	shǒuzhī	手指
foot	jiǎo	脚
hand	shǒu	手
head	tóu	头
heart	xīnzàng	心脏
hip	túnbù	臀部
kidney	shèn	肾
knee	xīgài	膝盖
leg	tuǐ	腿
liver	gān	肝
lung	fèi	肺
mouth	zuǐ	嘴
muscle	jīròu	肌肉
neck	bózi	脖子
nose	bízi	鼻子
rib	lèigǔ	肋骨
shoulder	jiānbǎng	肩膀
skin	pífū	皮肤
spine	jǐzhuī	脊椎
stomach	wèi	胃

teeth	yáchǐ	牙齿
throat	sǎngzi	嗓子
tongue	shétóu	舌头
tonsils	biǎntáoxiàn	扁桃腺
vein	jìngmài	静脉
wrist	wàn	腕

THEY MAY SAY ...

zěnme le?
What's the matter?

怎么了？

gǎndào téngtòng ma?
Do you feel any pain?

感到疼痛吗？

nǎr téng?
Where does it hurt?

哪儿疼？

nǐzài xíngjīng ma?
Are you menstruating?

你在行经吗？

nǐ zài fāshāo ma?
Do you have a temperature?

你在发烧吗？

nǐ zhèiyàng yǒu jǐtiān le?
How long have you been like this?

你这样有几天了？

yǐqián yǒu guò ma?
Have you had this before?

以前有过吗？

nǐ zài chī yào ma?
Are you on medication?

你在吃药吗？

nǐchōu yān ma?
Do you smoke?

你抽烟吗？

nǐ hē jiǔ ma?
Do you drink?

你喝酒吗？

nǐ xī dú ma?
Do you take drugs?

你吸毒吗？

nǐ duì shènme guòmǐn ma?
Are you allergic to anything?

你对什么过敏吗？

nǐ huáiyùn le ma?
Are you pregnant?

你怀孕了吗？

HEALTH

AT THE CHEMIST   在药房

You'd be wise to bring prescribed drugs with you. Alternatively, you could look into Chinese traditional herbal medicine, a form of treatment that's taken very seriously in China.

The best part of Chinese chemists is that they sell inexpensive over-the-counter antibiotics.

I need something for diarrhoea.
  wǒ yào zhì fùxiède yào   我要治腹泻的药。
I need something for a cold.
  wǒ yào zhì gǎnmào de yào   我要治感冒的药。
I need something for an insect bite.
  wǒ yào zhì chóng yào de yào   我要治虫咬的药。
Do I need a prescription for ...?
  ... yīnggāi shi dàifu   ... 应该是大夫
  kāi de ma?   开的吗？
How many times a day?
  měitiān chī jǐcì?   每天吃几次？

antibiotics	**kàngjūnsù**	抗菌素
antiseptic cream	**xiāodúgāo**	消毒膏
aspirin	**āsīpīlín**	阿斯匹林
baby's bottle	**nǎipíng**	奶瓶
baby powder	**fèizǐfěn**	痱子粉
bandage	**bēngdài**	绷带
Band-Aids	**chuàngkětiē**	创可贴
chlorine tablets	**lùpiàn**	氯片
comb	**shūzi**	梳子
condoms	**bìyùntào**	避孕套
contraceptive	**bìyùnyào**	避孕药

HEALTH

deodorant	chútǐxiùyè	除体臭液
hairbrush	fàshuā	发刷
insect repellant	chúchóngjì	除虫剂
iodine	diǎnjiǔ	碘酒
laxative	qīngxièjì	清泻剂
moisturising cream	rùnfūshuāng	润肤霜
nauseous	ěxīn	恶心
ointment	ruǎngāo	软膏
razor	tìxūdāo	剃须刀
rehydration salts	fùshuǐyán	复水盐
sanitary napkins	fùnǚwèishēngjīn	妇女卫生巾
shampoo	xǐfà xiāngbō	洗发香波
shaving cream	tìxū zàoyè	剃须皂液
soap	féizào	痱子
sunscreen	fángshàishuāng	防晒霜
talcum powder	shuǎngshēnfén	爽身粉
tampons	yuèjīng miánsāi	月经棉塞
tissues	shǒujīn zhǐ	手巾纸
toilet paper	wèishēngzhǐ	卫生纸
toothbrush	yá shuā	牙刷
toothpaste	yágāo	牙膏
vitamin	wéishēngsù	维生素

AT THE DENTIST 在牙医处

Is there a good dentist here?
zhèr yǒu hǎo 这儿有
yákē dàifu ma? 好牙科大夫吗？

I have a toothache.
wǒ yá téng 我牙疼。

at the ...	zài ...	在 ...
top	shàngmiàn	上面
bottom	xiàmiàn	下面
front	qiánmiàn	前面
back	hòumiàn	后面

HEALTH

I've lost a filling.
   wǒ de bǔyá tiánliào diào le   我的补牙填料掉了。

I've broken my tooth.
   wǒ de yá pò le   我的牙破了。

My gums hurt.
   wǒ de yáchuáng téng   我的牙床疼。

My gums are bleeding.
   wǒ de yáchuáng zài liúxuè   我的牙床在流血。

Ouch!
   āyá!   啊呀！

I don't want it extracted.
   qǐng búyào bá   请不要拔。

Please give me an anaesthetic.
   qǐng gěi wǒ dǎ máyào   请给我打麻药。

USEFUL WORDS   常用词语

bleed	chūxuè	出血
blood test	yànxuè	验血
faeces	dàbiàn	大便
injection	dǎ zhēn	打针
oxygen	yǎngqì	氧气
pus	nóng	脓
urine	niào	尿

HEALTH

SPECIFIC NEEDS 特别需求

DISABLED TRAVELLERS 残疾游客

Road traffic in China rarely gives way to pedestrians, so people whose sight, hearing or walking ability is impaired should be especially cautious. As buses and trains can be difficult for anyone to negotiate, travelling by car or taxi is probably the safest option.

I'm disabled/handicapped.
    wǒ shì cánjí rén   我是残疾人。

I need assistance.
    wǒ xūyào bāngzhu   我需要帮助。

What services do you have for disabled people?
    nǐmén xiàng cánjí rén   你们向残疾人
    tígòng shénme fúwù?   提供什么服务？

Is there wheelchair access?
    yǒu méiyǒu lúnyǐ tōngdào?   有没有轮椅通道？

I'm deaf. Can you speak louder please.
    wǒ ěr lóng, nǐ néng   我耳聋，你能
    dàshēng shuō ma?   大声说吗？

I can lipread.
    wǒ huì chún dú   我可唇读.

I have a hearing aid.
    wǒ dài zhùtīngqì   我戴助听器。

Does anyone here know ... sign language?
    yǒu rén dǒng ... shǒushìyǔ ma? 有人懂...手势语吗？

Are guide dogs permitted?
    yǔnxǔ dǎomángquǎn ma?   允许导盲犬吗？

disabled person	cánjí rén	残疾人
guide dog	dǎomángquǎn	导盲犬
wheelchair	lúnyǐ	轮椅

SPECIFIC NEEDS

GAY TRAVELLERS   同性恋游客

Although homosexuality is illegal in China, there are gay discos, bars and pubs in large cities, though they tend to keep a fairly low profile. It's generally not a good idea for gays and lesbians to flaunt their sexual preferences in public, as local officials could respond with a crackdown on local meeting places.

Where are the gay hangouts?
    tóngxìngliàn jùjíchù zài nǎr?   同性恋聚集处在哪儿？
Is there a gay district?
    yǒu tóngxìngliàn qūyù ma?   有同性恋区域吗？
Am I/Are we likely to be
harrassed here?
    wǒ/wǒmén zài zhèr   我/我们在这
    huì shòudào sāorǎo ma?   儿会受到骚扰吗？
Is there a local gay publication?
    běndì yǒu tóngxìngliàn   本地有同性恋
    chūbǎnwù ma?   出版物吗？

TRAVELLING WITH A FAMILY   与家人旅行

Many Chinese cities have spacious parks, zoos and amusement parks which can help keep children occupied. As children's prices are rarely available for foreign children, organising an International Student Identity Card for your child can help reduce costs.

Are there any facilities for babies?
    yǒu yīng'ér shèshī ma?   有婴儿设施吗？
Do you have a child-minding service?
    yǒu tuōér fúwù ma?   有托儿服务吗？
Where can I find a(n)
(English-speaking) babysitter?
    zài nǎr kěyǐ zhǎodào   在哪儿可以找到
    (shuō yīngwén de) bǎomǔ?   (说英文的)保姆？

I need a car with a child seat.

wǒ xūyào yīliàng yǒu yīng'ér zuòwèi de qìchē	我需要一辆有婴儿座位的汽车。

Are there any activities for children?

yǒu értóng cānjiā de huódòng ma?	有儿童参加的活动吗？

Is there a family discount?

yǒu jiātíng yōuhuì ma?	有家庭优惠吗？

Are children allowed?

yǔnxǔ háizi ma?	允许孩子吗？

Can you put an extra bed/cot in the room?

zài fángjiān lǐ jiā fàng yīzhāng chuáng/yòuérchuáng, hǎo ma?	在房间里加放一张床/幼儿床，好吗？

Could you make it a child's portion?

néng zuòchéng háizi xūyào de yīfèr ma?	能做成孩子需要的一份吗？

Is there a playground around here?

zhèr yǒu yóuxìchǎng ma?	这儿有游戏场吗？

ON BUSINESS   业务

We're attending a ...	wǒmén cānjiā ...	我们参加 ...
conference	tǎolùnhuì	讨论会
meeting	huìyì	会议
trade fair	jiāoyīhuì	交易会

HANDLING PAPER

When being handed a business card or a document from someone, it's respectful to receive it with both hands. Business cards should never be crumpled up or placed in one's pocket in a mindless way. At meetings, it's common to leave your counterpart's business card in front of you to refer to throughout discussions.

SPECIFIC NEEDS

I'm on a course.
  wǒ zài xuéxí   我在学习。
I have an appointment with ...
  wǒ hé ... yǒu yuēhuì   我和 ... 有约会。
Here's my business card.
  zhè shì wǒ de míngpiàn   这是我的名片。
I need an intrepreter.
  wǒ xūyào fānyì   我需要翻译。
I need to use a computer.
  wǒ xūyào shǐyòng diànnǎo   我需要使用电脑。
I need to send an email/fax.
  wǎ xūyào fā   我需要发电
  chuánzhēn /diànzǐ yóujiàn   子邮件/传真。

NAME CHOPS

The 'name chop' – a kind of seal that serves as a signature
– has been used in China for thousands of years. Chinese
documents are worthless without an official chop printed in
red ink. When an official is disgraced and removed from
their position, the first thing that's done is to remove their
chop. Choplessness renders one powerless.

---

appointment	yuēhuì	约会
business lunch	gōngzuò wǔcān	工作午餐
business partner	yèwù huǒbàr	业务伙伴
client	kèhù	客户
colleague	tóngshì	同事
courier	kuàidìyuán	快递员
distributor	xiāoshòu rén	销售人
email	diànzǐ yóujiàn	电子邮件
exhibition	zhǎnlǎn	展览
file	wénjiàn	文件

fax machine	**chuánzhēn jī**	传真机
Internet	**guójì hùliánwǎng**	国际互联网
Internet connection	**jiētōng hùliánwǎng**	接通互联网
manager	**jīnglǐ**	经理
mobile phone	**yídòng diànhuà**	移动电话
modem	**tiáozhì jiětiáoqì**	调制解调器
profit	**lìrùn**	利润
proposal	**jiànyì**	建议
sales representative	**xiāoshòu dàibiǎo**	销售代表

SPECIFIC NEEDS

TRACING ROOTS & HISTORY   寻根与历史

(I think) my ancestors
came from this area.
    (wǒ xiǎng) wǒ de zǔxiān   (我想)我的祖先
    láizì zhèige dìqū   来自这个地区。

I'm looking for my relatives.
    wǒ zài xúnzhǎo qīnqi   我在寻找亲戚。

I have/had a relative who
lives/lived around this area.
    wǒ yǒu yī ge   我有一个
    qīnqi zhù zài fùjin   亲戚住在附。

Is there anyone here by
the name of ...?
    zhèr yǒurén míngzi   这儿有人名
    jiào ... ma?   字叫 ... 吗?

I'd like to go to the cemetery.
    wǒ xiǎng qù gōngmù   我想去公墓。

TAOISM

It's said that Taoism, or dào jiào, is the only true 'home-grown' Chinese religion – Buddhism was imported from India and Confucianism is mainly a philosophy.

At the centre of Taoism is the concept of Dao. Dao cannot be perceived because it exceeds senses, thoughts and imagination; it can be known only through mystical insight which cannot be expressed with words. Dao is the way of the universe, the driving power in nature, the order behind all life, the spirit which cannot be exhausted. Dao is the way people should order their lives to keep in harmony with the natural order of the universe.

Just as there have been different interpretations of the 'way', there have also been different interpretations of De – the power of the universe.

Taoism split into two divisions, the 'Cult of the Immortals' and 'The Way of the Heavenly Teacher'. The Cult of the Immortals offered immortality through meditation, exercise, alchemy and various other techniques. The Way of the Heavenly Teacher had many gods, ceremonies, saints, special diets to prolong life and offerings to the ghosts. As time passed, Taoism increasingly became wrapped up in the supernatural, self-mutilation, witchcraft, exorcism, fortune telling, magic and ritualism.

TIME, DATES & FESTIVALS

时间、日期与
节日

TELLING THE TIME   说明时间

Once you've learnt the numbers, telling the time in Chinese is a piece of cake. After the hour, place the word **diǎn**, which literally means 'point', then the number of minutes past the hour (see Numbers & Amounts, page 187), and then the word **fēn**, 'minutes'. You may hear the word **zhōng**, which translates as 'o'clock', placed at the end of all this, but it's optional.

am	shàngwǔ	上午
pm	xiàwǔ	下午
o'clock	zhōng	钟
point	diǎn	点
minutes	fēnzhōng	分钟
quarter of an hour	yīkè zhōng	一刻钟
half (an hour)	bàn xiǎoshí	半小时
hour	xiǎoshí	小时
midnight	bànyè	半夜
minute	fēnzhōng	分钟
noon	zhōngwǔ	中午
second	miǎozhōng	秒钟
in the morning	zǎoshàng	早上
in the afternoon	xiàwǔ	下午
in the evening	wǎnshàng	晚上

TIME, DATES & FESTIVALS

What time is it?	xiànzài jǐdiǎn le?	现在几点了？
9 am	**zǎoshàng jiǔ diǎn** (lit: in-the-morning 9 point)	早上九点
12 noon	**zhōngwǔ shíèr diǎn** (lit: noon 12 point)	中午十二点。
1.10	**yī diǎn shí fēn** (lit: 1 point 10 minutes)	一点十分。
2.15	**liǎng diǎn shíwǔ fēn**	两点十五分。
3.20	**sān diǎn èrshí fēn** (lit: 3 point 20 minutes)	三点二十分。
4.30	**sì diǎn bàn** (lit 4 point half)	四点半。
5.40	**wǔdiǎn sìshífēn**	五点四十分。
6.45	**liù diǎn sìshíwǔ fēn** (lit: 6 point 45 minutes)	六点四十五分。

3 o'clock in the afternoon
xiàwǔ sān diǎnzhōng   下午三点钟
(lit: in-the-afternoon 3
point o'clock)
8.30 in the evening
wǎnshàng bā diǎnbàn   晚上八点半
(lit: in-the-evening
8 point half)

DAYS & WEEKS   星期

Either of the following words, which both mean 'week' and are
interchangeable, can be used in the names for days of the week

week	**xīngqī/lǐbài**	星期/礼拜

TIME, DATES & FESTIVALS

Monday	xīngqīyī	星期一
Tuesday	xīngqīèr	星期二
Wednesday	xīngqīsān	星期三
Thursday	xīngqīsì	星期四
Friday	xīngqīwǔ	星期五
Saturday	xīngqīliù	星期六
Sunday	xīngqītiān	星期天
	xīngqīrì	
	(tián and rì both mean 'day' and are interchangeable)	

MONTHS　　　　　　　　　　　　　　　　　　月份

January	yīyuè	一月
February	èryuè	二月
March	sānyuè	三月
April	sìyuè	四月
May	wǔyuè	五月
June	liùyuè	六月
July	qīyuè	七月
August	bāyuè	八月
September	jiǔyuè	九月
October	shíyuè	十月
November	shíyīyuè	十一月
December	shíèryuè	十二月

DATES　　　　　　　　　　　　　　　　　　　日期

Dates start with the year, followed by the month and finally the day of the month. Thus, 1 January 1999 is literally: one nine nine nine year, one month, one day. The use of haò for 'day' is interchangeable with the word rì, meaning day.

Refer to Numbers & Amounts, page 187, to work out the date for a particular day. The system is easy once you get the hang of it – for the year, the number is followed by nián. For the month, the number (one = January, nine = September) is followed by yuè. And for the day, the date followed by hào.

TIME, DATES & FESTIVALS

What date is it today?
  jīntiān jǐ hào?   今天几号？
It's 28 June.
  liù yuè èrshíbā hào   六月二十八号。
  (lit: six month 28th)
It's 6 October.
  shí yuè liù hào   十月六号。
  (lit: 10 month 6th)

Present 目前

immediately	**mǎshàng**	马上
now	**xiànzài**	现在
today	**jīntiān**	今天
tonight	**jīntiān wǎnshàng**	今天晚上
this morning	**jīntiān zǎoshàng**	今天早上
this afternoon	**jīntiān xiàwǔ**	今天下午
this week	**zhèige xīngqī**	这个星期
this month	**zhèige yuè**	这个月
this year	**jīnnián**	今年

LUNAR, SOLAR

In China, time is measured using both the solar and lunar calendars, with festivals and agriculture still following the lunar cycle. The traditional lunar calendar, or **nóng lì** (lit: agricultural calendar), differs from the solar calendar, **yáng lì**, by 11 days. The lunar calendar year is divided into 12 months, each with either 29 or 30 days. Each month begins with a new moon, while the 15th day always falls when the moon is full. An extra month is added every three years to bring the calendar in line with the solar calendar.

LUNAR, SOLAR

Before China adopted the seven day week, it calculated time based on cycles of 60 days. The Chinese 60-day cycle revolves around two interchanging wheels – one of 10 spokes called dìzhī or 'earthly branches', and one of 12 spokes called the tiāngān or 'heavenly stems'. The animals associated with the Chinese zodiac follow the Earthly Branches. The first day of the cycle is named after the first of the Heavenly Stems and the first of the Earthly Branches, the second day by the second of each, and so on until the cycle reaches the tenth day. After the last of the 10 earthly branches, the 11th day pairs with the first branch, the 11th heavenly stem and so on, until the full cycle of 60 days is completed.

TIME, DATES & FESTIVALS

The 10 Heavenly Stems
tiāngān 天干

jiǎ	甲
yǐ	乙
bǐng	丙
dīng	丁
wù	戊
jǐ	己
gēng	庚
xīn	辛
rén	壬
guǐ	癸

The 12 Earthly Branches
dìzhī 地支

zǐ	子	Rat
chǒu	丑	Ox
yín	寅	Tiger
mǎo	卯	Rabbit
chèn	辰	Dragon
sì	巳	Snake
wǔ	午	Horse
wèi	未	Sheep
shēn	申	Monkey
yǒu	酉	Rooster
xū	戌	Dog
hài	亥	Pig

In ancient China, the tiāngān dìzhī system was also used to designate cycles of 60 years. Years were named using a combination of stems and branches, along with the 'reign name' of the current emperor. When emperors came to power, they chose a name for their time of rule. Reign names tended to be optimistic, with typical names including 'Smooth Rule', 'Great Virtue' and 'Celestial Celebration'.

TIME, DATES & FESTIVALS

Past 过去

yesterday	zuótiān	昨天
day before yesterday	qiántiān	前天
yesterday morning	zuótiān zǎoshàng	昨天早上
yesterday afternoon	zuótiān xiàwǔ	昨天下午
last night/evening	zuótiān wǎnshang	昨天晚上
last week	shàngge xīngqī	上个星期
last month	shàngge yuè	上个月
last year	qùnián	去年

Future 将来

tomorrow	míngtiān	明天
day after tomorrow	hòutiān	后天
tomorrow morning	míngtiān zǎoshàng	明天早上
tomorrow afternoon	míngtiān xiáwǔ	明天下午
tomorrow evening/night	míngtiān wǎnshàng	明天晚上
next week	xiàge xīngqī	下个星期
next month	xiàge yuè	下个月
next year	míngnián	明年

USEFUL WORDS   常用词语

after	yǐhòu	以后
always	zǒngshì	总是
before	yǐqián	以前
century	shìjì	世纪
to count	jìsuàn	计算
day	rì	日
daytime	báitiān	白天
early	zǎo	早
evening	wǎnshàng	晚上
every day	měitiān	每天
forever	yǒngyuǎn	永远
month	yuè	月

never	cónglái méi	从来没
night	yè	夜
noon	zhōngwǔ	中午
recently	zuìjìn	最近
sunrise	rìchū	日出
sunset	rìluò	日落
weekend	zhōumò	周末
year	nián	年

TIME, DATES & FESTIVALS

FESTIVALS & HOLIDAYS   节日

Days off are something of a rarity in China, so festivals and public holidays are celebrated enthusiastically. Most of the big festivals are calculated according to the lunar calendar and fall on different dates each year.

The government has implemented a staggered work week for many institutions. Some people might get Saturday and Sunday off, while others take Tuesday and Wednesday off. It can seem that China has tremendous unemployment because each day looks like a weekend with so many people out on the streets.

WELL WISHING

Congratulations!	gōngxǐ gōngxǐ!	恭喜恭喜！
Happy birthday!	zhù nǐ shēngrì kuàilè!	祝你生日快乐！
Happy New Year!	xīnnián kuàilè!	新年快乐！
May you be happy and prosperous! (New Year's greeting)	gōngxǐ fācái!	恭喜发财！
Good luck!	zhùnǐ hǎoyùn!	祝你成功！
Fantastic!	zhēn bàng!	真棒！
Cheers!	gān bēi!	干杯！
To your health!	zhù nǐ jiànkāng!	祝你健康！
To your happiness!	zhù nǐ yúkuài!	祝你愉快！

duānwǔjié 端午节

the **duānwǔjié** festivities commemorate the drowning suicide of **Qūyuán**, 屈原, a virtuous poet and official of the 4th century BC. After being unjustly removed from his position as foreign ambassador for the Chu State, the depressed **Qūyuán** travelled through the **Húnán** region in search of a shaman or a Daoist priest to help relieve his grief. During his journey, he composed the first Chinese poems written in the first person, and created the sao, or 'sadness' style of literature from which all subsequent Chinese poetry can be traced.

TIME, DATES & FESTIVALS

Dragon boat races held in late May or early June re-enact the search for his body in the water, and rice pockets wrapped in banana leaves eaten during this festival symbolise the effort to feed the fish that might eat **Qūyuán**'s drowned body.

The name **duānwǔ**, 'double five', means the fifth day of the fifth month of the Chinese lunar calendar.

hūnjié 春节

also known as the Spring Festival, this is the Chinese New Year, held in late January or early February. It traditionally involves a large family celebration lasting several days, and trains and planes are booked solid during this time. At home, long noodles are eaten, symbolically giving long life to the family.

uóqìngjié 国庆节

National Day. Held on 1 October to commemorate the day Chairman **Máo** established the People's Republic in 1949.

uóqìng (shuāng shí) jié 国庆（双十）节

National Day (Taiwan). This 10 October celebration commemorates the overthrow of the Manchu-ruled Qing Dynasty in 1911.

HAND OVER THE RED PACKET!

On New Year's Day, children are traditionally given small red envelopes of money, and greet adults with the words:

Congratulations and prosper,
now hand over the red envelope!

gōngxǐ fācái, hóngbāo nálái
恭喜发财，红包拿来！

qīngmíngjié   清明节

The name of this holiday means 'Clear and Bright'. On th
day in April, people traditionally sweep and tidy the tombs o
their ancestors.

yuánxiāojié   元宵节

held shortly after the Spring Festival, this day marks the form
end of the New Year celebrations with firecrackers and speci
sweets, called **yuánxiāo, 元宵**

zhōngqiūjié   中秋节

the moon is huge in the heavens when it's closest to the earth
This is the most romantic of Chinese holidays, when peop
take time out to go on evening strolls and gaze at the moon
This is also the holiday that the Chinese government uses t
solve its **dà nán dà nǚ**, 'big male, big female' problem, puttin
together single adult men and women in their late 20s an
early 30s, hoping they find a magical mate under the spell o
the moon.

CHINESE DYNASTIES & REPUBLICS   中国朝代

In China, historical time is marked by dynasties. If you g
sightseeing, you'll constantly come across references to them.

Xià/Shāng   2100-1100 BC   夏/商

characterised by the practice of Shamanism, divination by oracl
bones, and the production of bronze ceremonial vessels

Zhōu   1100-221 BC   周

noted for the practice of ancestor worship, Shamanism
Confucianism, Taoism, and the production of ornate bronz
ceremonial vessels

Xīzhōu	1100-771	西周
	Western Zhou	
Chūnqiū	770-476 BC	春秋
	Spring & Autumn Period	
Zhàn guó	475-221 BC	战国
	Warring States Period	

TERRACOTTA ARMIES

A legacy of the Qín Dynasty is a thousands-strong army of life-sized terracotta warriors and horses, called **bīngmǎyǒng**, which were found placed in a series of underground vaults in Xian.

Qín	221-207 BC	秦

saw the unification of China, the production of the terracotta army buried in Xi'an, and the construction of the first parts of the Great Wall

Hàn	206 BC-220 AD	汉

known as a period of cultural flourishing, as well as Silk road trade with Asia and places as far afield as Rome. The name 'Han', which is used for the majority Chinese ethnic group who make up 92 per cent of the population, hearkens back to this glorious and united dynastic period.

Xīhàn	206 BC-24 AD	西汉
	Western Han	
Dōnghàn	25-220	东汉
	Eastern Han	

Sānguó	220-265	三国

Three Kingdoms Period

Jìn	265-420	晋
Xījìn	265-316	西晋
	Western Jin	
Dōngjìn	317-420	东晋
	Eastern Jin	

Nánběicháo	420-582	南北朝

Southern & Northern Dynasties Period

Suí	581-618	隋

Táng   **619-907**   唐

the most glorious period of Chinese cultural flourishing, including painting and ceramics, Buddhism, the poets Du Fu and Li Bai, internationalisation and Silk Road trade

Wǔdài   **907-960**   五代

Five Dynasties Period

Liáo   **916-1125**   辽

Sòng   **960-1279**   宋

this dynasty saw the renewal of Confucianism, commercial revolution and urban flourishing

Jīn   **1125-1234**   金

Yuán   **1271-1368**   元

period of Mongol rule, the Khans Ghenghis and Kublai, Marco Polo, and the emergence of Beijing as capital

Míng   **1368-1644**   明

period of conservatism, with the re-establishment of Chinese rule and the restriction of international trade. Build-up of maritime power.

Qīng   **1644-1911**   清

Manchu rule in Northwest China. The empire expands with the conquest of Xinjiang, Tibet and Mongolia. Opium addiction rife.

Republic of China   **1911-1949**   中华民国

development of democratic institutions. Civil war, corruption, Sun Yatsen, and Chiang Kaishek.

People's Republic of China   **1949-**   中华人民共和国

Máo's communist revolution

NUMBERS & AMOUNTS

数字与数量

The counting system in Mandarin is easy to learn. Multiples of 10 are made by stating the multiple and then 10 – so 20 is literally 'two ten'. If you learn the numbers from one to 10 you can count to 100 without having to learn any new vocabulary. The only exception is the number two – when counting, two is **èr** and when used with classifiers (see Classifiers in Grammar, page 25) it is **liǎng**.

CARDINAL NUMBERS

基数

0	líng	零
1	yī	一
2	èr	二
3	sān	三
4	sì	四
5	wǔ	五
6	liù	六
7	qī	七
8	bā	八
9	jiǔ	九
10	shí	十
11	shíyī	十一
12	shíèr	十二
13	shísān	十三
14	shísì	十四
15	shíwǔ	十五
16	shíliù	十六
17	shíqī	十七
18	shíbā	十八
19	shíjiǔ	十九
20	èrshí	二十
21	èrshíyī	二十一
22	èrshíèr	二十二
23	èrshísān	二十三

30	sānshí	三十
31	sānshíyī	三十一
40	sìshí	四十
50	wǔshí	五十
60	liùshí	六十
70	qīshí	七十
80	bāshí	八十
90	jiǔshí	九十
100	yībǎi	一百
101	yībǎilíngyī	一百零一
102	yībǎilíng'èr	一百零二
110	yībǎiyīshí	一百一十
189	yībǎibāshíjiǔ	一百八十九
200	liǎngbǎi/èrbǎi	两百 / 二百
300	sānbǎi	三百
1000	yīqiān	一千
10,000	yīwàn	一万
100,000	shíwàn	十万
1 million	yībǎiwàn	一百万
100 million	yīyì	一亿

NUMBERS

ORDINAL NUMBERS   序数

Simply prefix any number with dì, 第, and it becomes an ordinal

1st	dìyī	第一
2nd	dì'èr	第二
3rd	dìsān	第三
10th	dìshí	第十

COUNT DOWN

The Chinese counting system is based on units of 10. These multiply as follows:

10	shí	十
100	bǎi	百
1000	qiān	一千
10,000	wán	万
100,000	shí wán	十万
1 million	bǎi wán	百万
10 million	qiān wán	千万
100 million	wán wán; yì	万万; 亿
1 billion	shí yì	十亿

FRACTIONS   分数

1/4	sìfēnzhīyī	四分之一
1/3	sānfēnzhīyī	三分之一
	(lit: from three parts one)	
1/2	yībàn	一半
3/4	sìfēnzhīsān	四分之三
How much/many?	duōshǎo?	多少？
Enough!	gòu le!	够了！
once	yīcì	一次
twice	liǎngcœ	两次
three times	sāncœ	次
double	liǎngbèi	两倍
triple	sānbéi	倍
a pair	yīshuāng	一双
a dozen	yīdǎ	一打
about	zuǒyòu	左右

NUMBERS

a little (amount)	**yīdiǎnr**	一点儿
few	**shǎo**	少
many; a lot	**hěn duō**	很多
too much	**tái duō le**	太多了
abacus	**suánpán**	算盘
calculator	**jìsuánqì**	计算器
to count	**jìsuán**	计算

NUMBERS

EMERGENCIES 紧急情况

Help!	jiùmìng!	救命！
Police!	jǐngchá!	警察！
Thief!	xiǎotōu!	小偷！
Watch out!	xiǎoxīn!	小心！
Go away!	zǒu kāi!	走开！

I've been robbed.
  yǒu rén tōu le
  wǒ de dōngxī

有人偷了
我的东西。

I've been raped.
  wǒ bèi qiángjiān le

我被强奸了。

There's been an accident!
  chūshìle!

出事了！

I'm lost.
  wǒ mílù le

我迷路了。

Could you help me please?
  nǐ néng bùnéng bāng
  wǒ ge máng?

你能不能帮
我个忙？

I'm terribly sorry.
  bàoqiàn, bàoqiàn

抱歉、抱歉。

Where are the toilets?
  cèsuǒ/
  xǐshǒujiān
  zài nǎr?

厕所／
洗手间在
哪儿？

They took my ...
  tāmen tōuzǒu le wǒde ...

他们偷走了我的 ...

I've lost my ...	wǒ diūle ...	我丢了 ...
backpack	bèibāo	背包
bag	bāo	包
camera	zhàoxiàngjī	照相机
money	qián	钱
passport	hùzhào	护照
watch	shǒubiǎo	手表

HEALTH EMERGENCIES   紧急医疗

I need ...	wǒ xūyào ...	我需要 ...
a doctor	yīshēng	医生
to go to a hospital	qù yīyuàn	去医院

| Call a doctor! | qǐng jiào yīshēng! | 请叫医生！ |
| I'm ill. | wǒ shēngbìng le | 我生病了。 |

My blood group is
(A/B/O/AB) positive/negative.
  wǒde xuèxíng shì   我的血型是
  (A/B/O/AB) zhèng/fù   (A/B/O/AB) 正 / 负。
I have medical insurance.
  wǒ yǒu yīliáo bǎoxiǎn   我有医疗保险。

| next of kin | zuìjìn de qīnshǔ | 最近的亲属 |

DEALING WITH THE POLICE   与警察打交道

I didn't realise I was
doing anything wrong.
  wǒ bùzhīdào zuòcuò le shì   我不知道做错了事。
I didn't do it.
  búshì wǒ zuòde   不是我做的。
Could I please use the phone?
  wǒ kěyǐ dǎ ge   我可以打个
  diànhuà ma?   电话吗？

EMERGENCIES

THE POLICE MAY SAY ...

nǐ bèi zhǐkòng fànyǒu ...	你被指控犯有 ...	You'll be charged with ...
fǎn zhèngfǔ huódòng	反政府活动	anti-government activity
qīnfàn rénshēn	侵犯人身	assault
rǎoluàn zhì'ān	扰乱治安	disturbing the peace
cángyǒu (fēifǎ wùpǐn)	藏有（非法物品）	possession (of illegal substances)
fēifǎ rùjìng	非法入境	illegal entry
móushā	谋杀	murder
wèihuò qiānzhèng	未获签证	not obtaining a visa
yùqī jūliú	逾期居留	overstaying your visa
qiángjiān	强奸	rape
qiǎngjié	抢劫	robbery
zài shāngdiàn zhōng páqiè	在商店中扒窃	shoplifting
wéifǎn jiāotōng guīzé	违反交通规则	a traffic violation
wúzhèng gōngzuò	无证工作	working without a permit

I want to contact my embassy/consulate.

wǒ xī wàng gēn wǒguóde dàshǐguǎn/lǐngshìguǎn liánxì

我希望跟我国的大使馆 / 领事馆联系。

I'm a tourist.

wǒ shì yóukè.

我是游客。

What am I accused of?

zhǐkòng wǒ shénme?

指控我什么？

I don't understand.

wǒ bù míngbài.

我不明白。

I understand.

wǒ míngbài

我明白。

EMERGENCIES

Is there someone here who
speaks English?
> zhèr yǒu rén huì shuō
> yīngwén ma?

这儿有人会说
英文吗?

I'm sorry, I don't speak Mandarin.
> bàoqiàn, wǒ bú huì
> shuō pǔtōnghuà

抱歉, 我不会
说普通话。

arrested	bèibǔ	被捕
cell	láofáng	牢房
embassy/consulate	dàshǐguǎn/	大使馆／
	lǐngshìguǎn	领事馆
fine (payment)	fákuǎn	罚款
guilty	yǒuzuì	有罪
lawyer	lùshī	律师
not guilty	wúzuì	无罪
police officer	jǐngchá	警察
police station	pàichūsuǒ	派出所
prison	jiānyù	监狱
trial	shěnxùn	审讯

A

abacus	suànpán	算盘
abdomen	fùbù	腹部
able (to be); can	néng/kěyǐ	能／可以

Can I take your photo?
wǒ néng gěi nǐ zhàoxiàng ma?
我能给你照相吗?

Can you show me on the map?
nǐ kěyǐ zài dìtú shàng zhǐ gěi wǒ kàn ma?
你可以在地图上指给我看吗?

board	shàng ...	上 ...
(boat)	chuán	船
(car)	chē	车
(plane)	dēngjī	登机
abortion	liúchǎn	流产
about	dàyuē	大约
above	shàng	上
abroad	hǎiwài	海外
accept	shōu	收
accident	shìgù	事故
accommodation	zhùsù	住宿
ache	téng	疼
across	tōngguò	通过
activist	jījìn zhǔyì fènzǐ	激进主义分子
actor	yǎnyuán	演员
acupuncture	zhēnjiǔ	针灸
adaptor	chāzuò	插座
addiction	yǐn	瘾
address	dìzhǐ	地址
address book	tōngxùnbù	通讯簿
admire	zànshǎng	赞赏
admission	rùchǎng	入场
to admit	chéngrèn	承认
adult	chéngrén	成人
advantage	yōushì	优势
adventure	màoxiǎn	冒险
advice	jiànyì	建议
aeroplane	fēijī	飞机

afraid	pà	怕
to be afraid of **hàipà** 害怕		
afternoon	xiàwǔ	下午
in the afternoon (zài) xiàwǔ (在)下午		
this afternoon jīntiān xiàwǔ 今天下午		
after(wards)	yǐhòu	以后
again	zài	再
against	duì	对
age	niánlíng	年龄
ago	qián	前
a while ago yīhuìr qián 一会儿前		
agree	tóngyì	同意
I don't agree. wǒ bù tóngyì 我不同意.		
agriculture	nóngyè	农业
ahead	qiántóu	前头
aid (help)	bāngzhù	帮助
AIDS	àizībìng	艾滋病
air	kōngqì	空气
air-conditioned	kōngtiáo	空调
air pollution	kōngqìwūrǎn	空气污染
airmail	hángkōng	航空
airport	fēijīchǎng	飞机场
alarm clock	nàozhōng	闹钟
alcohol	jiǔ	酒
all	dōu	都
allergic	guòmǐn	过敏
an allergy	mǐn gǎn	敏感
to allow	yǔnxǔ	允许

It's allowed.
yǔnxǔ
允许.

English	Pinyin	Chinese
almost	chàbuduō	差不多
alone	dāndú	单独
already	yǐjīng	已经
also	yě	也
alter	gǎi	改
altitude	hǎibá	海拔
always	zǒngshì	总是
amateur	yèyú àihàozhě	业余爱好者
ambassador	dàshǐ	大使
among	qízhōng	其中
ancient	gǔdàide	古代的
and	hé	和
angry	shēngqì	生气
animal	dòngwù	动物
ankle	jiǎohuái	脚踝
annual	niándù	年度
answer	huídá	回答
ant	mǎyǐ	蚂蚁
antibiotics	kàngjūnsù	抗菌素
antique	gǔdiǎn	古
antiseptic cream	fángfǔjì	防腐剂
appendicitis	lán wéi yán	阑尾炎
apple	píngguǒ	苹果
appointment	yuēhuì	约会
approximately	dàyuē	大约
apricot	xìng	杏
archaeology	kǎogǔxué	考古学
architecture	jiànzhùxué	建筑学
argue	chǎojià	吵架
arm	gēbo	胳膊
arrive	dào	到
art	yìshù	艺术
artist	yìshùjiā	艺术家
arts & crafts	gōngyì měishù	工艺美术
ashtray	yānhuīgāng	烟灰缸
ask	wèn	问
aspirin	āsīpǐlín	阿斯匹林
asthma	xiàochuǎn	哮喘

at	zài	在
aunt	āyí	阿姨
automatic teller machine (ATM)	zìdòng qǔkuǎn jī	自动取款机
automatic	zìdòng	自动
autumn (fall)	qiūtiān	秋天

B

baby	yīng ér	婴儿
baby food	yīng ér shípǐn	婴儿食品
babysitter	línshí bǎomǔ	临时保姆
back (body)	bèi	背
back (rear)	hòubiān	后边
backpack	bèibāo	背包
bad	huài	坏
bag	dàizǐ	袋子
baggage	xínglǐ	行李
bakery	miànbāo diàn	面包店
balcony	yángtái	阳台
ball	qiú	球
ballpoint	yuánzhūbǐ	圆珠笔
bamboo	zhúzi	竹子
banana	xiāngjiāo	香蕉
band (musical)	yuèduì	乐队
bandage	bēngdài	绷带
Band-Aid	chuàngkětiē	创可贴
bank	yínháng	银行
banknote	chāopiào	钞票
banquet	yànhuì	宴会
baptism	xǐlǐ	洗礼
bar	jiǔbā	酒吧
barbershop	lǐfàdiàn	理发店
basket	lánzǐ	篮子
bath	yùgāng	浴缸
bathing suit	yǒuyǒngyī	游泳衣
bathroom	yùshì	浴室
batteries	diànchí	电池
beach	hǎitān	海滩
beancurd	dòufu	豆腐
beans	dòu	豆

beard	húzǐ	胡子
beautiful	piàoliàng	漂亮
because	yīnwèi	因为
bed	chuáng	床
bedbugs	chòuchōng	臭虫
	(lit: stink bugs)	
beef	niúròu	牛肉
beer	píjiǔ	啤酒
before	yǐqián	以前
beggar	qǐgài	乞丐
begin	kāishǐ	开始
behind	zài hòumiàn	在后面
bell	líng	铃
below	zài xiàmiàn	在下面
beside	zài pángbiān	在旁边
best	zuì hǎo	最好
better	bǐjiào hǎo	比较好
between	zài zhōngjiān	在中间
the Bible	shèngjīng	圣经
bicycle	zìxíngchē	自行车
big	dà	大
bill	zhàngdān	帐单
bird	niǎo	鸟
birth certificate	chūshēngzhèng	出生证
birthday	shēngrì	生日
biscuit	bǐnggān	饼干
bite (n, dog)	yǎo	咬
bite (n, insect)	dīng	叮
bitter	kǔde	苦的
black	hēi sè	黑色
B&W (film)	hēi bái	黑白
bladder	pángguāng	膀胱
blanket	tǎnzǐ	毯子
bleed	liúxuè	流血

Bless you! (when sneezing)
chángmìng bǎisuì!
长命百岁!

blister	shuǐpào	水泡
blood	xuè	血
blood group	xuèxíng	血型

blood pressure	xuèyā	血压
blood test	yànxuè	验血
blood transfusion	shūxuè	输血
blouse	nǚchènshān	女衬衫
blue	lánsè	蓝色
to board (ship, etc)	shàng	上
boat	chuán	船
body	shēntǐ	身体
boiled water	kāishuǐ	开水
bomb	zhàdàn	炸弹

Bon appétit!
zhù nǐ wèikǒu hǎo
祝你胃口好。

| bone | gǔtóu | 骨头 |

Bon voyage!
yīlùpíng'ān
一路平安。

book	shū	书
to book	yùdìng	预订
(make a booking)		

I'd like to book a room.
wǒ yào yùdìng fángjiān
我要预订房间。

bookshop	shūdiàn	书店
boots	xuēzi	靴子
border	biānjiè	边界
bored	mèn	烦
boring	mèn	闷
borrow	jiè	借
boss (n)	lǎobǎn	老板
botanical gardens	zhíwùyuán	植物园
botany	zhíwùxué	植物学
both	dōu	都
bottle	píng	瓶
bottle opener	kāipíngqì	开瓶器
(at the) bottom	(zài) dǐbù	(在)底部
bowel	dàcháng	大肠
bowl (n)	wǎn	碗
box	hézǐ	盒子

B

boy	nánháir	男孩儿
boyfriend	nán péngyǒu	男朋友
bra	rǔzhào	乳罩
bracelet	shǒuzhuó	手镯
brain	nǎozi	脑子
branch	zhītiáo	枝条
bread	miànbāo	面包
break (n)	nòng huài	弄坏
breakfast	zǎofàn	早饭
breast	rǔfáng	乳房
breathe	hūxī	呼吸
bribe (n)	huìlù	贿赂
to bribe	xínghuì	行贿
bridge	qiáo	桥
bright	míngliàng	明亮
bring	ná	拿
broken	huài le	坏了
brooch	xiōngzhēn	胸针
brother	xiōngdì	兄弟
brothel	jìyuàn	妓院
brown	hèsè	褐色
bruise	qīngzhǒng	青肿
brush (n)	shuāzǐ	刷子
bucket	shuǐtǒng	水桶
Buddhism	fójiào	佛教
bug	chong	虫
to build	jiànzào	建造
building (construction)	jiànzhùwù	建筑物
bulb	diàndēngpào	电灯泡
bull	gōngniú	公牛
burn (n)	shāoshāng	烧伤
bus	gōnggòngqìchē	公共汽车
bus stop	qìchēzhàn	汽车站
business	shāngyè	商业
busker	jiētóu yìrén	街头艺人
businessperson	shāngren	商人
busy	máng	忙
but	dànshì	但是
butter	huángyóu	黄油
butterfly	húdié	蝴蝶
buttons	niǔkòu	钮扣

D
I
C
T
I
O
N
A
R
Y

buy   mǎi   买

I'd like to buy ...
wǒ xiǎng mǎi ...
我想买 ...

Where can I buy a ticket?
zài nǎr mǎi piào?
在哪儿买票？

C

cabin	kècāng	客舱
cake	dàn gāo	蛋糕
cake shop	gāodiǎndiàn	糕点店
calendar	rìlì	日历
to call (phone)	dǎ diànhuà	打电话
to call (name)	jiào	叫
calligraphy	shūfǎ	书法
camel	luòtuo	骆驼
camera	zhàoxiàngjī	照相机
camp	yěyíng	野营

Can we camp here?
zhèr kěyǐ yěyíng ma?
这儿可以野营吗？

can (tin)	guàntóu	罐头
can opener	kāiguànqì	开罐器
can	néng	能
cannot	bùnéng	不能

We can do it.
wǒmen néng
我们能.

I can't do it.
wǒ bù néng
我不能.

canal	yùnhé	运河
cancel	qǔxiāo	取消
cancer	áizhèng	癌症
candle	làzhú	蜡烛
Cantonese (language)	guǎngdōng huà	广东话
cap (hat)	màozi	帽子
capital	shǒudū	首都

capitalism	zīběnzhǔyì	资本主义
car	chē	车
card (business)	míngpiàn	名片
card (credit, etc)	kǎpiàn	卡片
to care (about)	guānxīn	关心
to care (for someone)	dānxīn	耽心

Careful!
xiǎoxīn!
小心！

carpet	dìtǎn	地毯
carrot	húluóbo	胡萝卜
carry	tí/ná	提／拿
cartoons	mànhuà	漫画
cash (n)	xiànjīn	现金
cassette	cídài	磁带
cat	māo	猫
Catholic	tiānzhǔjiào	天主教
cave	shāndòng	山洞
CD	jīguāng chàngpiàn	激光唱片
to celebrate	qìngzhù	庆祝
cemetery	gōngmù	公墓
centimetre	límǐ	厘米
centre	zhōngxīn	中心
century	shìjì	世纪
ceramics	táoqì	陶器
certain	quèdìng	确定
certificate	zhèngshū	证书
chair	yǐzi	椅子
champagne	xiāngbīn	香槟
championship	guànjūn	冠军
chance	jīhuì	机会
to change (money)	duìhuàn	兑换
change (n)	língqián	零钱
changing rooms	gēngyīshì	更衣室
cheap	piányi	便宜
cheap hotel	piányi de bīnguǎn	便宜的宾馆
cheat (n)	qīpiàn	欺骗

Cheat!
piànrén!
骗人！

to check	jiǎnchá	检查
check-in (desk)	dēngjìtái	登记台

Checkmate!
jiāngsǐ!
将死 !

| checkpoint | biānfáng jiǎncházhàn | 边防检查站 |

Cheers!
gānbēi!
干杯!

cheese	nǎilào	奶酪
chemist (pharmacy)	yàodiàn	药店
chemistry	huàxué	化学
cheque	zhīpiào	支票
chess	xiàngqí	象棋
chessboard	qípán	棋盘
chicken	jī	鸡
child	háizi	孩子
chilli	làjiāo	辣椒
chocolate	qiǎokèlì	巧克力
chop (for name)	yìnzhāng	印章
chopsticks	kuàizi	筷子
to choose	tiāoxuǎn	挑选
Christian	jīdūjiào	基督教
Christmas	shèngdànjié	圣诞节
church	jiàotáng	教堂
cigarette papers	juǎnyān zhǐ	卷烟纸
cigarettes	xiāngyān	香烟
cinema	diànyǐng yuàn	电影院
circus	mǎxì	马戏
citizenship	gōngmín quán	公民权
city	chéngshì	城市
city centre	shì zhōngxīn	市中心
classical art	gǔdiǎn yìshù	古典艺术
classical theatre	gǔdiǎn jùchǎng	古典剧场
clean	gānjìng	干净
cleaning	qīngjié	清洁
cliff	xuányá	悬崖
to climb	pāndēng	攀登
clock	zhōng	钟
to close	guānbì	关闭

closed (shop, etc)	guānmén	关门
clothing	yīfu	衣服
cloud	yún	云
coach (bus)	chángtúqìchē	长途汽车
coast	hǎi àn	海岸
coat	dàyī	大衣
coat hanger	yījià	衣架
cockroach	zhāngláng	蟑螂
coconut	yēzi	椰子
coffee	kāfēi	咖啡
coins	yìngbì	硬币
a cold	gǎnmào	感冒
cold (adj)	lěng	冷

It's cold.
tiān lěng le
天冷了

to have a cold	gǎnmào le	感冒了
cold water	lěng shuǐ	冷水
colour	yánsè	颜色
comb	shūzi	梳子
to come	lái	来
comedy	xǐjù	喜剧
comfortable	shūfu	舒服
commune	gōngshè	公社
communist	gòngchǎndǎng yuán	共产党员
companion	tóngbàn	同伴
company (business)	gōngsī	公司
compass	zhǐnánzhēn	指南针
complex	fùzá	复杂
computer	diànnǎo	电脑
computer game	diànnǎo yóuxì	电脑游戏
comrade	tóngzhì	同志
concert	yīnyuèhuì	音乐会
condom	bìyùntào	避孕套
conductor	shòupiàoyuán	售票员
confectionary	gāodiǎn	糕点
to confirm (a booking)	quèrèn	确认

Congratulations!
gōngxǐ!
恭喜！

conservative	bǎoshǒu	保守
to be constipated	biànmì	便秘
constipation	biànmì	便秘
construction work	jiànzhù gōngchéng	建筑工程
consulate	lǐngshìguǎn	领事馆
contact lens	yǐnxíng yǎnjìng	隐型眼镜
contagious	chuánrǎn	传染
contraceptive	bìyùnyào	避孕药
contract	hétong	合同
conversation	huìhuà	会话
to cook	zuòfàn	做饭
cool (coll)	dǐngguāguā	顶呱呱
copper	tóng	铜
coral	shānhú	珊瑚
corner	jiǎo	角
corner (street)	lùkǒu	路口
correct	duì	对
corrupt	fǔbài	腐败
to cost	huāfèi	花费

How much does it cost to go to ...?
qù ... yào huā duōshǎo qián?
去 ... 要花多少钱？

It costs a lot.
yào huā hěn duō qián
要花很多钱.

cot	xiǎo chuáng	小床
cotton	miánbù	棉布
cotton wool	tuōzhǐmián	脱脂棉
cough	késou	咳嗽
cough drops	késou táng	咳嗽糖
count (n)	shùzì	数字
	(lit: numbers)	
to count	jìsuàn	计算
country (nation)	guójiā	国家
countryside	nóngcūn	农村
court (legal)	fǎyuàn	法院
court (tennis)	qiúchǎng	球场
cow	niú	牛
crab	pángxie	螃蟹
crafts	shǒuyì	手艺

crafty	jīlíng	机灵
crag (wall of rock)	xuányá	悬崖
cramp	chōujīn	抽筋
crazy	shénjīngbìng	神经病
cream	nǎiyóu	奶油
credit card	xìnyòngkǎ	信用卡
cricket	bǎnqiú	板球
cross (religious)	shízìjià	十字架
cross (angry)	shēngqì	生气
cross-country trail	yuèyě xiǎodào	越野小道
crossroads	shízìlùkǒu	十字路口
cup	bēizi	杯子
cupboard	guìzi	柜子
curator	guǎnzhǎng	馆长
current affairs	shíshì	时事
curtain	chuānglián	窗帘
customs	hǎiguān	海关
to cut	qièxuē	切削
to cycle	qíchē	骑车
cyclist	qíchē rén	骑车人
cystitis	pángguāng yán	膀胱炎

D

dad	bàba	爸爸
daily	rìchángde	日常的
dairy products	nǎizhìpǐn	奶制品
damp	cháoshī	潮湿
to dance	tiàowǔ	跳舞
dancing	tiàowǔ	跳舞
dangerous	wēixiǎn	危险
dark	àn	暗
date (appointment)	yuēhuì	约会
date (time)	rìqī	日期
date of birth	shēngrì	生日
daughter	nǚér	女儿
dawn	límíng	黎明
day	tiān	天

    day after tomorrow
    hòutiān
    后天

day before yesterday		
	qiántiān	
	前天	
dead	sǐ	死
deaf	lóng	聋
decide	juédìng	决定
decision	juédìng	决定
deck (of cards)	yī fù pái	一副牌
deck (of ship)	jiǎbǎn	甲板
deep	shēn	深
deer	lù	鹿
deforestation	luànkǎn lànfá	乱砍滥伐
delay	yánhuǎn	延缓
delicious	hǎochī	好吃
delirious	shénzhìhūnmí	神志昏迷
deliver	sòng	送
democracy	mínzhǔ	民主
demonstration	shìwēi	示威
dental floss	jiéyá xiàn	洁牙线
dentist	yáyī	牙医
denture	jiǎyá	假牙
deny	jùjué	拒绝
deodorant	chútǐxiùyè	除体臭液
to depart (leave)	líkāi	离开
department store	bǎihuò shāngdiàn	百货商店
departure	chūfā	出发
deposit (n)	yājīn	押金
desert	shāmò	沙漠
dessert	tiánpǐn	甜品
destination	mùdìdì	目的地
destroy	pòhuài	破坏
diabetes	tángniàobìng	糖尿病
dial tone	bōhào yīn	拨号音
diaper (nappy)	zhǐniàobù	纸尿布
diarrhoea	fùxiè	腹泻
diary	rìjì	日记
dice/die	tóuzi	骰子
dictionary	zìdiǎn	字典
to die	sǐ	死
different	bùyīyàng	不一样

difficult	nán	难
dining car	cānchē	餐车
dining room	cāntīng	餐厅
dinner	wǎnfàn	晚饭
direction	fāngxiàng	方向
dirty	zāng	脏
disabled	cánjírén	残疾人
discount	zhékòu	折扣
to discover	fāxiàn	发现
discrimination	qíshì	歧视
disease	jíbìng	疾病
disinfectant	xiāodújì	消毒剂
dislocate	tuōjiù	脱臼
dismissal	kāichú	开除
dissatisfied	bù mǎnyì	不满意
distributor	xiāoshòu rèn	销售人
disturb	dǎrǎo	打扰
diving	qiánshuǐ	潜水
diving equipment	qiánshuǐ shèshī	潜水设施
dizzy	tóuyūn	头晕
to do	zuò	做

What are you doing?
nǐ zài zuò shénme?
你在做什么？

I didn't do it.
búshì wǒ zuò de
不是我做的.

dock	mǎtóu	码头
doctor	dàifu/yīshēng	大夫／医生
documentary	jìshí	记实
dog	gǒu	狗
dole	jiùjì	救济
doll	wáwa	娃娃
dollar	yuán	元
door	mén	门
dope (marijuana)	dàmá	大麻
dormitory	sùshè	宿舍
double	shuāng	双
double bed	shuāngrén chuáng	双人床
double room	shuāngrénfáng	双人房

downstairs	lóuxià	楼下
downtown	shìzhōngxīn	市中心
dozen	dá	打
drawing pin	túdīng	图钉
dream	mèng	梦
dress	nǚ fú	女服
drink (n)	yǐnliào	饮料
to drink	hē	喝
drive (car)	kāi (chē)	开车
driver	sījī	司机
driver's licence	jiàshǐ zhízhào	驾驶执照
drug	dúpǐn	毒品
drug addiction	dúpǐn shàngyǐn	毒品上瘾
drug dealer	dúpǐn fànzi	毒品贩子
drugged	fúyòng dúpǐn hóu	服用毒品后
drums	gǔ	鼓
drunk	zuì	醉
dry	gān	干
dry white (wine)	gān hóng pútaojiǔ	干白葡萄酒
dry red (wine)	gān bái pútaojiǔ	干红葡萄酒
drycleaner	gānxǐdiàn	干洗店
duck	yā	鸭
dumplings	jiǎozi	饺子
dummy (pacifier)	nǎizuǐ	奶嘴
during ...	zài ... de shíhou	在 ... 的时候
dust	huīchén	灰尘
duty (customs)	shuì	税

E

each	měi	每
ear	ěrduo	耳朵
earache	ěrduo téng	耳朵疼
early	zǎo	早
It's still early.		
tiān hái zǎo		
天还早.		
earn	zhuàn	赚
earring	ěrhuán	耳环
ears	ěrduō	耳朵
Earth	dìqiú	地球

English	Pinyin	Chinese
earth (soil)	tǔdì	土地
earthquake	dìzhèn	地震
east	dōng	东
Easter	fùhuójié	复活节
easy	róngyì	容易
eat	chī	吃
economy	jīngjì	经济
education	jiàoyù	教育
eel	mànyú	鳗鱼
egg	jīdàn	鸡蛋
eggplant	qiézi	茄子
eight	bā	八
eighteen	shíbā	十八
eighty	bāshí	八十
elastic bandage	tánxìngbēngdài	弹性绷带
elbow	zhǒu	肘
election	xuǎnjǔ	选举
electricity	diàn	电
electric fan	diànfēngshàn	电风扇
elevator	fútī	扶梯
eleven	shíyī	十一
embarassed	bù hǎo yìsi	不好意思
embassy	dàshǐguǎn	大使馆
embroidery	cìxiù	刺绣
emergency	jǐnjí qíngkuàng	紧急情况
emperor	huángdì	皇帝
employee	zhígōng	职工
employer	gùzhǔ	雇主
empty	kōngde	空的
end (n)	jiéshù	结束
to end	jiéshù	结束
endangered species	bīnwēi wùzhǒng	濒危物种
engagement	yuēhuì	约会
engine	fādòngjī	发动机
engineer	gōngchéngshī	工程师
England	yīngguó	英国
English	yīngyǔ	英语
to enjoy (oneself)	xiǎngshòu	享受
enough	zúgòu	足够

Enough!
gòu le!
够了！

entrance	rùkǒu	入口
envelope	xìnfēng	信封
environment	huánjìng	环境
epileptic	diānxiánbìng huànzhě	癫痫病患者
equal (n)	píngděng	平等
equator	chìdào	赤道
equality	píngděng	平等
equipment	shèbèi	设备
Europe	ōuzhōu	欧洲
evening	wǎnshàng	晚上
event	shìjiàn	事件
every	měi	每
every day	měitiān	每天

for example
bǐfāngshuō
比方说

excellent	yōuxiù de	优秀的
to exchange	huàn	换
exchange rate	duìhuànl	兑换率
excluded	páichú	排除
excuse me	duìbùqǐ	对不起
exhausted	lèihuài le	累坏了
exhibition	zhǎnlǎn	展览
exit	chūkǒu	出口
expensive	guì	贵
experience	jīngyàn	经验
export (n/v)	chūkǒu	出口
express (letter)	kuàidì	快递
express (train)	tèkuài	特快
extension cord	yáncháng xiànlù	延长线路
eye	yǎnjīng	眼睛
eye drops	yǎnyàoshuǐ	眼药水

F

face	liǎn	脸
factory	gōngchǎng	工厂
factory worker	gōngrén	工人
to fall	shuāidǎo	摔倒
fall (autumn)	qiūtiān	秋天

false	jiǎde	假的
family	jiā	家
famous	yǒumíng	有名
fan (handheld)	shànzi	扇子
fan (electric)	diànshàn	电扇
far	yuǎn	远
fare	piàojià	票价
farm	nóngchǎng	农场
farmer	nóngchǎng zhǔ	农场主
fast	kuài	快
fat	pàng	胖
father	fùqin	父亲
faucet	shuǐlóngtóu	水龙头
fault	cuò	错
faulty	cuòwù de	错误的
fee	fèi	费
to feel	juéde	觉得
feelings	gǎnjué	感觉
ferry	dùchuán	渡船
festival	jiérì	节日
fever	fāshāo	发烧
few	shǎo	少
fiancée/fiancé	wèihūnqī/	未婚妻 /
	wèihūnfu	未婚夫
fiction	xiǎoshuō	小说
field	tiándì	田地
fifty	wǔshí	五十
fight	dǎdòu	打斗
to fight	dǎdòu	打斗
to fill in (form)	tiánxiě	填写
film (cinema)	diànyǐng	电影
film (photographic)	jiāojuǎn	胶卷
to find	zhǎo	找
fine (penalty)	fákuǎn	罚款
finger	shǒuzhǐ	手指
fire	huǒzāi	火灾
firewood	mùchái	木柴
first	dìyī	第一
first-aid kit	jíjiùxiāng	急救箱
first class	tóuděng	头等

fish	yú	鱼
fish shop	yúdiàn	鱼店
five	wǔ	五
fizzy drink	qìshuǐ	汽水
flag	qí	旗
flash (camera)	shǎnguāngdēng	闪光灯
flashlight	shǒudiàntǒng	手电筒
flat	píng	平
flea	tiàozǎo	跳蚤
flight	hángbān	航班
flood	shuǐzāi	水灾
flour	miànfěn	面粉
flower	huā	花
flu	gǎnmào	感冒
to fly	fēi	飞
fog	wù	雾
folk music	mínjiān yīnyuè	民间音乐
follow	gēnsuí	跟随
food	shíwù	食物
food poisoning	shíwùzhōngdú	食物中毒
foot	jiǎo	脚
football (soccer)	zúqiú	足球
footpath	rénxíng xiǎodào	人行小道
forest	sēnlín	森林
forget	wàngjì	忘记

I forget.
wǒ wàng le
我忘了.

Forget about it!; Don't worry!
suàn le, méi guānxi!
算了，没关系！

forgive	yuánliàng	原谅
fork	chāzi	叉子
form (document)	biǎo	表
fortnight	liǎngzhōu	两周
fortune teller	suànmìng xiānsheng	算命先生
fountain	quán	泉
four	sì	四
forty	sìshí	四十
France	fǎguó	法国

ee (cost)	miǎnfèi	免费
ee (time)	yǒu kòng	有空
ee (vacant)	méirén	没人
ee market	zìyóu shìchǎng	自由市场
rench	fǎyǔ	法语
esh	xīnxiān	新鲜
iend	péngyǒu	朋友
iendly	yǒuhǎo	友好
iendship Store	yǒuyìshāngdiàn	友谊商店
front of	zài qiánmiàn	在前面
om	cóng	从
ozen foods	bīngdòng shípǐn	冰冻食品
uit	shuǐguǒ	水果
uit juice	guǒzhī	果汁
uit picking	zhāi shuǐguǒ	摘水果
ull	mǎn	满
un	hǎowánr	好玩儿
or fun	nàozhe wán	闹着玩
to have fun		
wán de gāoxìng		
玩得高兴		
to make fun of		
kāi wánxiào		
开玩笑		
uneral	zànglǐ	葬礼
unny	hǎoxiào	好笑
uture	jiānglái	将来
urniture	jiājù	家具

G

ame	yóuxì	游戏
arbage	lājī	垃圾
arden	huāyuán	花园
arlic	suàn	蒜
as	méiqì	煤气
ate	mén	门
ay	tóngxìngliàn	同性恋
n general	zǒngtǐ	总体
enuine	zhēnde	真的

geology	dìzhìxué	地质学

Get lost!
gǔn kāi!
滚开 !

gift	lǐwù	礼物
ginger	jiāng	姜
girl	nǚ háizi	女孩子
girlfriend	nǚ péngyǒu	女朋友
give	gěi	给

Could you give me ...?
nǐ néng gěi wǒ ... ma?
你能给我 ... 吗?

glass	bēizi	杯子
glasses (spectacles)	yǎnjìng	眼镜
glove	shǒutào	手套
glue	jiāoshuǐ	胶水
to go	qù	去

Let's go.
wǒmén zǒu ba
我们走吧。

We'd like to go to ...
wǒmén xiǎng qù ...
我们想去 ...

Go straight ahead.
yīzhí wǎng qián zǒu
一直往前走。

to go out	chūqù	出去
to go out with	tán péngyǒu	谈朋友
goal	mùbiāo	目标
goalkeeper	shǒumén yuán	守门员
goat	shānyáng	山羊
God	shàngdì	上帝
gold	jīn	金
good	hǎo	好

Good afternoon.
xiàwǔ hǎo
下午好。

Goodbye.
zàijiàn
再见。

Good evening/night.
wǎnshàng hǎo/wǎn'ān
晚上好／晚安.

Good luck!
zhù nǐ hǎo yùn!
祝你好运！

Good morning.
zǎoshàng hǎo
早上好.

oods	huòwù	货物
oose	é	鹅
overnment	zhèngfǔ	政府
ram	kè	克
randchild	sūnzi	孙子
randfather	zǔfù	祖父
randmother	zǔmǔ	祖母
rape	pútáo	葡萄
raphic art	huìhuà yìshù	绘画艺术
rass	cǎo	草
rave	fénmù	坟墓
reasy	yóuwūde	油污的
reat	měimiào de	美妙的

Great!
hǎo jí le!
好极了！

reen	lǜsè	绿色
reengrocer	shūcài shuǐguǒ diàn	蔬菜水果店
reen tea	lǜchá	绿茶
rey	huīsè	灰色
rocery	fùshídiàn	副食店
roup	tuántǐ	团体
o guess	cāixiǎng	猜想
uide (n)	dǎoyóu	导游
uidebook	lǚ yóuzhǐnán	旅游指南
uidedog	dǎománg quǎn	导盲犬
uided trek	lǐnglù yuǎnzú	领路远足
uitar	jítā	吉它
ym	jiànshēnfáng	健身房
ymnastics	tǐcāo	体操
ynaecologist	fùkēyīshēng	妇科医生

H

hair	tóufa	头发
hairbrush	fàshuā	发刷
hairdressers	lǐfàdiàn	理发店
half	bàn	半
ham	huǒtuǐ	火腿
hammer	chuízi	锤子
hammock	diàochuáng	吊床
hand	shǒu	手
handbag	shǒutíbāo	手提包
handicrafts	gōngyìpǐn	工艺品
handkerchief	shǒupà	手帕
handmade	shǒugōngzhìde	手工制的
handsome	yīngjùn	英俊
happy	gāoxìng	高兴

Happy birthday!
zhù nǐ shēngrì kuàilè!
祝你生日快乐！

harbour	gǎngwān	港湾
hard (difficult)	nán	难
hard (not soft)	yìng	硬
hard seat	yìngzuò	硬座
hard sleeper	yìngwò	硬卧
harrassment	sāorǎo	骚扰
hash	suìshí	碎食
hate	hèn	恨
have	yǒu	有

Do you have ...?
nǐmèn yǒu ... ma?
你们有 ... 吗？

I have ...
wǒ yǒu ...
我有 ...

hayfever	huāfěnzhèng	花粉症
he	tā	他
head	tóu	头
headache	tóuténg	头疼
health	jiànkāng	健康

To your health!
zhù nǐ jiànkāng!
祝你健康！

...ar	tīngjiàn	听见
...aring aid	zhùtīngqì	助听器
...art	xīnzàng	心脏
...ater	qǔnuǎnqì	取暖器
...eating	nuǎnqì	暖气
...avy	zhòng	重

Hello.
nǐ hǎo
你好.

Hello! (answering telephone)
wéi
喂！

...elmet	tóukuī	头盔
help	bāngmáng	帮忙

Help!
jiùmìng!
救命！

...er	tāde	她的
...erbs	cǎoyào	草药
...erbalist	cǎoyào yīshēng	草药医生
...ere	zhèr	这儿
...eroin	hǎiluòyīn	海洛因
...eroin addict	hǎiluòyīn shàngyǐn	海洛因上瘾
...gh	gāo	高
...gh school	zhōngxué	中学
...ke	túbùlǚxíng	徒步旅行
...king	túbù lǚxíng	徒步旅行
...king boots	túbù lǚxíng xuē	徒步旅行靴
...king routes	túbù lǚxíng lùxiàn	徒步旅行路线
...ill	xiǎoshān	小山
...indu	yìndù jiào	印度教
...ire	zū	租
...is	tāde	他的
...istory	lìshǐ	历史
...o hitchhike	dāchē	搭车
...IV positive	HIV chéng yángxìng	HIV 呈阳性

holiday	jiàqī	假期
home	jiā	家
homeless	wújiākěguī	无家可归
homeopathy	shùnshì liáofǎ	顺势疗法
homesick	xiǎngjiā	想家
homosexual	tóngxìngliàn	同性恋
honest	chéngshí	诚实
honey	fēngmì	蜂蜜
honeymoon	mìyuè	蜜月
hope	xīwàng	希望
hors d'oeuvres	kāiwèicài	开胃菜
horse	mǎ	马
horse riding	qí mǎ	骑马
hospital	yīyuàn	医院
hot	rè	热

    It's hot.
    tiān hěn rè
    天很热。

hotel	lǚguǎn	旅馆
hot water	rèshuǐ	热水
hour	xiǎoshí	小时
house	fángwū	房屋
housework	jiāwù	家务
how	zěnme	怎么

    How do I get to ...?
    ... zěnme qù?
    ... 怎么去?

    How do you say ...?
    ... zěnme shuō?
    ... 怎么说?

human rights	rénquán	人权
hundred	bǎi	百
hungry	è	饿
hurry	jímáng	急忙
in a hurry	jíjímángmáng	急急忙忙
hurt (adj)	téng	疼
husband	zhàngfu	丈夫

	wǒ	我
ce	bīng	冰
ce cream	bīngqílín	冰淇淋
dea	zhǔyì	主意
dentification	shēnfèn	身份
dentification card	shēnfènzhèng	身份证
diot	báichī	白痴
f	rúguǒ	如果
l	bìng le	病了
legal	fēifǎ	非法
mmediately	mǎshàng	马上
mmigration	yímín	移民
mport (n/v)	jìnkǒu	进口
mportant	zhòngyào	重要

It's important.
hěn zhòngyào
很重要.

It's not important.
bú zhòngyào
不重要.

mpossible	bù kěnéng	不可能
ncluded	bāokuò	包括
nclude	bāokuò	包括
nconvenient	bùfāngbiàn	不方便
ncorrect	búduì	不对
ncrease	zēngjiā	增加
ndigestion	xiāohuàbùliáng	消化不良
ndividual	gètǐ de	个体的
ndustry	gōngyè	工业
nequality	bù píngděng	不平等
nfected	gǎnrǎn	感染
nfectious	chuánrǎn	传染
nflammation	fāyán	发炎
nflation	tōnghuò péngzhàng	通货膨胀
nformal	fēizhèngshì	非正式
nformation office	wènxùnchù	问讯处
njection	zhùshè	注射
njured	shòushāng le	受伤了
nk	mòshuǐ	墨水

insect	chóngzi	虫子
insect repellent	chúchóngjì	除虫剂
inside	lǐmiàn	里面
instructor	jiàoliàn	教练
insurance	bǎoxiǎn	保险
intelligent	cōngmíng	聪明
interested	gǎn xìngqù	感兴趣
interesting	yǒuqù	有趣
international	guójì	国际
interview	miàntán	面谈
introduce	jièshào	介绍
investment	tóuzī	投资
invite	yāoqíng	邀请
island	dǎo	岛
itch	yǎng	痒
ivory	xiàngyá	象牙

J

jacket	duǎnshàngyī	短上衣
jade	yù	玉
jail	jiānyù	监狱
jam	guǒjiàng	果酱
jar	guànzi	罐子
jasmine tea	mòlihuāchá	茉莉花茶
jazz	juéshìyīnyuè	爵士音乐
jealous	jídù	嫉妒
jeans	niúzǎikù	牛仔裤
jewellery	zhūbǎo	珠宝
Jewish	yóutài rén	犹太人
job	gōngzuò	工作
job advertisement	jiùyè guǎnggào	就业广告
journalist	jìzhě	记者
journey	lǚtú	旅途
juice	zhī	汁
to jump	tiào	跳
jumper (sweater)	máoyī	毛衣
jungle	cónglín	丛林

key	yàoshi	钥匙
keyboard	jiànpán	键盘
kick	tī	踢
kidney	shèn	肾
kill	shā	杀
kilogram	gōngjīn	公斤
kilometre	gōnglǐ	公里
kind (type)	zhǒng	种
kindergarten	yòuéryuán	幼儿园
king	guówáng	国王
kiss (n/v)	wěn	吻
kitchen	chúfáng	厨房
kite	fēngzheng	风筝
knapsack	bèibāo	背包
knee	xīgài	膝盖
knife	dāozi	刀子
know (person)	rènshi	认识
know (something)	zhīdào	知道

I don't know.
wǒ bù zhīdào
我不知道。

lace	wǎngyǎn zhīwù	网眼织物
lacquerware	qīqì	漆器
lake	hú	湖
lamb (meat)	yángròu	羊肉
lamp	diàndēng	电灯
land	tǔdì	土地
landscape	fēngjǐng	风景
landslide	shānbēng	山崩
language	yǔyán	语言
large	dà	大
last (final)	zuìhòu	最后
last month	shàng ge yuè	上个月
last night	zuótiān wǎnshàng	昨天晚上
last week	shàng ge xīngqī	上个星期

last year	qùnián	去年
late	wǎn	晚
to laugh	xiào	笑
laundry (place)	xǐyīdiàn	洗衣店
law	fǎ l	法律
lawyer	lùshī	律师
laxative	qīngxièjì	倾泻剂
lazy	lǎnduò	懒惰
leader	língdǎo	领导
learn	xué	学
leather	pígé	皮革
leave	zǒu	走
leave (train/bus)	kāichē	开车
leech	shuǐzhì	水蛭
to be left (behind/over)	liúxià	留下
left (direction)	zuǒbiān	左边
left-luggage office	xínglǐ jìcúnchù	行李寄存处
left-wing	zuǒyì	左翼
leg	tuǐ	腿
leg (in race)	sàichéng	赛程
legal	héfǎ	合法
legalisation	héfǎ huà	合法化
legislation	lìfǎ	立法
lemon	níngméng	柠檬
lend	jiè	借
lens (camera)	jìngtóu	镜头
lens (glasses)	jìngpiàn	镜片
lens cap	jìngtóugài	镜头盖
lesbian	nǚ tóngxìngliàn	女同性恋
less	shǎo yīdiǎnr	少一点儿
letter	xìn	信
liar	shuōhuǎngzhě	说谎者
library	túshūguǎn	图书馆
lid	gài	盖
lice	shīzi	虱子
to lie	sǎhuǎng	撒谎
life	shēnghuó	生活
lift (elevator)	diàntī	电梯
to lift	tíqǐ	提起
light (colour)	qiǎn	浅
light (electric)	diàndēng	电灯

light (weight)	qīng	轻
lighter	dǎhuǒjī	打火机
lightning	shǎndiàn	闪电
to like	xǐhuān	喜欢
lip	zuǐchún	嘴唇
lipstick	kǒuhóng	口红
listen	tīng	听
litre	shēng	升
little (adj)	yīdiǎnr	一点儿
a little (amount)	yīxiē	一些
a little bit	yīdiǎnr	一点儿
to live (life)	shēnghuó	生活
Long live …!		
… wànsuì!		
… 万岁！		
to live (somewhere)	zhù	住
liver	gān	肝
lobster	lóngxiā	龙虾
local	běndì	本地
lock	suǒ	锁
to lock	suǒshàng	锁上
long	cháng	长
long-distance call	chángtú diànhuà	长途电话
look	kàn	看
to look after	zhàogu	照顾
to look for	xúnzhǎo	寻找
loose change	língqián	零钱
lose	diū	丢
a lot	hěn duō	很多
loud	chǎo	吵
to love	ài	爱
lover	qíngrén	情人
low	dī	低
luck	yùnqì	运气
lucky	xìngyùn	幸运
luggage	xínglǐ	行李
lump (swelling)	zhǒngkuài	肿块
lunch	zhōngfàn	中饭
lung	fèi	肺
luxury	háohuá	豪华
lychees	lìzhī	荔枝

M

machine	jīqì	机器
mad	fāfēng	发疯
made (of)	zhìzào	制造
magazine	zázhì	杂志
mahjong	májiàng	麻将
to mail	jì	寄
mailbox	xìnxiāng	信箱
main	zhǔyào	主要
main road	gàndào	干道
main square	zhǔ guǎngchǎng	主广场
majority	dà bùfen	大部分
to make	zhìzuò	制做
makeup	huàzhuāng	化妆
man	nánrén	男人
manager	jīnglǐ	经理
Mandarin (language)	pǔtōnghuà	普通话
mango	mángguǒ	芒果
manual worker	gōngrén	工人
many	hěn duō	很多
map	dìtú	地图

Can you show me on the map?
nǐ néng zài dìtú shàng zhǐ gěi wǒ kàn ma?
你能在地图上指给我看吗？

marble	dàlǐshí	大理石
market	shìchǎng	市场
married	yǐhūn	已婚
massage	ànmó	按摩
match (sport)	bǐsài	比赛
matches	huǒchái	火柴
matter	shì	事

It doesn't matter.
méi shì
没事。

What's the matter?
(shénme) shì?
什么事？

| mattress | chuángdiàn | 床垫 |
| maybe | yěxǔ | 也许 |

me	wǒ	我
meal	fàn	饭
to measure	liáng	量
meat	ròu	肉
mechanic	jìgōng	技工
medicine	yào	药
meditation	mòxiǎng	默想
meet	jiànmiàn	见面
melon	guā	瓜
memorial hall	jì niàn guǎn	纪念馆
mend	xiūlǐ	修理
menstruation	yuèjīng	月经
menu	càidān	菜单
message	liúhuà	留话
metal	jīnshǔ	金属
method	fāngfǎ	方法
metre	mǐ	米
midday	zhōngwǔ	中午
middle	zhōngjiān	中间
midnight	wǔyè	午夜
military	jūnduì	军队
military service	bīngyì	兵役
milk	niúnǎi	牛奶
million	bǎiwàn	百万
mineral water	kuàngquánshuǐ	矿泉水
mint	bòhe	薄荷
minute	fēnzhōng	分钟

Just a minute.
děng yìhuǐr
等一会儿。

in (five) minutes
(wǔ) fēnzhōng yǐhòu
(五)分钟以后

mirror	jìngzi	镜子
miscarriage	liúchǎn	流产
Miss	xiǎojiě	小姐
miss (long for)	xiǎng	想
mist	bówù	薄雾
mistake	cuòwù	错误
to mix	hùnhé	混合

mobile phone	yídòng diànhuà	移动电话
modem	tiáozhì jiětiáoqì	调制解调器
modern	xiàndài	现代
money	qián	钱
monkey	hóuzi	猴子
monosodium glutimate (MSG)	wèijīng	味精
month	yuè	月
this month	zhè ge yuè	这个月
monument	jì niàn bēi	纪念碑
moon	yuèliang	月亮
more	duō yīdiǎnr	多一点儿
morning	zǎoshàng	早上
mosque	qīngzhēnsì	清真寺
mother	mǔqīn	母亲
mother-in-law	yuèmǔ/pópo	岳母／婆婆
motorbike	mótuóchē	摩托车
motorway (tollway)	gāosù gōnglù (shōufèi gōnglù)	高速公路 （收费公路）
mountain	shān	山
mountain bike	dēngshānchē	登山车
mountain hut	shānzhōng xiǎo wū	山中小屋
mountain path	shānzhōng xiǎolù	山中小路
mountain range	shānmài	山脉
mountaineering	dēngshān yùndòng	登山运动
mouth	zuǐ	嘴
to move	dòng	动
movie	diànyǐng	电影
Mr	xiānsheng	先生
Mrs	tàitai	太太
MSG (monosodium glutimate)	wèijīng	味精
mud	ní	泥
muscle	jīròu	肌肉
museum	bówùguǎn	博物馆
music	yīnyuè	音乐
musical instrument	yuèqì	乐器
Muslim	qīngzhēn	清真
must	bìxū	必须
mutton	yángròu	羊肉
my	wǒde	我的

nail (finger)	zhǐjiǎ	指甲
nail clippers	zhǐjiǎdāo	指甲刀
name	xìngmíng	姓名
nappy (diaper)	niàobù	尿布
nappy rash	niàobù zhěn	尿布疹
national park	guójiā gōngyuán	国家公园
nationality	guójí	国籍
natural	zìrán de	自然的
nature	zìránjiè	自然界
naturopath	zìrán liáofǎ yīshī	自然疗法医师
nausea	èxīn	恶心
near	jìn	近
nearby hotel	fùjìn de bīnguǎn	附近的宾馆
necessary	bìyào de	必要的
neck	bózi	脖子
necklace	xiàngliàn	像链
to need	xūyào	需要
needle (sewing)	féngyīzhēn	缝衣针
needle (syringe)	zhùshè zhēntóu	注射针头
negative (film)	dǐpiàn	底片
neither	yě bù	也不
never	cónglái méiyǒu	从来没有
new	xīn	新
news	xīnwén	新闻
newspaper	bàozhǐ	报纸
New Year's Day	yuándàn	元旦
New Year's Eve	yuándàn chúxī	元旦除夕
next	xià	下
next month	xià ge yuè	下个月
next to	páng biānr	旁边儿
next week	xià ge xīngqī	下个星期
next year	míngnián	明年
nice	hǎo	好
night	yè	夜
nine	jiǔ	九
nineteen	shíjiǔ	十九
ninety	jiǔshí	九十
no	bù	不
noisy	chǎo	吵

non-direct	fēi zhíjiē	非直接
none	wúyī	无一
noodles	miàntiáo	面条
noon	zhōngwǔ	中午
normal	zhèngcháng	正常
north	běi	北
nose	bízi	鼻子
notebook	bǐjìběn	笔记本
note paper	xìnzhǐ	信纸
nothing	yīwúsuǒyǒu	一无所有
novel	xiǎoshuō	小说
novelist	xiǎoshuōjiā	小说家
now	xiànzài	现在
nuclear energy	hé'néng	核能
nuclear testing	hé shìyàn	核试验
number	hàomǎ	号码
nurse	hùshi	护士

O

obvious	míngxiǎn	明显
occupation	zhíyè	职业
ocean	hǎiyáng	海洋
offence	fànfǎ xíngwéi	犯法行为
office	bàn gōng shì	办公室
officer	jūnguān	军官
office work	bàn gōng shì gōngzuò	办公室工作
office worker	zhíyuán	职员
offside	yuèwèi	越位
often	chángcháng	常常
oil	yóu	油
oil (cooking)	xiāngyóu	香油
oil (crude)	shíyóu	石油
ointment	yàogāo	药膏
OK.		
hǎo		
好。		
old (person)	lǎo	老
old (thing)	jiù	旧
old city	lǎochéng	老城
Olympic Games	àoyùnhuì	奥运会

n	zài shàngmiàn	在上面
n time	zhǔnshí	准时
nce	yīcì	一次
ne	yīge	一个
ne-way ticket	dānchéng piào	单程票
nion	yángcōng	洋葱
nly	zhǐ	只
pen (sign)	zhèngzài yíngyè	正在营业
pen (v/adj)	kāimén	开门
pera	xìjù	戏剧
pera house	jùyuàn	剧院
peration	shǒushù	手术
pinion	yìjiàn	意见
pium	yāpiàn	鸦片
pportunity	jīhuì	机会
pposite	duìmiàn	对面
r	háishì	还是
range (colour)	júhóng sè	桔红色
range (fruit)	júzi	橘子
range juice	júzizhī	桔子汁
rder (meal)	diǎn cài	点菜
o order (someone to do something)	mìnglìng	命令
rdinary	pǔtōng	普通
rganise	zǔzhī	组织
rganisation	zǔzhī	组织
riginal	yuánxiān	原先的
ther	biéde	别的
utside	zài wàimiàn	在外面
ver	zài shàngmiàn	在上面
veralls	gōngzhuāngkù	工装裤
vercoat	dàyī	大衣
verdose	guòliàng	过量
vernight	zhěngyè	整夜
verseas	hǎiwài	海外
we	qiàn	欠
x	gōngniú	公牛
xygen	yǎngqì	氧气
yster	háo	蚝
zone layer	chòuyǎngcéng	臭氧层

P

pacifier (dummy)	nǎizuǐ	奶嘴
packet (cigarettes)	bāo	包
paddy field	dàotián	稻田
padlock	guàsuǒ	挂锁
page	yè	页
pagoda	bǎotǎ	宝塔
pain	téngtòng	疼痛
painful	hén téng	很疼
painkillers	zhǐtòng yào	止痛药
to paint	huà huàr	画画儿
painter	huàjiā	画家
painting	huà	画
pair	yīshuāng	一双
palace	gōngdiàn	宫殿
palpitation	xīnjì	心悸
paper	zhǐ	纸
(writing) paper	xìnzhǐ	信纸
parallel	píngxíngde	平行的
paraplegic	jiétān	截瘫
parcel	bāoguǒ	包裹
parents	fùmǔqīn	父母亲
park	gōngyuán	公园
to park	tíngchē	停车
party (n)	shèjiāo jùhuì	社交聚会
party (fiesta)	jùhuì	聚会
party (political)	dǎngpài	党派
passport	hùzhào	护照
passport number	hùzhào hàomǎ	护照号码
past	guòqù	过去
pastry	gāodiǎn	糕点
pastry shop	gāodiǎnpù	糕点铺
path	xiǎolù	小路
patient	bìngrén	病人
pavillion	tíngzi	亭子
to pay	fùqián	付钱
pea	wāndòu	豌豆
peace	hépíng	和平
peach	táozi	桃子
peanut	huāshēng	花生

ENGLISH – MANDARIN

pear	lí	梨
pearl	zhēnzhū	珍珠
pedestrian	xíngrén	行人
pen	bǐ	笔
pencil	qiānbǐ	铅笔
penicillin	qīngméisù	青霉素
penknife	xiǎodāo	小刀
people	rén	人
pepper	hújiāo	胡椒
per cent	bǎifēnzhī	百分之
perfect	wánměi	完美
performance	yǎnchū	演出
period (menstrual)	yuèjīng	月经
period (of time)	shíqī	时期
period pain	yuèjīng tòng	月经痛
permanent collection	gùdìng shōucángpǐn	固定收藏品
permission	yúnxǔ	允许
permit	xǔkězhèng	许可证
person	rén	人
personal	sīrénde	私人的
personality	gèxìng	个性
perspire	chūhàn	出汗
petrol	qìyóu	汽油
pharmacy	yàodiàn	药店
phone book	diànhuà bù	电话簿
phone booth	diànhuà tíng	电话亭
phonecard	diànhuà kǎ	电话卡
photo	zhàopiàn	照片

Can I take a photo?
wǒ kěyǐ zhàoxiàng ma?
我可以照相吗？

photocopy	fùyìn	复印
photography	shèyǐng	摄影
pickaxe	dīngzìgǎo	丁字镐
to pick up	jiǎnqǐ	捡起
pie	bǐng	饼
piece	kuài	快
pig	zhū	猪
pill	piàn	片
pill (contraceptive)	bìyùnyào	避孕药

pillow	zhěntóu	枕头
pillowcase	zhěntào	枕套
pineapple	bōluó	菠萝
pink	fěnhóng sè	粉红色
pipe	yāndǒu	烟斗
place	dìfāng	地方
place of birth	chūshēngdì	出生地
plane	fēijī	飞机
planet	xīngqiú	星球
plant	zhíwù	植物
to plant	zhòngzhí	种植
plastic	sùliào	塑料
plate	pánzi	盘子
platform (station)	zhàntái	站台
play (theatre)	xìjù	戏剧
to play (a game)	wánr	玩儿
to play (music)	tánzòu	弹奏
to play cards	dǎ pái	打牌
player (sports)	yùndòngyuán	运动员
please	qǐng	请
plug (bath)	sāizi	塞子
plug (electricity)	chātóu	插头
plum	lǐzi	李子
pocket	kǒudài	口袋
poet	shīrén	诗人
poetry	shīgē	诗歌
to point	zhǐ	指
poison	dúyào	毒药
police	jǐngchá	警察
police station	pàichūsuǒ	派出所
politics	zhèngzhì	政治
pollen	huāfěn	花粉
pollution	wūrǎn	污染
pond	chítáng	池塘
pool (swimming)	yóuyǒngchí	游泳池
poor	qióng	穷
popular	liúxíng	流行
porcelain	cíqì	瓷器
pork	zhūròu	猪肉
port	mǎtóu	码头
portrait sketcher	huàxiàng shī	画像师

possible	kěnéng	可能
	It's (not) possible. bù kěnéng 不可能。	
to post	jì	寄
postage	yóufèi	邮费
postage stamp	yóupiào	邮票
postcard	míngxìnpiàn	明信片
postcode	yóuzhèng biānmǎ	邮政编码
post office	yóujú	邮局
potato	tǔdòu	土豆
pot (ceramic)	hú	壶
pot (dope)	dúpǐn	毒品
pottery	táoqì	陶器
poverty	pínqióng	贫穷
power	lìliàng	力量
practical	shíjì	实际
prawn	duìxiā	对虾
prayer	dǎogào	祷告
prayer book	qídǎo shū	祈祷书
prefer	bǐjiào xǐhuān	比较喜欢
pregnant	huáiyùn	怀孕
prehistoric art	shǐqián yìshù	史前艺术
prepare	zhǔnbèi	准备
prescription	yàofāng	药方
present (gift)	lǐwù	礼物
present (time)	mùqián	目前
presentation	zèngsòng	赠送
president	zǒngtǒng	总统
pressure	yālì	压力
pretty	piàoliang	漂亮
prevent	fángzhǐ	防止
price	jiàqián	价钱
priest	jiàoshì	教士
prime minister	zǒnglǐ	总理
prison	jiānyù	监狱
prisoner	fànrén	犯人
private	sīrén	私人
privatisation	sīyíng huà	私营化
probably	dàgài	大概

problem	wèntí	问题
processing (film)	chōngxǐ	冲洗
to produce	shēngchǎn	生产
producer	shēngchǎn zhě	生产者
product	chǎnpǐn	产品
profession	zhíyè	职业
professional	zhuānyè de	专业的
profit	lìrùn	利润
programme	jiémù	节目
projector	jìhuà rén	计划人
to promise	dāying	答应
pronunciation	fāyīn	发音
property	cáichǎn	财产
prostitute	jìnǚ	妓女
protect	bǎohù	保护
protected forest	fánghù lín	防护林
protected species	shòu bǎohù	受保护物种
	wùzhǒng	
protest	kàngyì	抗议
to protest	kàngyì	抗议
province	shěng	省
psychology	xīnlǐxué	心理学
public toilet	gōngyòng cèsuǒ	公用厕所
to pull	lā	拉
to pump	bèng	泵
puncture	cìpò	刺破
to punish	chéngfá	惩罚
puppy	xiǎo gǒu	小狗
pure	chúnde	纯的
purple	zǐ sè	紫色
pus	nóng	脓
to push	tuī	推
to put	fàng	放

Q

qualifications	xuélì	学历
quality	zhìliàng	质量
quantity	shùliàng	数量
quarantine	jiǎnyì	检疫

quarrel (n/v)	chǎojià	吵架
quarter	sìfēnzhīyī	四分之一
queen	nǚwáng	女王
question	wèntí	问题
queue	páiduì	排队
quick	kuài	快
quiet	ānjìng	安静
quilt	bèizi	被子
to quit	tuìchū	退出

R

rabbit	tùzi	兔子
race (breed)	rénzhǒng	人种
race (sport)	bǐsài	比赛
racing bike	sàichē	赛车
racism	zhǒngzúpiānjiàn	种族偏见
racquet	wǎngqiú pāi	网球拍
radiator	sànrèqì	散热器
radio	shōuyīnjī	收音机
railway station	huǒchēzhàn	火车站
to rain	xiàyǔ	下雨

It's raining.
xià yǔ le
下雨了。

raincoat	yǔyī	雨衣
rape (assault)	qiángjiān	强奸
rare	nándé	难得
rash	zhěnzi	疹子
raspberry	shùméi	树莓
rat	hàozi	耗子
raw	shēngde	生的
razor	tìdāo	剃刀
razor blades	tìdāo piàn	剃刀片
read	kànshū	看书
ready	hǎo le	好了
real	zhēn de	真的
to realise	rènshi dào	认识到
really	zhēn de	真的
reason	yuányīn	原因

receipt	shōujù	收据
to receive	shōudào	收到
recent(ly)	zuìjìn	最近
reception desk	fúwùtái	服务台
recommend	tuījiàn	推荐
recording	lùyīn	录音
recyclable	huíshōu lìyòng	回收利用
recycling	huíshōu	回收
record (disk)	chàngpiàn	唱片
red	hóng sè	红色
referee	cáipàn	裁判
reference	tuījiàn xìn	推荐信
reflection (mirror)	fǎnshè	反射
reflection (thinking)	xiǎngfǎ	想法
refrigerator	bīngxiāng	冰箱
refugee	nànmín	难民
refund (n/v)	tuìkuǎn	退款
to refuse	jùjué	拒绝
region	dìqū	地区
regional	dìqū	地区
registered (mail)	guàhào	挂号
relation(ship)	guānxi	关系
religion	zōngjiào	宗教
remember	jìdé	记得
to rent/hire	zū	租
to repair	xiū	修
to repeat	chóngfù	重复
to report	bàogào	报告
representative	dàibiǎo	代表
reptile	páxíngdòngwù	爬行动物
republic	gònghéguó	共和国
reservation	yùdìng	预定
to reserve	yùdìng	预定
resignation	tuìzhí	退职
respect	zūnjìng	尊敬
responsibility	zérèn	责任
rest (relaxation)	xiūxi	休息
rest (what's left)	shèngyú	剩余
to rest	xiūxi	休息
restaurant	fànguǎn	饭馆
resumé	jiǎnlì	简历

retired	tuìxiū	退休
return (give back)	huán	还
return (go back)	huíqú	回去
return (come back)	huílái	回来
return trip	láihuí piào	来回票
reverse charges	duìfāngfùfèi	对方付费
review	fùxí	复习
revolution	gémìng	革命
rib	lèigǔ	肋骨
rice (uncooked)	mǐ	米
rice (cooked)	báifàn	白饭
rich (wealthy)	fùyǒu	富有
rich (food)	yóunì	油腻
to ride (a horse)	qí	骑
right (side)	yòubiān	右边
to be right	zhèngquè	正确

You're right.
nǐ shuō de duì
你说的对。

civil rights	mínquán	民权
right now	mǎshàng	马上
right-wing	yòuyì	右翼
right (correct)	duì	对
ring (jewellery)	jièzhǐ	戒指
ring (of phone)	dǎ	打

I'll give you a ring.
wǒ gěi nǐ dǎ diànhuà
我给你打电话。

ring (sound)	língshēng	铃声
ripe	chéngshú	成熟
rip-off	qiāo zhúgàng	敲竹杠
river	hé	河
road	lù	路
road map	gōnglù tú	公路图
to rob	qiǎngjié	抢劫
rock climbing	pānyán	攀岩
(wall of) rock	yánshí	岩石
rock group	yáogǔn yuèduì	摇滚乐队
romance	làngmàn	浪漫
roof	wūdǐng	屋顶

room	fángjiān	房间
room number	fángjiān hàomǎ	房间号码
rope	shéngzi	绳子
round	yuán de	圆的
roundabout	yuánhuán	圆环
route	lùjìng	路径
rubbish	lājī	垃圾
rug	xiǎo dìtǎn	小地毯
ruins	jiùzhǐ	旧址
to run	pǎobù	跑步

S

sad	bēiāi	悲哀
safe (adj)	ānquán	安全
safe (n)	bǎoxiǎnxiāng	保险箱
safety pin	biézhēn	别针
sailor	shuǐshǒu	水手
salary	gōngzī	工资
(on) sale	liánjià chūshòu	廉价出售
sales department	xiāoshòu bù	销售部
salt	yán	盐
same	yīyàng	一样
sandals	liángxié	凉鞋
sandwich	sānmíngzhì	三明治
sanitary napkins	wèishēngjīn	卫生巾
satisfied	mǎnyì	满意
sausage	xiāngcháng	香肠
to say	shuō	说
scald	tàngshāng	烫伤
scarf	wéijīn	围巾
scenery	fēngjǐng	风景
school	xuéxiào	学校
science	kēxué	科学
scientist	kē xué jiā	科学家
scissors	jiǎndāo	剪刀
scrambled egg	chǎojīdàn	炒鸡蛋
to score	défēn	得分
scoreboard	jìfēn pái	记分牌
screen (for room)	píngfēng	屏风
screwdriver	qǐzi	起子

scroll	juànzhóu	卷轴
sea	hǎi	海
seafood	hǎixiān	海鲜
seasick	yùnchuán	晕船
season	jìjié	季节
seat	zuòwèi	座位
seatbelt	ānquándài	安全带
second (not first)	dì èr	第二
second (time)	miǎo	秒
second class	èrděng	二等
secret	mìmì	秘密
secretary	mìshū	秘书
see	kàn	看
see (meet)	jiànmiàn	见面

I see. (understand)
wǒ míngbái le
我明白了.

See you later.
zàijiàn
再见.

See you tomorrow.
míngtiān jiàn
明天见.

self-employed	gètǐhù	个体户
selfish	zìsī	自私
self-service	zìwǒ fúwù	自我服务
sell	mài	卖
send (post)	jì	寄
sentence (language)	jùzi	句子
sentence (prison)	pànjué	判决
to separate	fēnlǐ	分离
serious	yánsù	严肃
serious (injury)	yánzhòng	严重
service (religious)	fúwù	服务
seven	qī	七
seventeen	shíqī	十七
seventy	qīshí	七十
several	jǐ ge	几个
sew	féng	缝
sex	xìng	性

sexism	xìngbié piānjiàn	性别偏见
sexy	mírén/xìnggǎn de	迷人/性感的
shade	yīnliáng	荫凉
shadow	yīnliáng	荫凉
shampoo	xǐfàjì	洗发剂
shape	xíngzhuàng	形状
to share (with)	fēnxiǎng	分享
shave	guāliǎn	刮脸
she	tā	她
sheep	yáng	羊
sheet (bed)	bèidān	被单
shell	bèiké	贝壳
ship	chuán	船
to ship	zhuāngyùn	装运
shirt	chènshān	衬衫
shoe	xié	鞋
shoelace	xiédài	鞋带
shoe polish	xiéyóu	鞋油
shop	shāngdiàn	商店
to go shopping	gòuwù	购物
shopping area	shāngyèqū	商业区
shore	àn	岸
short (length)	duǎn	短
short (height)	ǎi	矮
shortage	duǎnquē	短缺
shorts	duǎnkù	短裤
shoulder	jiānbǎng	肩膀
to show	zhǎnshì	展示

Can you show me on the map?
nǐ néng zài dìtú shàng zhǐ gěi wǒ kàn ma?
你能在地图上指给我看吗?

shower	línyù	淋浴
shrimp	xiā	虾
to shut	guān	关
shut (adj)	guān mén	关门
shy	hàixiū	害羞
sick	shēngbìng	生病
sickness	bìng	病
side	pángbiānr	旁边儿
sightseeing	yóulǎn	游览

sign	biāozhì	标志
to sign	qiānzì	签字
signature	qiānmíng	签名
silk	sīchóu	丝绸
silk factory	sīchóuchǎng	丝绸厂
silver	yín	银
simple	jiǎndān	简单
since	cóng	从
sing	chànggē	唱歌
single (unmarried)	dānshēn	单身儿
single room	dānrénfáng	单人房
single ticket	dānchéngpiào	单程票
sister (older)	jiějie	姐姐
sister (younger)	mèimei	妹妹
sit	zuò	坐
situation	qíngkuàng	情况
six	liù	六
sixteen	shíliù	十六
sixty	liùshí	六十
size	dàxiǎo	大小
size (clothes)	chǐcùn	尺此
skin	pífu	皮肤
skirt	qúnzi	裙子
sky	tiānkōng	天空
to sleep	shuìjiào	睡觉
sleeping car	wòchē	卧车
sleeping pill	ānmiányào	安眠药
sleepy	píjuàn	疲倦
sleeve	xiùzi	袖子
slide (film)	huàndēngpiàn	幻灯片
slipper	tuōxié	拖鞋
slow	màn	慢
small	xiǎo	小
small change	língqián	零钱
smelly	chòu	臭
smile	xiào	笑
to smoke	chōuyān	抽烟
snack	xiǎochī	小吃
snake	shé	蛇
to snow	xiàxuě	下雪
soap	féizào	肥皂

S

D
I
C
T
I
O
N
A
R
Y

soap opera	féizào jù	肥皂剧
soccer	zúqiú	足球
socialism	shèhuìzhǔyì	社会主义
sock	wàzi	袜子
soft	ruǎn	软
soft seat	ruǎnzuò	软座
soft sleeper	ruǎnwò	软卧
soil	nítǔ	泥土
some	yìxiē	一些
somebody	yǒurén	有人
someone	yǒurén	有人
something	mǒushì	某事
sometimes	yǒushí	有时
son	érzi	儿子
song	gēqǔ	歌曲
soon	bùjiǔ	不久
sorry	duìbùqǐ	对不起

I'm sorry.
duìbùqǐ
对不起。

soup	tāng	汤
south	nán	南
souvenir	jìniànpǐn	纪念品
souvenir shop	jìniànpǐn shāngdiàn	纪念品商店
soya sauce	jiàngyóu	酱油
space (outer)	tàikōng	太空
to speak	shuō	说
special	tèbié	特别
specialist	zhuānjiā	专家
speed (n)	sùdù	速度
speed limit	xiànsù	限速
spicy	là	辣
spider	zhīzhū	蜘蛛
spine	jǐzhuī	脊椎
spoon	sháozi	勺子
sport	tǐyù yùndòng	体育运动
to sprain	niǔshāng	扭伤
spring (season)	chūntiān	春天
spring (coil)	tánhuáng	弹簧
square (shape)	fāngxíng	方形

square (plaza)	guǎngchǎng	广场
squid	yóuyú	鱿鱼
stadium	tǐyù chǎng	体育场
stairs	lóutī	楼梯
stale	bùxīnxiān	不新鲜
stamp	yóupiào	邮票
standard (usual)	pǔtōng	普通
standard of living	shēnghuó shuǐpíng	生活水平
star	xīngxīng	星星
to start	kāishǐ	开始
station	zhàn	站
stationery	wénjù	文具
statistics	tǒngjì	统计
statue	diāoxiàng	雕像
to stay (remain)	tíngliú	停留
to stay (somewhere)	zhù	住
steal	tōu	偷
steamed	qīngzhēng de	清蒸的
steamed bread	mántóu	馒头
steep	dǒu	陡
step	táijiē	台阶
stick	mùgùn	木棍
stomach	wèi	胃
stone	shítóu	石头
stoned	shénzhì huǎnghū	神志恍惚
to stop	tíng	停

Stop!
zhànzhù!
站住!

store (shop)	shāngdiàn	商店
storm	fēngbào	风暴
storey	lóu	楼
story (narrative)	gùshi	故事
stove	huǒlú	火炉
straight ahead	yīzhí	一直
strange	qíguài	奇怪
stranger	mòshēngrén	陌生人
strawberry	cǎoméi	草莓
stream	xīliú	溪流
street	jiē	街

strike (union)	bàgōng	罢工
on strike	bàgōng	罢工
string	shéngzi	绳子
stroll	sànbù	散步
student	xuésheng	学生
to study	xué	学
stupid	bèn	笨
sturdy	jiēshi	结实
subtitles	zìmù	字幕
suburb	jiāoqū	郊区
subway	dìtiě	地铁
success	chénggōng	成功
to suffer	huànbìng	患病
sugar	táng	糖
suit	xīfú	西服
suitcase	xiāngzi	箱子
suite	tàofáng	套房
summer	xiàtiān	夏天
sun	tàiyáng	太阳
sunblock	fángshàishuāng	防晒霜
sunburn	shàishāng	晒伤
sunglasses	mòjìng	墨镜
sunrise	rìchū	日出
sunset	rìluò	日落
sunscreen lotion	fángshàishuāng	防晒霜
supermarket	chāojíshìchǎng	超级市场
sure	yīdìng	一定
surface mail	pǔtōng	普通
surname	xìng	姓
surprise (n)	jīngqí	惊奇
to survive	xìngcún	幸存
swamp	zhǎozé	沼泽
sweater (jumper)	máoyī	毛衣
sweet	tián	甜
to swim	yóuyǒng	游泳
swimming pool	yóuyǒngchí	游泳池
swimsuit	yóuyǒngyī	游泳衣
swollen	zhǒngle	肿了
syringe	zhùshèqì	注射器
system	xìtǒng	系统

T

table	zhuōzi	桌子
table tennis	pīngpāngqiú	乒乓球
tailor	cáiféngdiàn	裁缝店
to take (away)	ná zǒu	拿走
to take (the train)	zuò chē	坐车
to take photographs	zhàoxiàng	照相
takeaway	dàizǒu	带走
talcum powder	shuǎngshēnfěn	爽身粉
talk	shuōhuà	说话
tall	gāo	高
tangerine	gānjú	柑橘
Taoism	dàojiào	道教
tap	shuǐlóngtóu	水龙头
tape recorder	lùyīnjī	录音机
tasty	hǎochī	好吃
tax	shuì	税
taxi	chūzūqìchē	出租汽车
tea	chá	茶
tea cup	chábēi	茶杯
teacher	jiàoshī	教师
tea pot	cháhú	茶壶
team	duì	队
teaspoon	tāngchí	汤匙
technique	jìshù	技术
teeth	yáchǐ	牙齿
telegram	diànbào	电报
telephone	diànhuà	电话
telephone directory	diànhuàbù	电话簿
telephoto lens	shèyuǎn jìngtóu	摄远镜头
television	diànshìjī	电视机
telex	diànchuán	电传
tell	gàosu	告诉
temperature	wēndù	温度
tennis	wǎngqiú	网球
tennis court	wǎngqiú chǎng	网球场
tent	zhàngpeng	帐篷
tent pegs	zhàngpeng zhuāng	帐篷桩
test	cèshì	测试
tetanus	pòshāngfēng	破伤风

thanks	xièxie	谢谢

Thank you.
xièxie nǐ
谢谢你.

that	nèige	那个
theatre	jùchǎng	剧场
there	nèr	那儿
thick	hòu	厚
thief	zéi	贼
thigh	dàtuǐ	大腿
thin (slim)	shòu	瘦
think	kǎolǜ	考虑
thirsty	kǒukě	口渴
thirteen	shísān	十三
thirty	sānshí	三十
this	zhèige	这个
thousand	qiān	千
thread	xiàn	线
three	sān	三
throat	sǎngzi	嗓子
through	jīngguò	经过
thumb	mǔzhǐ	拇指
thunder	léi	雷
ticket	piào	票
ticket collector	chápiào yuán	查票员
ticket office	shòupiàochù	售票处
tide	cháo	潮
tight (clothes)	jǐn	紧
time	shíjiān	时间
on time	zhǔnshí	准时
timetable	shíkèbiǎo	时刻表
tin (can)	guàntóu	罐头
tin opener	kāiguànqì	开罐器
tip (gratuity)	xiǎofèi	小费
tired	lèi	累
tissue paper	miànzhǐ	面纸
toast	kǎomiànbāo	烤面包
tobacco	yāncǎo	烟草
tobacco kiosk	xiāngyān diàn	香烟店
today	jīntiān	今天

T

toe	jiǎozhǐ	脚趾
together	yīqǐ	一起
toilet	cèsuǒ	厕所
toilet paper	wèishēngzhǐ	卫生纸
tomato	xīhóngshì	西红柿
tomb	fénmù	坟墓
tomorrow	míngtiān	明天
tomorrow afternoon/ evening	míngtiān xiàwǔ/ wǎnshang	明天下午 / 晚上
tomorrow morning	míngtiān zǎoshàng	明天早上
tonight	jīnwǎn	今晚
too	tài	太

too expensive
tài guì le
太贵了

too much
tài duō le
太多了

too many
tài duō le
太多了

tooth	yá	牙
toothbrush	yáshuā	牙刷
toothpaste	yágāo	牙膏
toothpick	yáqiān	牙签
top	dǐng	顶
torch (flashlight)	shǒudiàntǒng	手电筒
tour group	lǚxíngtuán	旅行团
tourist	lǚkè	旅客
tourist information office	yóukè wènxùn chù	游客问讯处
towards	xiàng	向
towel	máojīn	毛巾
tower	tǎ	塔
town	shìzhèn	市镇
toy	wánjù	玩具
track (car-racing)	pǎodào	跑道
track (footprints)	zújì	足迹
track (sports)	tiánjìng	田径
track (path)	xiǎodào	小道
trade (n/v)	màoyì	贸易

D I C T I O N A R Y

traffic	jiāotōng	交通
traffic light	hóngùdēng	红绿灯
to trail	lùjìng	路径
train	huǒchē	火车
train station	huǒchē zhàn	火车站
tram	diànchē	电车
transfer (bank)	zhuǎnzhàng	转帐
translate	fānyì	翻译
translator	fānyì	翻译
travel	lǚxíng	旅行
travel agency	lǚxíngshè	旅行社
travellers cheque	lǚxíng zhīpiào	旅行支票
travelling bag	lǚxíng bāo	旅行包
travel sickness	lǚxíng xuànyùn	旅行眩晕
tree	shù	树
trek	yuǎnzú	远足
trendy (person)	shímáo	时髦
trip	lǚxíng	旅行
trousers	chángkù	长裤
truck	kǎchē	卡车

It's true.
zhēn de
真的.

trust	xìnrèn	信任
to trust	xiāngxìn	相信
to try	shì	试
to turn (change direction)	guǎiwān	拐弯

Turn left.
wàng zuǒ guǎi
往左拐.

Turn right.
wàng yòu guǎi
往右拐.

turtle	hǎiguī	海龟
TV (set)	diànshì (jī)	电视(机)
tweezers	nièzi	镊子
twelve	shíèr	十二
twice	liǎngcì	两次

U

twins	shuāngbāotāi	双胞胎
two	èr	二
type	dǎzì	打字
typical	diǎnxíng	典型
typhus	bānzhěnshānghán	斑疹伤寒
tyres	lúntāi	轮胎

U

ugly	chǒulòu	丑陋
ulcer	kuìyáng	溃疡
umbrella	yǔsǎn	雨伞
uncle	shūshu	叔叔
uncomfortable	bùshūfu	不舒服
under	zài xiàmiàn	在下面
underground (subway)	dìtiě	地铁
understand	dǒng	懂
underwear	nèiyī	内衣
unemployed	shīyè	失业
USA	měiguó	美国
unions	gōnghuì	工会
universe	yǔzhòu	宇宙
university	dàxué	大学
unleaded	wúqiān	无铅
until	dào	到
unusual	yìhūxúncháng	异乎寻常
up	shàng	上
upstairs	lóushàng	楼上
urgent	jǐnjí	紧急
urine	niào	尿
use	yòng	用
useful	yǒuyòng	有用

V

vacancy	kōngfángjiān	空房间
vacant	kōngde	空的
vaccination	miǎnyì	免疫
vacuum flask	bǎowēnpíng	保温瓶
valley	shāngǔ	山谷
valuable	guìzhòng	贵重

value	jiàqián	价钱
vegetable	shūcài	蔬菜
vegetarian	chīsùde	吃素的

I'm vegetarian.
wǒ chī sù
我吃素。

venereal disease	xìngbìng	性病
very	hěn	很
video camera	shèxiàngjī	摄像机
view	guānkàn	观看
village	cūnzhuāng	村庄
vinegar	cù	醋
virus	bìngdú	病毒
visa	qiānzhèng	签证
visit	fǎngwèn	访问
vitamins	wéishēngsù	维生素
vomit	ǒutù	呕吐
to vote	tóupiào	投票
vulgar	cūsú	粗俗

W

waist	yāo	腰
wait	děng	等
waiter	fúwùyuán	服务员
waiting room	hòuchēshì	候车室
wage	gōngzī	工资
to wake	jiàoxǐng	叫醒
to walk	zǒulù	走路
wall	qiáng	墙
wallet	qiánbāo	钱包
to want	yào	要
war	zhànzhēng	战争
wardrobe	yīguì	衣柜
warm	nuǎnhuo	暖和
wash	xǐ	洗
washing powder	xǐyīfěn	洗衣粉
watch (wrist)	biǎo	表
water	shuǐ	水
water bottle (drinking)	shuǐpíng	水瓶
waterfall	pùbù	瀑布

watermelon	xīguā	西瓜
wave (sea)	làng	浪
way (method)	fāngfǎ	方法
way (road)	lù	路

Tell me the way to …
dào … zěnme zǒu
到 … 怎么走。

Which way?
něi ge fāngxiàng?
哪个方向？

Way Out.
chūkǒu
出口。

we	wǒmén	我们
weak	ruò	弱
wealthy	yǒuqián	有钱
to wear	chuān	穿
weather	tiānqi	天气
weather forecast	tiānqi yùbào	天气预报
wedding	hūnlǐ	婚礼
week	xīngqī	星期
weekend	zhōumò	周末
weigh	chēng	称
weight	zhòngliàng	重量
welcome	huānyíng	欢迎
welfare	shēnxīn jiànkāng	身心健康
well (for water)	jǐng	井
well (health)	jiànkāng	健康
vest	xī	西
western style	xīshì	西式
westernised	xīhuà	西化
wet	shī	湿
what	shénme	什么

What's he saying?
tā shuō shénme?
他说什么？

What time is it?
jǐ diǎn le?
几点了？

wheel	lúnzi	轮子
wheelchair	lúnyǐ	轮椅
when	shénme shíhòu	什么时候

When does it leave?
shénme shíhòu líkāi?
什么时候离开？

| where | nǎr | 哪儿 |

Where's the bank?
yínháng zài nǎr?
银行在哪儿？

which	něige	哪个
white	báisè	白色
who	shéi/shuí	谁

Who is it?
shéi?
谁？

Who are they?
tāmén shì shuí?
他们是谁？

| why | wèishénme | 为什么 |

Why is the museum closed?
bówùguǎn wèishénme bù kāimén?
博物馆为什么不开门？

wide	kuān	宽
wife	qīzi	妻子
wildlife	yěshēngdòngwù	野生动物
win	yíng	赢
wind	fēng	风
window	chuānghu	窗户
windscreen	dǎngfēng bōli	挡风玻璃
wine	pútaojiǔ	葡萄酒
wings	chìbǎng	翅膀
winter	dōngtiān	冬天
wire	diànxiàn	电线
to wish	xīwàng	希望
with	yǔ	与
withdraw (from bank)	qǔ	取
within	zài lǐmiàn	在里面

within an hour
yī xiǎoshí nèi
一小时内

without	méiyǒu	没有
wok	guō	锅
woman	nǚ rén	女人
wonderful	bàng jí le	棒极了
wood	mùtóu	木头
wool	chúnmáo	纯毛
word	cí	词
work	gōngzuò	工作
workout	duànliàn	锻炼
work permit	gōngzuò xǔkě	工作许可
workshop	yántǎohuì	研讨会
world	shìjiè	世界
worried	dānxīn	耽心
worse	shǒuwàn	手腕
wristwatch	shǒubiǎo	手表
write	xiě	写
writer	zuòjiā	作家
writing paper	xìnzhǐ	信纸
wrong	cuòde	错的

I'm wrong. (my fault)
shì wǒ de cuò
是我的错。

I'm wrong. (not right)
wǒ cuò le
我错了。

X

x-ray	X guāngpiàn	X 光片

Y

year	nián	年
this year	jīnnián	今年
yellow	huángsè	黄色
yes	duì	对
yesterday	zuótiān	昨天

yesterday afternoon/ evening	zuótiān xiàwǔ/ wǎnshang	昨天下午 /晚上
yesterday morning	zuótiān zǎoshang	昨天早上
yogurt	suānnǎi	酸奶
you	nǐ	你
young	niánqīng	年轻
youth (collective)	qīngnián	青年
youth hostel	qīngnián lǚshè	青年旅社

Z

zero	líng	零
zodiac	huángdào dài	黄道带
zoo	dòngwùyuán	动物园
zoology	dòngwùxué	动物学

When two Pinyin words have the same spelling, they're organised according to tone in the following order:

ā	high
á	rising
ǎ	falling-rising
à	falling

A

ǎi	short (height)	矮
ài	to love	爱
àizībìng	AIDS	艾滋病
áizhèng	cancer	癌症
àn	dark	暗
àn	shore	岸
ānjìng	quiet	安静
ānmiányào	sleeping pill	安眠药
ànmó	massage	按摩
ānquán	safe (adj)	安全
ānquándài	seatbelt	安全带
àoyùnhuì	Olympic Games	奥运会
āsīpīlín	aspirin	阿斯匹林
āyí	aunt	阿姨

B

bā	eight	八
bàba	dad	爸爸
bàgōng	strike; on strike	罢工
bǎi	hundred	百
báichī	idiot	白痴
báifàn	rice (cooked)	白饭
bǎifēnzhī	per cent	百分之
bǎihuò shāngdiàn	department store	百货商店
báisè	white	白色
bǎiwàn	million	百万
bàn	half	半

bàng jí le	wonderful	棒极了
bāngmáng	to help	帮忙
bàn gōng shì	office	办公室
bàn gōngshì gōngzuò	office work	办公室工作
bāngzhù	aid (help)	帮助
bānzhěnshānghán	typhus	斑疹伤寒
bǎnqiú	cricket	板球
bāo	wrap; packet (cigarettes)	包
bàogào	to report	报告
bāoguǒ	parcel	包裹
bāokuò	include	包括
bāokuò	included	包括
bǎohù	protect	保护
bǎoshǒu	conservative	保守
bǎotǎ	pagoda	宝塔
bǎowēnpíng	vacuum flask	保温瓶
bǎoxiǎn	insurance	保险
bǎoxiǎnxiāng	safe (n)	保险箱
bàozhǐ	newspaper	报纸
bāshí	eighty	八十
běi	north	北
bèi	back (body)	背
bēiāi	sad	悲哀
bèibāo	backpack	背包
bèidān	sheet (bed)	被单
bèiké	shell	贝壳
bèizi	quilt	被子
bēizi	cup/glass	杯子
bèn	stupid	笨
běndì	local	本地
bèng	pump	泵
bēngdài	bandage	绷带
bǐ	pen	笔
biǎo	form (document); wristwatch	表
biānfáng jiǎncházhàn	checkpoint	边防检查站
biānjiè	border	边界
biànmì	constipation; to be constipated	便秘
biāozhì	sign	标志

iéde	other	别的
iézhēn	safety pin	别针
ijiào hǎo	better	比较好
ijiào xǐhuān	prefer	比较喜欢
ijìběn	notebook	笔记本
inwēi wùzhǒng	endangered species	濒危物种
ìng	ice	冰
ǐng	pie	饼
ìng	sickness	病
ìngdòng shípǐn	frozen foods	冰冻食品
ìngdú	virus	病毒
ǐnggān	biscuit	饼干
ìng le	ill	病了
īngqílín	ice cream	冰淇淋
ìngrén	patient	病人
īngxiāng	refrigerator	冰箱
īngyì	military service	兵役
ǐsài	match/race (sport)	比赛
ìxū	must	必须
ìyào de	necessary	必要的
ìyùntào	condom	避孕套
ìyùnyào	contraceptive	避孕药
ìyùnyào	Pill (contraceptive)	避孕药
ízi	nose	鼻子
ōhào yīn	dial tone	拨号音
òhe	mint	薄荷
ōluó	pineapple	菠萝
ówù	mist	薄雾
ówùguǎn	museum	博物馆
ózi	neck	脖子
ù	no	不
ùduì	incorrect	不对
ùfāngbiàn	inconvenient	不方便
ù hǎo yìsi	embarassed	不好意思
ùjiǔ	soon	不久
ù kěnéng	impossible	不可能
ù mǎnyì	dissatisfied	不满意
ùnéng	cannot	不能
ù píngděng	inequality	不平等

bùshūfu	uncomfortable	不舒服
bùxīnxiān	stale	不新鲜
bùyīyàng	different	不一样

C

cǎo	grass	草
cǎoméi	strawberry	草莓
cǎoyào yīshēng	herbalist	草药医
cǎoyào	herbs	草药
cáichǎn	property	财产
càidān	menu	菜单
cáiféngdiàn	tailor	裁缝店
cáipàn	referee	裁判
cāixiǎng	to guess	猜想
cānchē	dining car	餐车
cánjírén	disabled	残疾人
cāntīng	dining room	餐厅
cèshì	test	测试
cèsuǒ	toilet	厕所
chábēi	tea cup	茶杯
chàbuduō	almost	差不多
cháhú	tea pot	茶壶
cháng	long	长
chángcháng	often	常常
chànggē	sing	唱歌儿
chángkù	trousers	长裤
chàngpiàn	record (disk)	唱片
chángtú diànhuà	long-distance call	长途电话
chángtúqìchē	coach (bus)	长途汽车
chǎnpǐn	product	产品
cháo	tide	潮
chǎo	loud/noisy	吵
chǎojià	argue	吵架
chǎojīdàn	scrambled egg	炒鸡蛋
chāojíshìchǎng	supermarket	超级市场
chāopiào	banknote	钞票
chápiào yuán	ticket collector	查票员
cháoshī	damp	潮湿
chātóu	plug (electricity)	插头
chāzi	fork	叉子

chāzuò	adaptor	插座
chénggōng	success	成功
chéngrén	adult	成人
chéngrèn	to admit	承认
chéngshí	honest	诚实
chéngshì	city	城市
chéngshú	ripe	成熟
chènshān	shirt	衬衫
chī	eat	吃
chǐcùn	size (clothes)	尺寸
chìdào	equator	赤道
chīsùde	vegetarian	吃素的
chítáng	pond	池塘
chóng	bug	虫
chóngfù	to repeat	重复
chōngxǐ	processing (film)	冲洗
chóngzi	insect	虫子
chòu	smelly	臭
chòuchóng	bedbugs	臭虫
chōujīn	cramp	抽筋
chǒulòu	ugly	丑陋
chōuyān	to smoke	抽烟
chòuyǎngcéng	ozone layer	臭氧层
chuān	to wear	穿
chuán	boat/ship	船
chuáng	bed	床
chuángdiàn	mattress	床垫
chuānghu	window	窗户
chuàngkětiē	Band-Aid	创可贴
chuānglián	curtain	窗帘
chuánrǎn	contagious	传染
chúchóngjì	insect repellent	除虫剂
chūfā	departure	出发
chúfáng	kitchen	厨房
chūhàn	perspire	出汗
chuízi	hammer	锤子
chūkǒu	exit/export	出口
chúnde	pure	纯的
chúnmáo	wool	纯毛
chūntiān	spring (season)	春天

chūqù	to go out	出去
chūshēngdì	place of birth	出生地
chūshēngzhèng	birth certificate	出生证
chūzūqìchē	taxi	出租汽车
chútǐxiùyè	deodorant	除体臭液
cí	word	词
cídài	cassette	磁带
cìpò	puncture	刺破器
cíqì	porcelain	瓷器
cìxiù	embroidery	刺绣
cóng	from/since	从
cónglái méiyǒu	never	从来没有
cónglín	jungle	丛林
cōngmíng	intelligent	聪明
cù	vinegar	醋
cūnzhuāng	village	村庄
cuò	fault	错
cuòde	wrong	错的
cuòwù	mistake	错误
cuòwù de	faulty	错误的
cūsú	vulgar	粗俗

D

dá	dozen	打
dǎ	ring (of phone)	打
dà	big/large	大
dà bùfèn	majority	大部分
dāchē	to hitchhike	搭车
dàcháng	bowel	大肠
dǎ diànhuà	to call (phone)	打电话
dǎdòu	fight; to fight	打斗
dàgài	probably	大概
dǎhuǒjī	lighter	打火机
dàibiǎo	representative	代表
dàifu	doctor	大夫
dàizǒu	takeaway	带走
dàizi	bag	袋子
dàlǐshí	marble	大理石
dàmá	dope (marijuana)	大麻
dānchéng piào	one-way/single ticket	单程票

āndú	alone	单独
àn gāo	cake	蛋糕
ǎngfēng bōli	windscreen	挡风玻璃
àngpài	party (political)	党派
ānrénfáng	single room	单人房
ānshēn	single (unmarried)	单身
ànshì	but	但是
ānxīn	to care (for someone)	耽心
ǎo	island	岛
ào	arrive/until	到
àogào	prayer	祷告
àojiào	Taoism	道教
ǎománg quǎn	guidedog	导盲犬
àotián	paddy field	稻田
ǎoyóu	guide(n)	导游
āozi	knife	刀子
árǎo	disturb	打扰
àshǐ	ambassador	大使
àshǐguǎn	embassy	大使馆
àtuǐ	thigh	大腿
àxiǎo	size	大小
àxué	university	大学
àyūe	about	大约
àyī	overcoat	大衣
áiying	promise	答应
àyuē	approximately	大约
àzì	to type	打字
éfēn	to score	得分
ēngjìtái	check-in (desk)	登记台
ēngshān yùndòng	mountaineering	登山运动
ēngshānchē	mountain bike	登山车
ng	wait	等
	low	低
àn	electricity	电
ǎn cài	order (meal)	点菜
ǎnxíng	typical	典型
ànbào	telegram	电报
ànchē	tram	电车
ànchí	batteries	电池
ànchuán	telex	电传
àndēng	lamp	电灯

D
I
C
T
I
O
N
A
R
Y

diàndēng	light (electric)	电灯
diàndēngpào	bulb	电灯泡
diànfēngshàn	electric fan	电风扇
diànhuà	telephone	电话
diànhuà bù	telephone directory	电话簿
diànhuà kǎ	phonecard	电话卡
diànhuà tíng	phone booth	电话亭
diànnǎo	computer	电脑
diànnǎo yóuxì	computer game	电脑游戏
diànshàn	fan (electric)	电扇
diànshì	TV	电视
diànshìjī	television	电视机
diàntī	lift (elevator)	电梯
diànxiàn	wire	电线
diānxiánbìng huànzhè	epileptic	癫痫病患者
diànyǐng	film (cinema)	电影
diànyǐng	movie	电影
diànyǐng yuàn	cinema	电影院
diàochuáng	hammock	吊床
diāoxiàng	statue	雕像
(zài) dǐbù	(at the) bottom	(在)底部
dì èr	second (not first)	第二
dìfang	place	地方
dīng	bite (n, insect)	叮
dǐng	top	顶
dǐngguāguā	cool (coll)	顶呱呱
dīngzìgǎo	pickaxe	丁字镐
dǐpiàn	negative (film)	底片
dìqū	region(al)	地区
dìqiú	Earth	地球
dìtǎn	carpet	地毯
dìtiě	underground (subway)	地铁
dìtú	map	地图
diū	lose	丢
dìyī	first	第一
dìzhǐ	address	地址
dìzhèn	earthquake	地震
dìzhìxué	geology	地质学
dōng	east	东
dǒng	understand	懂

òng	to move	动
ōngtiān	winter	冬天
òngwù	animal	动物
òngwùxué	zoology	动物学
òngwùyuán	zoo	动物园
ōu	all/both	都
ǒu	steep	陡
òu	beans	豆
òufǔ	beancurd	豆腐
uǎn	short (length)	短
uǎnkù	shorts	短裤
uǎnquē	shortage	短缺
uǎnshàngyī	jacket	短上衣
uànliàn	workout	锻炼
ùchuán	ferry	渡船
uì	against/correct/yes	对
uì	team	队
uìbùqǐ	excuse me; sorry	对不起
uìfāngfùfèi	reverse-charge	对方付费
uìhuàn	to change (money)	兑换
uìhuànlǜ	exchange rate	兑换率
uìmiàn	opposite	对面
uìxiā	prawn	对虾
uō yīdiǎnr	more	多一点儿
úpǐn	drug	毒品
úpǐn fànzi	drug dealer	毒品贩子
úpǐn shàngyǐn	drug addiction	毒品上瘾
úyào	poison	毒药

F

	goose	鹅
	hungry	饿
r	two	二
rděng	second class	二等
rduo	ear	耳朵
rduō	ears	耳朵
rduo téng	earache	耳朵疼
rhuán	earring	耳环
rzi	son	儿子
xīn	nausea	恶心

F

fādòngjī	engine	发动机
fāfēng	mad	发疯
fǎguó	France	法国
fákuǎn	fine (penalty)	罚款
fǎlǜ	law	法律
fàn	meal	饭
fànfǎ xíngwéi	offence	犯法行为
fàng	to put	放
fāngfǎ	way/method	方法
fángfǔjì	antiseptic cream	防腐剂
fánghù lín	protected forest	防护林
fángjiān hàomǎ	room number	房间号码
fángjiān	room	房间
fángshàishuāng	sunscreen lotion	防晒霜
fànguǎn	restaurant	饭馆
fángwū	house	房屋
fāngxiàng	direction	方向
fāngxíng	square (shape)	方形
fǎngwèn	visit	访问
fángzhǐ	prevent	防止
fànrén	prisoner	犯人
fǎnshè	reflection (mirror)	反射
fānyì	translate/translator	翻译
fāshāo	fever	发烧
fāshuā	hairbrush	发刷
fāxiàn	to discover	发现
fāyīn	pronunciation	发音
fāyán	inflammation	发炎
fǎyǔ	French	法语
fǎyuàn	court (legal)	法院
fēi	to fly	飞
fèi	fee	费
fèi	lung	肺
fēifǎ	illegal	非法
fēijī	aeroplane	飞机
fēijīchǎng	airport	飞机场
féizào	soap	肥皂
féizào jù	soap opera	肥皂剧
fēizhèngshì	informal	非正式

fēi zhíjiē	non-direct	非直接
fēng	wind	风
féng	sew	缝
fēngbào	storm	风暴
fēngjǐng	landscape/scenery	风景
fēngmì	honey	蜂蜜
féngyīzhēn	needle (sewing)	缝衣针
fēngzheng	kite	风筝
fēnlí	to separate	分离
fēnxiǎng	to share (with)	分享
fēnzhōng	minute	分钟
fěnhóng sè	pink	粉红色
fénmù	grave/tomb	坟墓
fójiào	Buddhism	佛教
fǔbài	corrupt	腐败
fùbù	abdomen	腹部
fùhuójié	Easter	复活节
fùjìn de bīnguǎn	nearby hotel	附近的宾馆
fùmǔqīn	parents	父母亲
fùqián	to pay	付钱
fùqin	father	父亲
fùshídiàn	grocery	副食店
fútī	elevator	扶梯
fúwù	service (religious)	服务
fúwùtái	reception desk	服务台
fúwùyuán	waiter	服务员
fùxí	review	复习
fùxiè	diarrhoea	腹泻
fùyǒu	rich (wealthy)	富有
fùyìn	photocopy	复印
fúyòng dúpǐn hóu	drugged	服用毒品后
fùzá	complex	复杂

G

gǎi	alter	改
gài	lid	盖
gān	dry	干
gān	liver	肝
gàndào	main road	干道

gǎngwān	harbour	港湾
gānjìng	clean	干净
gānjú	tangerine	柑橘
gǎnjué	feelings	感觉
gǎnmào le	to have a cold	感冒了
gǎnmào	a cold/'flu	感冒
gǎnrǎn	infected	感染
gānxǐdiàn	drycleaner	干洗店
gǎn xìngqù	interested	感兴趣
gāo	high/tall	高
gāodiǎn	confectionary/pastry	糕点
gāodiǎndiàn	cake shop	糕点店
gāodiǎnpù	pastry shop	糕点铺
gāosù gōnglù	motorway	高速公路
gàosu	tell	告诉
gāoxìng	happy	高兴
gēbo	arm	胳膊
gěi	give	给
gémìng	revolution	革命
gèng huài	worse	更坏
gēngyīshì	changing rooms	更衣室
gēnsuí	follow	跟随
gēqǔ	song	歌曲
gètǐ de	individual	个体的
gètǐhù	self-employed	个体户
gèxìng	personality	个性
gòngchǎndǎng yuán	communist	共产党员
gōngchǎng	factory	工厂
gōngchéngshī	engineer	工程师
gōngdiàn	palace	宫殿
gōnggòngqìchē	bus	公共汽车
gònghéguó	republic	共和国
gōnghuì	unions	工会
gōngjīn	kilogram	公斤
gōnglǐ	kilometre	公里
gōnglù tú	road map	公路图
gōngmín quán	citizenship	公民权
gōngmù	cemetery	公墓
gōngniú	bull/ox	公牛

gōngrén	factory/manual worker	工人
gōngshè	commune	公社
gōngsī	company (business)	公司
gōngyè	industry	工业
gōngyì měishù	arts & crafts	工艺美术
gōngyìpǐn	handicrafts	工艺品
gōngyòng cèsuǒ	public toilet	公用厕所
gōngyuán	park	公园
gōngzī	salary	工资
gōngzhuāngkù	overalls	工装裤
gōngzuò	job/work	工作
gōngzuò xǔkě	work permit	工作许可
gǒu	dog	狗
gòuwù	to go shopping	购物
gǔ	drums	鼓
guā	melon	瓜
guǎiwān	to turn (change direction)	拐弯
guǎngchǎng	square (plaza)	广场
guàhào	registered (mail)	挂号
guāliǎn	shave	刮脸
guān	to shut	关
guānbì	to close	关闭
guān mén	shut (adj)	关门
guǎngdōng huà	Cantonese (language)	广东话
guànjūn	championship	冠军
guānkàn	view	观看
guānmén	closed (shop, etc)	关门
guàntóu	can/tin	罐头
guānxì	relation(ship)	关系
guānxīn	to care (about)	关心
guǎnzhǎng	curator	馆长
guànzi	jar	罐子
guàsuǒ	padlock	挂锁
gǔdàide	ancient	古代的
gǔdiǎn	antique	古
gǔdiǎn jùchǎng	classical theatre	古典剧场
gǔdiǎn yìshù	classical art	古典艺术
gùdìng shōucángpǐn	permanent collection	固定收藏品
guì	expensive	贵
guìzhòng	valuable	贵重

guìzi	cupboard	柜子
guō	wok	锅
guǒjiàng	jam	果酱
guójì	international	国际
guójì	nationality	国籍
guójiā	country (nation)	国家
guójiā gōngyuán	national park	国家公园
guòliàng	overdose	过量
guòmǐn	allergic	过敏
guòqù	past	过去
guówáng	king	国王
guǒzhī	fruit juice	果汁
gùshi	story (narrative)	故事
gǔtóu	bone	骨头
gùzhǔ	employer	雇主

H

hǎi	sea	海
hǎi àn	coast	海岸
hǎibá	altitude	海拔
hǎiguī	turtle	海龟
hǎiguān	customs	海关
hǎiluòyīn shàngyǐn	heroin addict	海洛因上瘾
hǎiluòyīn	heroin	海洛因
háishì	or	还是
hǎitān	beach	海滩
hǎiwài	abroad/overseas	海外
hǎixiān	seafood	海鲜
hàixiū	shy	害羞
hǎiyáng	ocean	海洋
hǎo	good/nice	好
hǎochī	delicious/tasty	好吃
hǎo le	ready	好了
hǎowánr	fun	好玩儿
hǎoxiào	funny	好笑
háizi	child	孩子
hángbān	flight	航班
hángkōng	airmail	航空
háo	oyster	蚝
háohuá	luxury	豪华

hàomǎ	number	号码
hàozi	rat	耗子
hé shìyàn	nuclear testing	核试验
hé	and	和
hé	river	河
hē	to drink	喝
hénéng	nuclear energy	核能
héfǎ	legal	合法
héfǎ huà	legalisation	合法化
hēi bái	B&W (film)	黑白
hēi sè	black	黑色
hěn	very	很
hèn	hate	恨
hěn duō	a lot	很多
hén téng	painful	很疼
hépíng	peace	和平
hèsè	brown	褐色
hétóng	contract	合同
hézǐ	box	盒子
HIV chéng yángxìng	HIV positive	HIV 呈阳性
hóng sè	red	红色
hónglǜ dēng	traffic light	红绿灯
hòu	thick	厚
hòubiān	back (rear)	后边
hòuchēshì	waiting room	候车室
hóuzi	monkey	猴子
hú	lake	湖
hú	pot (ceramic)	壶
huà	painting	画
huā	flower	花
huāxī	breathe	呼吸
huāfèi	to cost	花费
huāfěn	pollen	花粉
huāfěnzhèng	hayfever	花粉症
huà huàr	to paint	画画儿
huài	bad	坏
huài le	broken	坏了
huáiyùn	pregnant	怀孕
huàjiā	painter	画家
huán	return (give back)	还

huàn	to exchange	换
huànbìng	to suffer	患病
huàndēngpiàn	slide (film)	幻灯片
huángdào dài	zodiac	黄道带
huángdì	emperor	皇帝
huángsè	yellow	黄色
huángyóu	butter	黄油
huánjìng	environment	环境
huānyíng	welcome	欢迎
huāshēng	peanut	花生
huàxiàng shī	portrait sketcher	画像师
huàxué	chemistry	化学
huāyuán	garden	花园
huàzhuāng	makeup	化妆
húdié	butterfly	蝴蝶
huīchén	dust	灰尘
huídá	answer	回答
huìhuà	conversation	会话
huìhuà yìshù	graphic art	绘画艺术
huílái	return (come back)	回来
huìlù	bribe (n)	贿赂
huíqù	return (go back)	回去
huīsè	grey	灰色
huíshōu	recycling	回收
huíshōu lìyòng	recyclable	回收利用
hújiāo	pepper	胡椒
húluóbo	carrot	胡萝卜
hùnhé	to mix	混合
hūnlǐ	wedding	婚礼
huǒchái	matches	火柴
huǒchē	train	火车
huǒchē zhàn	railway station	火车站
huǒlú	stove	火炉
huǒtuǐ	ham	火腿
huòwù	goods	货物
huǒzāi	fire	火灾
hùshi	nurse	护士
hùzhào	passport	护照
hùzhào hàomǎ	passport number	护照号码
húzǐ	beard	胡子

jī	chicken	鸡
jì	send (post)	寄
jiā	family/home	家
jiábǎn	deck (of ship)	甲板
jiǎde	false	假的
jiājù	furniture	家具
jiānbǎng	shoulder	肩膀
jiǎnchá	to check	检查
jiǎndān	simple	简单
jiǎndāo	scissors	剪刀
jiāng	ginger	姜
jiānglái	future	将来
jiàngyóu	soya sauce	酱油
jiànkāng	health/well	健康
jiǎnlì	resumé	简历
jiànmiàn	meet/see	见面
jiànpán	keyboard	键盘
jiǎnqǐ	to pick up	捡起
jiànshēnfáng	gym	健身房
jiǎnyì	quarantine	检疫
jiànyì	advice	建议
jiānyù	prison	监狱
jiànzào	to build	建造
jiànzhúwú	building (construction)	建筑物
jiànzhù gōngchéng	construction work	建筑工程
jiànzhùxué	architecture	建筑学
jiǎo	corner	角
jiǎo	foot	脚
jiào	to call (name)	叫
jiǎohuái	ankle	脚踝
jiāojuǎn	film (photographic)	胶卷
jiàoliàn	instructor	教练
jiāoqū	suburb	郊区
jiàoshī	teacher	教师
jiàoshì	priest	教士
jiāoshuǐ	glue	胶水
jiàotáng	church	教堂
jiāotōng	traffic	交通
jiàoxǐng	to wake	叫醒
jiàoyù	education	教育

jiǎozhǐ	toe	脚趾
jiǎozi	dumplings	饺子
jiàqī	holiday	假期
jiàqián	price/value	价钱
jiàshǐ zhízhào	driver's licence	驾驶执照
jiāwù	housework	家务
jiǎyá	denture	假牙
jíbìng	disease	疾病
jīdàn	egg	鸡蛋
jìdé	remember	记得
jídù	jealous	嫉妒
jīdūjiào	Christian	基督教
jiē	street	街
jiè	borrow/lend	借
jiějie	sister (older)	姐姐
jiémù	programme	节目
jiérì	festival	节日
jièshào	introduce	介绍
jiēshi	sturdy	结实
jiéshù	end (n/v)	结束
jiétān	paraplegic	截瘫
jiētóu yìrén	busker	街头艺人
jiéyá xiàn	dental floss	洁牙线
jièzhǐ	ring (jewellery)	戒指
jìfēn pái	scoreboard	记分牌
jǐ ge	several	几个
jìgōng	mechanic	技工
jīguāng chàngpiàn	CD	激光唱片
jìhuà rén	projector	计划人
jīhuì	chance/opportunity	机会
jìjié	season	季节
jíjímángmáng	in a hurry	急急忙忙
jījìn zhǔyì fènzǐ	activist	激进主义分子
jíjiùxiāng	first-aid kit	急救箱
jīlíng	crafty	机灵
jímáng	hurry	急忙
jīn	gold	金
jǐn	tight (clothes)	紧
jìn	near	近
jǐng	well (for water)	井
jīngguò	through	经过

īnglǐ	manager	经理
īngjì	economy	经济
īngpiàn	lens (glasses)	镜片
īngqí	surprise (n)	惊奇
īngtóu	lens (camera)	镜头
īngtóugài	lens cap	镜头盖
īngyàn	experience	经验
īngzi	mirror	镜子
ì niàn bēi	monument	纪念碑
ì niàn guǎn	memorial hall	纪念馆
ìniànpǐn	souvenir	纪念品
ìniànpǐn shāngdiàn	souvenir shop	纪念品商店
īnkǒu	to import	进口
īnnián	this year	今年
īnshǔ	metal	金属
īntiān	today	今天
īnǚ	prostitute	妓女
īnwǎn	tonight	今晚
īqì	machine	机器
īròu	muscle	肌肉
īngchá	police	警察
īnjí	urgent	紧急
īnjí qíngkuàng	emergency	紧急情况
ìshí	documentary	记实
ìshù	technique	技术
ìsuàn	to count	计算
ítā	guitar	吉它
iǔ	alcohol	酒
iǔ	nine	九
iù	old (thing)	旧
iǔbā	bar	酒吧
iùjì	dole	救济
iǔshí	ninety	九十
iùyè guǎnggào	job advertisement	就业广告
iùzhǐ	ruins	旧址
ìyuàn	brothel	妓院
ìzhě	journalist	记者
ǐzhuī	spine	脊椎
uǎnyān zhǐ	cigarette papers	卷烟纸

juànzhóu	scroll	卷轴
jùchǎng	theatre	剧场
juéde	to feel	觉得
juédìng	decide/decision	决定
juéshìyīnyuè	jazz	爵士音乐
júhóng sè	orange (colour)	桔红色
jùhuì	party (fiesta)	聚会
jùjué	deny/refuse	拒绝
jūnduì	military	军队
jūnguān	officer	军官
jùyuàn	opera house	剧院
júzi	orange (fruit)	橘子
jùzi	sentence (language)	句子
júzizhī	orange juice	桔子汁

K

kǎchē	truck	卡车
kāfēi	coffee	咖啡
kāi	drive (car)	开车
kāichē	leave (train/bus)	开车
kāichú	dismissal	开除
kāiguànqì	can/tin opener	开罐器
kāimén	open; to open	开门
kāipíngqì	bottle opener	开瓶器
kāishǐ	begin/start	开始
kāishuǐ	boiled water	开水
kāiwèicài	hors d'oeuvres	开胃菜
kàn	look/see	看
kàngjūnsù	antibiotics	抗菌素
kàngyì	protest; to protest	抗议
kànshū	read	看书
kǎogǔxué	archaeology	考古学
kǎo lǜ	think	考虑
kǎomiànbāo	toast	烤面包
kǎpiàn	cards	卡片
kè	gram	克
kècāng	cabin	客舱
kěnéng	possible	可能
késou	cough	咳嗽
késou táng	cough drops	咳嗽糖

L

kēxué	science	科学
kēxué jiā	scientist	科学家
kěyǐ	able (to be); can	可以
kōngde	empty/vacant	空的
kōngfángjiān	vacancy	空房间
kōngqì	air	空气
kōngqìwūrǎn	air pollution	空气污染
kōngtiáo	air-conditioned	空调
kǒudài	pocket	口袋
kǒuhóng	lipstick	口红
kǒukě	thirsty	口渴
kuài	fast/piece/quick	快
kuàidì	express (letter)	快递
kuàizi	chopsticks	筷子
kuān	wide	宽
kuàngquánshuǐ	mineral water	矿泉水
kǔde	bitter	苦的
kuìyáng	ulcer	溃疡

L

lā	to pull	拉
là	spicy	辣
lái	to come	来
láihuí piào	return trip	来回票
lājī	garbage/rubbish	垃圾
làjiāo	chilli	辣椒
lǎnduò	lazy	懒惰
làng	wave	浪
làngmàn	romance	浪漫
lánsè	blue	蓝色
lán wěi yán	appendicitis	阑尾炎
lánzǐ	basket	篮子
lǎo	old (person)	老
lǎobǎn	boss (n)	老板
lǎochéng	old city	老城
làzhú	candle	蜡烛
léi	thunder	雷
lèi	tired	累
lèigǔ	rib	肋骨
lèihuài le	exhausted	累坏了

D
I
C
T
I
O
N
A
R
Y

lěng	cold (adj)	冷
lěng shuǐ	cold water	冷水
lí	pear	梨
liǎn	face	脸
liǎngcì	twice	两次
liǎngzhōu	fortnight	两周
liáng	to measure	量
liángxié	sandals	凉鞋
liánjià chūshòu	(on) sale	廉价出售
lìfǎ	legislation	立法
lǐfàdiàn	barbershop/hairdressers	理发店
líkāi	to depart (leave)	离开
lìliàng	power	力量
límǐ	centimetre	厘米
lǐmiàn	inside	里面
límíng	dawn	黎明
líng	bell	铃
líng	zero	零
lǐngdǎo	leader	领导
lǐnglù yuǎnzú	guided trek	领路远足
língqián	loose change	零钱
língshēng	ring (sound)	铃声
línshí bǎomǔ	babysitter	临时保姆
lǐngshìguǎn	consulate	领事馆
línyù	shower	淋浴
lìrùn	profit	利润
lìrùn lǜ	profitability	利润率
lìshǐ	history	历史
liù	six	六
liúchǎn	abortion/miscarriage	流产
liúhuà	message	留话
liùshí	sixty	六十
liúxià	to be left (behind/over)	留下
liúxíng	popular	流行
liúxuè	bleed	流血
lǐwù	gift	礼物
lìzhī	lychees	荔枝
lǐzi	plum	李子
lóng	deaf	聋

lóngxiā	lobster	龙虾
lóu	storey	楼
lóushàng	upstairs	楼上
lóutī	stairs	楼梯
lóuxià	downstairs	楼下
lù	deer	鹿
lù	road/way	路
lǜ chá	green tea	绿茶
lǚguǎn	hotel	旅馆
lǚkè	tourist	旅客
lǜsè	green	绿色
lǚtú	journey	旅途
lǚxíng	travel/trip	旅行
lǚxíng bāo	travelling bag	旅行包
lǚxíngshè	travel agency	旅行社
lǚxíng xuànyùn	travel sickness	旅行眩晕
lǚxíng zhīpiào	travellers cheque	旅行支票
lǚxíngtuán	tour group	旅行团
lǜ shī	lawyer	律师
luànkǎn lànfá	deforestation	乱砍滥伐
lùjìng	route	路径
lùkǒu	corner (street)	路口
lúntāi	tyres	轮胎
lúnyǐ	wheelchair	轮椅
lúnzi	wheel	轮子
luòtuo	camel	骆驼
lùyīn	recording	录音
lùyīnjī	tape recorder	录音机
lǚ yóuzhǐnán	guidebook	旅游指南

M

mǎ	horse	马
mǎi	buy	买
mài	sell	卖
májiàng	mahjong	麻将
mǎn	full	满
màn	slow	慢
máng	busy	忙
mángguǒ	mango	芒果

mànhuà	cartoons	漫画
mántóu	steamed bread	慢头
mǎnyì	satisfied	满意
mànyú	eel	鳗鱼
māo	cat	猫
máojīn	towel	毛巾
màoxiǎn	adventure	冒险
máoyī	jumper (sweater)	毛衣
màoyì	trade	贸易
màozi	cap (hat)	帽子
mǎshàng	immediately	马上
mǎtóu	dock/port	码头
mǎxì	circus	马戏
mǎyǐ	ant	蚂蚁
měi	each/every	每
měiguó	USA	美国
mèimei	sister (younger)	妹妹
měimiào de	great	美妙的
méiqì	gas	煤气
méirén	free (vacant)	没人
měitiān	every day	每天
méiyǒu	without	没有
mèn	bored/boring	烦
mén	door/gate	门
mèng	dream	梦
mǐ	rice (uncooked)/metre	米
miànbāo	bread	面包
miànbāo diàn	bakery	面包店
miánbù	cotton	棉布
miǎnfèi	free (cost)	免费
miànfěn	flour	面粉
mǐn gǎn	an allergy	敏感
miǎnyì	vaccination	免疫
miàntán	interview	面谈
miàntiáo	noodles	面条
miànzhǐ	tissue paper	面纸
miǎo	second (time)	秒
mìmi	secret	秘密
míngliàng	bright	明亮

míngling	to order (command)	命令
míngnián	next year	明年
míngpiàn	card (business)	名片
míngtiān	tomorrow	明天
míngtiān wǎnshàng	tomorrow evening	明天晚上
míngtiān xiàwǔ	tomorrow afternoon	明天下午
míngxiǎn	obvious	明显
míngxìnpiàn	postcard	明信片
mínjiān yīnyuè	folk music	民间音乐
mínquán	civil rights	民权
mínzhǔ	democracy	民主
mírén de	sexy	迷人的
mìshū	secretary	秘书
mìyuè	honeymoon	蜜月
mòjìng	sunglasses	墨镜
mòlihuāchá	jasmine tea	茉莉花茶
mòshēngrén	stranger	陌生人
mòshuǐ	ink	墨水
mótuóchē	motorbike	摩托车
mǒushì	something	某事
mòxiǎng	meditation	默想
mùbiāo	goal	目标
mùchái	firewood	木柴
mùdìdì	destination	目的地
mùgùn	stick	木棍
mùqián	present (time)	目前
mǔqīn	mother	母亲
mùtóu	wood	木头
mǔzhǐ	thumb	拇指

N

ná	bring	拿
nǎilào	cheese	奶酪
nǎiyóu	cream	奶油
nǎizhìpǐn	dairy products	奶制品
nǎizuǐ	dummy (pacifier)	奶嘴
nán	difficult	难
nán	south	南
nándé	rare	难得

nánháir	boy	男孩儿
nànmín	refugee	难民
nán péngyǒu	boyfriend	男朋友
nánrén	man	男人
nàozhe wán	for fun	闹着玩
nàozhōng	alarm clock	闹钟
nǎozǐ	brain	脑子
nǎr	where	哪儿
ná zǒu	to take (away)	拿走
něige	which	哪个
nèige	that	那个
nèiyī	underwear	内衣
néng	can	能

wǒ néng gěi nǐ zhàoxiàng ma?
我能给你照相吗？
Can I take your photo?

nér	there	那儿
ní	mud	泥
nǐ	you	你
niǎo	bird	鸟
nián	year	年
niándù	annual	年度
niánlíng	age	年龄
niánqīng	young	年轻
niào	urine	尿
niàobù zhěn	nappy rash	尿布疹
niàobù	nappy (diaper)	尿布
níngméng	lemon	柠檬
nítǔ	soil	泥土
niú	cow	牛
niǔkòu	buttons	钮扣
niúnǎi	milk	牛奶
niúròu	beef	牛肉
niǔshāng	to sprain	扭伤
niúzǎikù	jeans	牛仔裤
nóng	pus	脓
nóngchǎng zhǔ	farmer	农场主
nóngchǎng	farm	农场
nóngcūn	countryside	农村
nòng huài	break (n)	弄坏

nóngyè	agriculture	农业
nuǎnhuo	warm	暖和
nuǎnqì	heating	暖气
nǔchènshān	blouse	女衬衫
nǔér	daughter	女儿
nǔ fú	dress	女服
nǔ háizi	girl	女孩子
nǔ péngyǒu	girlfriend	女朋友
nǔ rén	woman	女人
nǔ tóngxìngliàn	lesbian	女同性恋
nǔwáng	queen	女王

O

| ǒutù | vomit | 呕吐 |
| ōuzhōu | Europe | 欧洲 |

P

pà	afraid	怕
pàichūsuǒ	police station	派出所
páichú	excluded	排除
páiduì	queue	排队
pāndēng	to climb	攀登
pàng	fat	胖
páng biānr	next to; side	旁边儿
pángguāng	bladder	膀胱
pángguāng yán	cystitis	膀胱炎
pángxie	crab	螃蟹
pànjué	sentence (prison)	判决
pānyán	rock climbing	攀岩
pánzi	plate	盘子
pǎobù	to run	跑步
pǎodào	track (car-racing)	跑道
páxíngdòngwù	reptile	爬行动物
péngyǒu	friend	朋友
piàn	pill	片
piányi	cheap	便宜
piányi de bīnguǎn	cheap hotel	便宜的宾馆
piào	ticket	票

piàojià	fare	票价
piàoliàng	beautiful/pretty	漂亮
pífu	skin	皮肤
pígé	leather	皮革
píng	flat	平
píngděng	equal/equality	平等
píngfēng	screen (for room)	屏风
píngguǒ	apple	苹果
pīngpāngqiú	table tennis	乒乓球
píngxíngde	parallel	平行的
pínqióng	poverty	贫穷
pòhuài	destroy	破坏
pópo	mother-in-law	婆婆
pòshāngfēng	tetanus	破伤风
pùbù	waterfall	瀑布
pútáo	grape	葡萄
pútáojiǔ	wine	葡萄酒
pǔtōng	ordinary; standard; surface mail	普通
pǔtōnghuà	Mandarin (language)	普通话

Q

qī	seven	七
qí	flag	旗
qí	to ride (a horse)	骑
qiān	thousand	千
qián	ago	前
qián	money	钱
qiǎn	light (colour)	浅
qiánbāo	wallet	钱包
qiānbǐ	pencil	铅笔
qiáng	wall	墙
qiángjiān	rape (assault)	强奸
qiǎngjié	to rob	抢劫
qiānmíng	signature	签名
qiánshuǐ	diving	潜水
qiánshuǐ shèshī	diving equipment	潜水设施
qiántóu	ahead	前头

qiānzhèng	visa	签证
qiānzì	to sign	签字
qiáo	bridge	桥
qiǎokèlì	chocolate	巧克力
qiāo zhúgàng	rip-off	敲竹杠
qíchē	to cycle; cycling	骑车
qíchē rén	cyclist	骑车人
qìchēzhàn	bus stop	汽车站
qídǎo shū	prayer book	祈祷书
qiēxuē	to cut	切削
qiézi	eggplant	茄子
qǐgài	beggar	乞丐
qíguài	strange	奇怪
qí mǎ	horse riding	骑马
qīng	light (weight)	轻
qǐng	please	请
qīngjié	cleaning	清洁
qíngkuàng	situation	情况
qīngméisù	penicillin	青霉素
qīngnián	youth (collective)	青年
qīngnián lǚshè	youth hostel	青年旅社
qíngrén	lover	情人
qīngxièjì	laxative	倾泻剂
qīngzhēn	Muslim	清真
qīngzhēng de	steamed	清蒸的
qīngzhēnsì	mosque	清真寺
qīngzhǒng	bruise	青肿
qìngzhù	to celebrate	庆祝
qióng	poor	穷
qípán	chessboard	棋盘
qīpiàn	cheat (n)	欺骗
qīqì	lacquerware	漆器
qīshí	seventy	七十
qíshì	discrimination	歧视
qìshuǐ	fizzy drink	汽水
qiú	ball	球
qiúchǎng	court (tennis)	球场
qiūtiān	autumn (fall)	秋天
qìyóu	petrol	汽油
qízhōng	among	其中

qīzi	wife	妻子
qǐzi	screwdriver	起子
qǔ	withdraw (from bank)	取
qù	to go	去
quán	fountain	泉
quèdìng	certain	确定
quèrèn	to confirm (a booking)	确认
qùnián	last year	去年
qǔnuǎnqì	heater	取暖器
qúnzi	skirt	裙子
qǔxiāo	cancel	取消

R

rè	hot	热
rén	person/people	人
rénquán	human rights	人权
rènshi	know (person)	认识
rènshi dào	to realise	认识到
rénxíng xiǎodào	footpath	人行小道
rénzhǒng	race (breed)	人种
rèshuǐ	hot water	热水
rìchū	sunrise	日出
rìchángde	daily	日常的
rìjì	diary	日记
rìlì	calendar	日历
rìluò	sunset	日落
rìqī	date (time)	日期
róngyì	easy	容易
ròu	meat	肉
ruǎn	soft	软
ruǎnwò	soft sleeper	软卧
ruǎnzuò	soft seat	软座
rùchǎng	admission	入场
rǔfáng	breast	乳房
rúguǒ	if	如果
rùkǒu	entrance	入口
ruò	weak	弱
rǔzhào	bra	乳罩

S

sǎhuǎng	to lie	撒谎
sàichē	racing bike	赛车
sàichéng	leg (in race)	赛程
sāizi	plug (bath)	塞子
sān	three	三
sànbù	stroll/walk	散步
sǎngzi	throat	嗓子
sānmíngzhì	sandwich	三明治
sànrèqì	radiator	散热器
sānshí	thirty	三十
sāorǎo	harrassment	骚扰
sēnlín	forest	森林
shā	kill	杀
shàishāng	sunburn	晒伤
shāmò	desert	沙漠
shān	mountain	山
shānbēng	landslide	山崩
shǎndiàn	lightning	闪电
shāndòng	cave	山洞
shàng	above; to board; up	上
shàng chuán	aboard	上船
shàng ge xīngqī	last week	上个星期
shàng ge yuè	last month	上个月
shàngdì	God	上帝
shāngdiàn	shop/store	商店
shāngkǒu	wound	伤口
shāngren	businessperson	商人
shāngǔ	valley	山谷
shǎnguāngdēng	flash (camera)	闪光灯
shāngyè	business	商业
shāngyèqū	shopping area	商业区
shānhú	coral	珊瑚
shānmài	mountain range	山脉
shānyáng	goat	山羊
shānzhōng xiǎo lù	mountain path	山中小路
shānzhōng xiǎo wū	mountain hut	山中小屋

shànzi	fan (handheld)	扇子
shǎo	few	少
shāoshāng	burn (n)	烧伤
shǎo yīdiǎnr	less	少一点儿
sháozi	spoon	勺子
shé	snake	蛇
shèbèi	equipment	设备
shèhuìzhǔyì	socialism	社会主义
shéi	who	谁
shēn	deep	深
shèn	kidney	肾
shēnfèn	identification	身份
shēnfènzhèng	identification card	身份证
shēng	litre	升
shěng	province	省
shēngbìng	sick	生病
shēngchǎn	to produce	生产
shēngchǎn zhě	producer	生产者
shèngdànjié	Christmas	圣诞节
shēngde	raw	生的
shēnghuó	to live; life	生活
shēnghuó shuǐpíng	standard of living	生活水平
shèngjīng	the Bible	圣经
shēngqì	angry	生气
shēngrì	birthday; date of birth	生日
shèngyú	rest (what's left)	剩余
shéngzi	rope/string	绳子
shénjīngbìng	crazy	神经病
shénme	what	什么
shénme shíhòu	when	什么时候
shēntǐ	body	身体
shēnxīn jiànkāng	welfare	身心健康
shénzhì huǎnghū	stoned	神志恍惚
shénzhì hūnmí	delirious	神志昏迷
shèxiàngjī	video camera	摄像机
shèyǐng	photography	摄影
shèyuǎn jìngtóu	telephoto lens	摄远镜头
shì	to try	试
shíbā	eighteen	十八
shìchǎng	market	市场

shíèr	twelve	十二
shìgù	accident	事故
shìjì	century	世纪
shíjì	practical	实际
shíjiǔ	nineteen	十九
shíjiān	time	时间
shìjiàn	event	事件
shìjiè	world	世界
shíkèbiǎo	timetable	时刻表
shíliù	sixteen	十六
shímáo	trendy (person)	时髦
shíqī	period (of time)	时期
shíqī	seventeen	十七
shǐqián yìshù	prehistoric art	史前艺术
shísān	thirteen	十三
shíshì	current affairs	时事
shítóu	stone	石头
shìwēi	demonstration	示威
shíwù	food	食物
shíwùzhōngdú	food poisoning	食物中毒
shíyī	eleven	十一
shíyóu	oil (crude)	石油
shìzhèn	town	市镇
shì zhōngxīn	city centre	市中心
shízìjià	cross (religious)	十字架
shízìlùkǒu	crossroads	十字路
shōu	accept	收
shǒu	hand	手
shòu	thin (slim)	瘦
shòu bǎohù wùzhǒng	protected species	受保护物种
shǒubiǎo	wristwatch	手表
shōudào	to receive	收到
shǒudiàntǒng	torch (flashlight)	手电筒
shǒudū	capital	首都
shōufèi gōnglù	tollway	收费公路
shǒugōngzhìde	handmade	手工制的
shōujù	receipt	收据
shǒumén yuán	goalkeeper	守门员
shǒupà	handkerchief	手帕
shòupiàochù	ticket office	售票处
shòupiàoyuán	conductor	售票员

shòushāng le	injured	受伤了
shǒushù	operation	手术
shǒutào	glove	手套
shǒutíbāo	handbag	手提包
shǒuwàn	wrist	手腕
shǒuyì	crafts	手艺
shōuyīnjī	radio	收音机
shǒuzhǐ	finger	手指
shǒuzhuó	bracelet	手镯
shū	book	书
shù	tree	树
shuāidǎo	to fall	摔倒
shuāng	double	双
shuāngbāotāi	twins	双胞胎
shuāngrén chuáng	double bed	双人床
shuāngrén fáng	double room	双人房
shuǎngshēnfěn	talcum powder	爽身粉
shuāzi	brush (n)	刷子
shūcài	vegetable	蔬菜
shūcài shuǐguǒ diàn	greengrocer	蔬菜水果店
shūdiàn	bookshop	书店
shūfǎ	calligraphy	书法
shūfu	comfortable	舒服
shuí	who	谁
shuǐ	water	水
shuì	duty (customs); tax	税
shuǐguǒ	fruit	水果
shuìjiào	to sleep	睡觉
shuǐlóngtóu	tap (faucet)	水龙头
shuǐpào	blister	水泡
shuǐpíng	water bottle (drinking)	水瓶
shuǐshǒu	sailor	水手
shuǐtǒng	bucket	水桶
shuǐzāi	flood	水灾
shuǐzhì	leech	水蛭
shùliàng	quantity	数量
shùméi	raspberry	树莓
shùnshì liáofǎ	homeopathy	顺势疗法
shuō	to say/speak	说
shuōhuǎngzhě	liar	说谎者
shuōhuà	talk	说话

shūshu	uncle	叔叔
shūxuè	blood transfusion	输血
shūzi	comb	梳子
shùzì	count (n)	数字
sǐ	dead; to die	死
sì	four	四
sīchóu	silk	丝绸
sīchóuchǎng	silk factory	丝绸厂
sìfēnzhīyī	quarter	四分之一
sījī	driver	司机
sīrén	private	私人
sīréndé	personal	私人的
sìshí	forty	四十
sīyíng huà	privatisation	私营化
sòng	deliver	送
suàn	garlic	蒜
suànmìng xiānshēng	fortune teller	算命先
suānnǎi	yogurt	酸奶
suànpán	abacus	算盘
sùdù	speed	速度
suìshí	hash	碎食
sùliào	plastic	塑料
sūnzi	grandchild	孙子
suǒ	lock	锁
suǒshàng	to lock	锁上
sùshè	dormitory	宿舍

T

tā	he	他
tā	she	她
tǎ	tower	塔
tāde	her	她的
tāde	his	他的
tài	too	太
táijiē	step	台阶
tàikōng	space (outer)	太空
tàitai	Mrs	太太
tàiyáng	sun	太阳
tāng	soup	汤
táng	sugar	糖

tāngchí	teaspoon	汤匙
tángniàobìng	diabetes	糖尿病
tàngshāng	scald	烫伤
tánhuáng	spring (coil)	弹簧
tán péngyǒu	to go out with	谈朋友
tánxìngbēngdài	elastic bandage	弹性绷带
tǎnzi	blanket	毯子
tánzòu	to play (music)	弹奏
tàofáng	suite	套房
táoqì	pottery	陶器
táozi	peach	桃子
tèbié	special	特别
tèkuài	express (train)	特快
téng	ache/hurt	疼
téngtòng	pain	疼痛
tī	to kick	踢
tí	carry	提
tiān	day	天
tián	sweet	甜
tiándì	field	田地
tiánjìng	track (sports)	田径
tiānkōng	sky	天空
tiánpǐn	dessert	甜品
tiānqi (yùbào)	weather (forecast)	天气(预报)
tiánxiě	to fill in (form)	填写
tiānzhǔjiào	Catholic	天主教
tiào	to jump	跳
tiàowǔ	to dance	跳舞
tiāoxuǎn	to choose	挑选
tiàozǎo	flea	跳蚤
tiáozhì jiětiáoqì	modem	调制解调器
tìdāo (piàn)	razor (blades)	剃刀(片)
tǐcāo	gymnastics	体操
tīng	listen	听
tíng	to stop	停
tíngchē	to park	停车
tīngjiàn	hear	听见
tíngliú	to stay (remain)	停留
tíngzi	pavillion	亭子
tíqǐ	to lift	提起

ǐyù chǎng	stadium	体育场
ǐyù yùndòng	sport	体育运动
óng	copper	铜
óngbàn	companion	同伴
ōngguò	across	通过
ōnghuò péngzhàng	inflation	通货膨胀
ǒngjì	statistics	统计
óngxìngliàn	homosexual	同性恋
ōngxùnbù	address book	通讯簿
óng zhù sùshè	to share a dorm	同住宿舍
óngyì	agree	同意
óngzhì	comrade	同志
ōu	steal	偷
óu	head	头
óuděng	first class	头等
óufa	hair	头发
óukuī	helmet	头盔
óupiào	vote	投票
óuténg	headache	头疼
óuyūn	dizzy	头晕
óuzi	dice/die	骰子
óuzī	investment	投资
uī	to push	推
uǐ	leg	腿
uījiàn xìn	reference	推荐信
uījiàn	recommend	推荐
uántǐ	group	团体
úbù lǚxíng	hike/hiking	徒步旅行
úbù lǚxíng lùxiàn	hiking routes	徒步旅行路线
úbù lǚxíng xuē	hiking boots	徒步旅行靴
ǔdì	earth/land	土地
údīng	drawing pin	图钉
ǔdòu	potato	土豆
uìchū	to quit	退出
uìkuǎn	refund (n/v)	退款
uìxiū	retired	退休
uìzhí	resignation	退职
uōjiù	dislocate	脱臼
uōxié	slipper	拖鞋
uōzhīmián	cotton wool	脱脂棉

| túshūguǎn | library | 图书馆 |
| tùzi | rabbit | 兔子 |

W

wǎn	bowl (n)	碗
wǎn	late	晚
wāndòu	pea	豌豆
wǎnfàn	dinner	晚饭
wàngjì	forget	忘记
wǎngqiú	tennis	网球
wǎngqiú chǎng	tennis court	网球场
wǎngqiú pāi	tennis racquet	网球拍
wǎngyǎn zhīwù	lace	网眼织物
wánjù	toy	玩具
wánměi	perfect	完美
wánr	to play (a game)	玩儿
wǎnshàng	evening	晚上
wáwa	doll	娃娃
wàzi	sock	袜子
wèi	stomach	胃
wèihūnfū	fiancé	未婚夫
wèihūnqī	fiancée	未婚妻
wéijīn	scarf	围巾
wèijīng	monosodium glutimate (MSG)	味精
wèishēngjīn	sanitary napkins	卫生巾
wéishēngsù	vitamins	维生素
wèishēngzhǐ	toilet paper	卫生纸
wèishénme	why	为什么
wēixiǎn	dangerous	危险
wěn	kiss	吻
wèn	ask	问
wēndù	temperature	温度
wénjù	stationery	文具
wèntí	problem/question	问题
wènxùnchù	information office	问讯处
wǒ	I/me	我
wòchē	sleeping car	卧车
wǒde	my	我的
wǒmén	we	我们
wǔ	five	五

ù	fog	雾
ūdǐng	roof	屋顶
újiākěguī	homeless	无家可归
úqiān	unleaded	无铅
ūrǎn	pollution	污染
ǔshí	fifty	五十
ǔyè	midnight	午夜
úyī	none	无一

X

guāngpiàn	x-ray	X光片
ī	west	西
ǐ	wash	洗
iā	shrimp	虾
ià	next	下
ǎng	miss (long for)	想
ǎngfǎ	reflection (thinking)	想法
ǎngjiā	homesick	想家
ǎngshòu	to enjoy (oneself)	享受
ǎo	small	小
ǎo chuáng	cot	小床
ǎo dìtǎn	rug	小地毯
ǎo gǒu	puppy	小狗
ǎochī	snack	小吃
ǎodāo	penknife	小刀
ǎodào	track (path)	小道
ǎofèi	tip (gratuity)	小费
ǎojiě	Miss	小姐
ǎolù	path	小路
ǎoshān	hill	小山
ǎoshí	hour	小时
ǎoshuō	fiction	小说
ǎoshuō	novel	小说
ǎoshuōjiā	novelist	小说家
à ge xīngqī	next week	下个星期
à ge yuè	next month	下个月
àn	thread	线
àndài	modern	现代
àng	towards	向
āngbīn	champagne	香槟

xiāngcháng	sausage	香肠
xiāngjiāo	banana	香蕉
xiàngliàn	necklace	像链
xiàngqí	chess	象棋
xiāngxìn	to trust	相信
xiàngyá	ivory	象牙
xiāngyān	cigarettes	香烟
xiāngyān diàn	tobacco kiosk	香烟店
xiāngyóu	oil (cooking)	香油
xiāngzi	suitcase	箱子
xiànjīn	cash (n)	现金
xiānshēng	Mr	先生
xiànsù	speed limit	限速
xiànzài	now	现在
xiào	smile; to laugh	笑
xiàochuǎn	asthma	哮喘
xiāodújì	disinfectant	消毒剂
xiāohuàbùliáng	indigestion	消化不良
xiāoshòu bù	sales department	销售部
xiāoshòu rèn	distributor	销售人
xiàtiān	summer	夏天
xiàwǔ	afternoon	下午
xiàxuě	to snow	下雪
xiàyǔ	to rain	下雨
xié	shoe	鞋
xiě	write	写
xiédài	shoelace	鞋带
xièxie	thanks	谢谢
xiéyóu	shoe polish	鞋油
xǐfàjì	shampoo	洗发剂
xīfú	suit	西服
xīgài	knee	膝盖
xīguā	watermelon	西瓜
xīhóngshì	tomato	西红柿
xīhuà	westernised	西化
xǐhuān	to like	喜欢
xǐjù	comedy	喜剧
xìjù	opera/play	戏剧
xǐlǐ	baptism	洗礼
xīliú	stream	溪流
xìn	letter	信

xīn	new	新
xìnfēng	envelope	信封
xìng	apricot	杏
xìng	sex	性
xìng	surname	姓
xìngbié piānjiàn	sexism	性别偏见
xìngbìng	venereal disease	性病
xìngcún	to survive	幸存
xínghuì	to bribe	行贿
xínglǐ	luggage	行李
xínglǐ jìcúnchù	left-luggage office	行李寄存处
xìngmíng	name	姓名
xīngqī	week	星期
xīngqiú	planet	星球
xíngrén	pedestrian	行人
xīngxīng	star	星星
xìngyùn	lucky	幸运
xíngzhuàng	shape	形状
xīnjì	palpitation	心悸
xīnlǐxué	psychology	心理学
xìnrèn	trust	信任
xīnwén	news	新闻
xīnxiān	fresh	新鲜
xīnzàng	heart	心脏
xìnxiāng	mailbox	信箱
xìnyòngkǎ	credit card	信用卡
xìnzhǐ	writing paper	信纸
xiōngdì	brother	兄弟
xiōngzhēn	brooch	胸针
xīshì	western style	西式
xìtǒng	system	系统
xiū	to repair	修
xiūlǐ	mend	修理
xiùzi	sleeve	袖子
xīwàng	to hope	希望
xǐyīdiàn	laundry (place)	洗衣店
xǐyīfěn	washing powder	洗衣粉
xuǎnjǔ	election	选举
xuányá	cliff/crag	悬崖
xué	learn/study	学

xuè	blood	血
xuélì	qualifications	学历
xuésheng	student	学生
xuéxiào	school	学校
xuèxíng	blood group	血型
xuèyā	blood pressure	血压
xuēzi	boots	靴子
xǔkězhèng	permit	许可证
xúnzhǎo	to look for	寻找
xūyào	to need	需要

Y

yā	duck	鸭
yá	tooth	牙
yáchǐ	teeth	牙齿
yágāo	toothpaste	牙膏
yājīn	deposit	押金
yālì	pressure	压力
yán	salt	盐
yāncǎo	tobacco	烟草
yáncháng xiànlù	extension cord	延长线路
yǎnchū	performance	演出
yāndǒu	pipe	烟斗
yáng	sheep	羊
yǎng	itch	痒
yángcōng	onion	洋葱
yǎngqì	oxygen	氧气
yángròu	lamb (meat)	羊肉
yángròu	mutton	羊肉
yángtái	balcony	阳台
yánhuǎn	delay	延缓
yānhuīgāng	ashtray	烟灰缸
yànhuì	banquet	宴会
yǎnjīng	eye	眼睛
yǎnjìng	glasses (spectacles)	眼镜
yánsè	colour	颜色
yánsù	serious	严肃
yántǎohuì	workshop	研讨会
yànxuè	blood test	验血

yǎnyàoshuǐ	eye drops	眼药水
yǎnyuán	actor	演员
yánzhòng	serious (injury)	严重
yāo	waist	腰
yǎo	bite (n, dog)	咬
yào	medicine	药
yào	to want	要
yàodiàn	chemist (pharmacy)	药店
yàofāng	prescription	药方
yáogǔn yuèduì	rock group	摇滚乐队
yàogāo	ointment	药膏
yāoqǐng	invite	邀请
yàoshi	key	钥匙
yāpiàn	opium	鸦片
yáqiān	toothpick	牙签
yáshuā	toothbrush	牙刷
yáyī	dentist	牙医
yě	also	也
yè	night	夜
yè	page	页
yě bù	neither	也不
yěshēngdòngwù	wildlife	野生动物
yěxǔ	maybe	也许
yěyíng	camp	野营
yèyú àihàozhě	amateur	业余爱好者
yēzi	coconut	椰子
yīcì	once	一次
yìdiǎnr	little (adj); a little bit	一点儿
yídìng	sure	一定
yídòng diànhuà	mobile phone	移动电话
yīfu	clothing	衣服
yī fù pái	deck (of cards)	一副牌
yīge	one	一个
yīguì	wardrobe	衣柜
yǐhòu	after(wards)	以后
yǐhūn	married	已婚
yìhūxúncháng	unusual	异乎寻常
yījià	coat hanger	衣架
yìjiàn	opinion	意见
yǐjīng	already	已经

yímín	immigration	移民
yín	silver	银
yǐn	addiction	瘾
yìndù jiào	Hindu	印度教
yíng	win	赢
yìng	hard (not soft)	硬
yìngbì	coins	硬币
yīng ér	baby	婴儿
yīng ér shípǐn	baby food	婴儿食品
yīngguó	England	英国
yīngjùn	handsome	英俊
yīngyǔ	English	英语
yìngwò	hard sleeper	硬卧
yìngzuò	hard seat	硬座
yínháng	bank	银行
yīnliáng	shade/shadow	荫凉
yǐnliào	drink (n)	饮料
yīnwèi	because	因为
yǐnxíng yǎnjìng	contact lens	隐型眼镜
yīnyuè	music	音乐
yīnyuèhuì	concert	音乐会
yìnzhāng	chop (for name)	印章
yīqǐ	together	一起
yǐqián	before	以前
yīshēng	doctor	医生
yīshuāng	pair	一双
yìshùjiā	artist	艺术家
yīwúsuǒyǒu	nothing	一无所有
yīxiē	some; a little (amount)	一些
yīyàng	same	一样
yīyuàn	hospital	医院
yìzhí	straight ahead	一直
yǐzi	chair	椅子
yòng	use	用
yóu	oil	油
yǒu	have	有
yòubiān	right (side)	右边
yòuéryuán	kindergarten	幼儿园
yóufèi	postage	邮费
yǒuhǎo	friendly	友好

yóujú	post office	邮局
yóukè wènxùn chù	tourist information office	游客问讯处
yǒu kòng	free (time)	有空
yóulǎn	sightseeing	游览
yǒulì	strong	有力
yǒumíng	famous	有名
yóunì	rich (food)	油腻
yóupiào	postage stamp	邮票
yǒuqián	wealthy	有钱
yǒuqù	interesting	有趣
yǒurén	somebody	有人
yōushì	advantage	优势
yǒushí	sometimes	有时
yóutài rén	Jewish	犹太人
yóuwūde	greasy	油污的
yóuxì	game	游戏
yōuxiù de	excellent	优秀的
yòuyì	right-wing	右翼
yǒuyìshāngdiàn	Friendship Store	友谊商店
yóuyǒng	to swim	游泳
yóuyǒngchí	swimming pool	游泳池
yóuyǒngyī	bathing suit	游泳衣
yǒuyòng	useful	有用
yóuyú	squid	鱿鱼
yóuzhèng biānmǎ	postcode	邮政编码
yú	fish	鱼
yǔ	with	与
yù	jade	玉
yuán	dollar	元
yuǎn	far	远
yuǎnzú	trek	远足
yuán de	round	圆的
yuándàn	New Year's Day	元旦
yuándàn chúxī	New Year's Eve	元旦除夕
yuánhuán	roundabout	圆环
yuánliàng	forgive	原谅
yuánxiān	original	原先
yuányīn	reason	原因
yuánzhūbǐ	ballpoint	圆珠笔
yúdiàn	fish shop	鱼店

yùdìng	reservation; to reserve	预定
yuè	month	月
yuèduì	band (musical)	乐队
yuēhuì	date (appointment)	约会
yuèjīng	menstruation	月经
yuèjīng tòng	period pain	月经痛
yuèliang	moon	月亮
yuèmǔ	mother-in-law	岳母
yuèqì	musical instrument	乐器
yuèwèi	offside	越位
yuèyě xiǎodào	cross-country trail	越野小道
yùgāng	bath	浴缸
yún	cloud	云
yùnchuán	seasick	晕船
yùndòngyuán	player (sports)	运动员
yùnhé	canal	运河
yùnqì	luck	运气
yǔnxǔ	permission; to allow	允许
yǔsǎn	umbrella	雨伞
yùshì	bathroom	浴室
yǔyán	language	语言
yǔyī	raincoat	雨衣
yǔzhòu	universe	宇宙

Z

zài	again	再
zài	at	在
zài ... de shíhòu	during ...	在 ... 的时候
zài hòumiàn	behind	在后面
zài lǐmiàn	within	在里面
zài pángbiān	beside	在旁边
zài qiánmiàn	in front of	在前面
zài shàngmiàn	on/over	在上面
zài wàimiàn	outside	在外面
zài xiàmiàn	below	在下面
zài zhōngjiān	between	在中间
zāng	dirty	脏
zànglǐ	funeral	葬礼
zànshǎng	admire	赞赏

zǎo	early	早饭
zǎofàn	breakfast	早饭
zǎoshàng	morning	早上
zázhì	magazine	杂志
zéi	thief	贼
zēngjiā	increase	增加
zèngsòng	presentation	赠送
zěnme	how	怎么
zérèn	responsibility	责任
zhàdàn	bomb	炸弹
zhāi shuǐguǒ	fruit picking	摘水果
zhàn	station	站
zhàngdān	bill	帐单
zhàngfu	husband	丈夫
zhānglàng	cockroach	蟑螂
zhàngpeng	tent	帐篷
zhàngpengzhuāng	tent pegs	帐篷桩
zhǎnlǎn	exhibition	展览
zhǎnshì	to show	展示
zhàntái	platform (station)	站台
zhànzhēng	war	战争
zhǎo	to find	找
zhàogu	to look after	照顾
zhàopiàn	photo	照片
zhàoxiàng	to take photographs	照相
zhàoxiàngjī	camera	照相机
zhǎozé	swamp	沼泽
zhèige	this	这个
zhèi ge xīngqī	this week	这个星期
zhèi ge yuè	this month	这个月
zhékòu	discount	折扣
zhēn de	real/really/genuine	真的
zhèngcháng	normal	正常
zhèngfǔ	government	政府
zhèngquè	to be right	正确
zhèngshū	certificate	证书
zhèngzài yíngyè	open (sign)	正在营业
zhèngzhì	politics	政治
zhēnjiǔ	acupuncture	针灸
zhēnzhū	pearl	珍珠
zhěngyè	overnight	整夜

zhěntào	pillowcase	枕套
zhěntóu	pillow	枕头
zhěnzi	rash	疹子
zhèr	here	这儿
zhī	juice	汁
zhǐ	only	只
zhǐ	paper	纸
zhǐ	to point	指
zhīdào	know (something)	知道
zhídé	worthwhile	值得
zhígōng	employee	职工
zhǐjiǎ	nail (finger)	指甲
zhǐjiǎdāo	nail clippers	指甲刀
zhìliàng	quality	质量
zhǐnánzhēn	compass	指南针
zhīniàobù	diaper (nappy)	尿布
zhīpiào	cheque	支票
zhītiáo	branch	枝条
zhǐtòng yào	painkillers	止痛药
zhíwù	plant	植物
zhíwùxué	botany	植物学
zhíwùyuán	botanical gardens	植物园
zhíyè	occupation/profession	职业
zhíyuán	office worker	职员
zhìzào	made (of)	制造
zhīzhū	spider	蜘蛛
zhìzuò	to make	制做
zhōng	clock	钟
zhǒng	kind (type)	种
zhòng	heavy	重
zhōngfàn	lunch	中饭
zhōngjiān	middle	中间
zhǒngkuài	lump (swelling)	肿块
zhǒngle	swollen	肿了
zhòngliàng	weight	重量
zhōngwǔ	midday	中午
zhōngxīn	centre	中心
zhōngxué	high school	中学
zhòngyào	important	重要
zhòngzhí	to plant	种植

zhǒngzúpiānjiàn	racism	种族偏见
zhǒu	elbow	肘
zhōumò	weekend	周末
zhū	pig	猪
zhù	to live/stay (somewhere)	住
zhuàn	earn	赚
zhuāngyùn	to ship	装运
zhuānjiā	specialist	专家
zhuānyè de	professional	专业的
zhuǎnzhàng	transfer (bank)	转帐
zhūbǎo	jewellery	珠宝
zhǔ guǎngchǎng	main square	主广场
zhǔnbèi	prepare	准备
zhǔnshí	on time	准时
zhuōzi	table	桌子
zhūròu	pork	猪肉
zhùshè	injection	注射
zhùshèqì	syringe	注射器
zhùshè zhēntóu	needle (syringe)	注射针头
zhùsù	accommodation	住宿
zhùtīngqì	hearing aid	助听器
zhǔyào	main	主要
zhǔyì	idea	主意
zhúzi	bamboo	竹子
zīběnzhǔyì	capitalism	资本主义
zìdiǎn	dictionary	字典
zìdòng	automatic	自动
zìdòng qǔkuǎn jī	automatic teller machine (ATM)	自动取款机
zìmù	subtitles	字幕
zìrán de	natural	自然的
zìrán liáofǎ yīshī	naturopath	自然疗法医师
zìránjiè	nature	自然界
zǐ sè	purple	紫色
zìsī	selfish	自私
zìwǒ fúwù	self-service	自我服务
zìxíngchē	bicycle	自行车
zìyóu shìchǎng	free market	自由市场
zōngjiào	religion	宗教
zǒnglǐ	prime minister	总理

zǒngshì	always	总是
zǒngtǐ	in general	总体
zǒngtǒng	president	总统
zǒu	leave	走
zǒulù	walk	走路
zū	to rent/hire	租
zǔfù	grandfather	祖父
zuǐ	mouth	嘴
zuì	drunk	醉
zuì hǎo	best	最好
zuìhòu	last (final)	最后
zuìjìn	recent(ly)	最近
zújì	track (footprints)	足迹
zǔmǔ	grandmother	祖母
zūnjìng	respect	尊敬
zuǐchún	lip	嘴唇
zúgòu	enough	足够
zuò	sit	坐
zuò	to do	做
zuǒbiān	left (direction)	左边
zuò chē	to take (the train)	坐车
zuòfàn	to cook	做饭
zuòjiā	writer	作家
zuótiān	yesterday	昨天
zuótiān wǎnshàng	last night	昨天晚上
zuótiān xiàwǔ	yesterday afternoon	昨天下午
zuótiān zǎoshang	yesterday morning	昨天早上
zǔzhī	organise/organisation	组织

MANDARIN FINDER

COMPLETE LIST OF LONELY PLANET BOOKS

AFRICA Africa – the South • Africa on a shoestring • Arabic (Egyptian) phrasebook • Arabic (Moroccan) phrasebook • Cairo • Cape Town • Central Africa • East Africa • Egypt • Egypt travel atlas • Ethiopian (Amharic) phrasebook • The Gambia & Senegal • Kenya • Kenya travel atlas • Malawi, Mozambique & Zambia • Morocco • North Africa • South Africa, Lesotho & Swaziland • South Africa, Lesotho & Swaziland travel atlas • Swahili phrasebook • Trekking in East Africa • Tunisia • West Africa • Zimbabwe, Botswana & Namibia • Zimbabwe, Botswana & Namibia travel atlas
Travel Literature: The Rainbird: A Central African Journey • Songs to an African Sunset: A Zimbabwean Story • Mali Blues: Traveling to an African Beat

AUSTRALIA & THE PACIFIC Australia • Australian phrasebook • Bushwalking in Australia • Bushwalking in Papua New Guinea • Fiji • Fijian phrasebook • Islands of Australia's Great Barrier Reef • Melbourne • Micronesia • New Caledonia • New South Wales & the ACT • New Zealand • Northern Territory • Outback Australia • Papua New Guinea • Pidgin phrasebook • Queensland • Rarotonga & the Cook Islands • Samoa • Solomon Islands • South Australia • South Pacific phrasebook • Sydney • Tahiti & French Polynesia • Tasmania • Tonga • Tramping in New Zealand • Vanuatu • Victoria • Western Australia
Travel Literature: Islands in the Clouds • Sean & David's Long Drive

CENTRAL AMERICA & THE CARIBBEAN Bahamas and Turks & Caicos • Barcelona • Bermuda • Central America on a shoestring • Costa Rica • Cuba • Dominican Republic & Haiti • Eastern Caribbean • Guatemala, Belize & Yucatán: La Ruta Maya • Jamaica • Mexico • Mexico City • Panama
Travel Literature: Green Dreams: Travels in Central America

EUROPE Amsterdam • Andalucía • Austria • Baltic States phrasebook • Berlin • Britain • British phrasebook • Central Europe • Central Europe phrasebook • Croatia • Czech & Slovak Republics • Denmark • Dublin • Eastern Europe • Eastern Europe phrasebook • Edinburgh • Estonia, Latvia & Lithuania • Europe • Finland • France • French phrasebook • Germany • German phrasebook • Greece • Greek phrasebook • Hungary • Iceland, Greenland & the Faroe Islands • Ireland • Italian phrasebook • Italy • Lisbon • London • Mediterranean Europe • Mediterranean Europe phrasebook • Paris • Poland • Portugal • Portugal travel atlas • Prague • Provence & the Côte D'Azur • Romania & Moldova • Russia, Ukraine & Belarus • Russian phrasebook • Scandinavian & Baltic Europe • Scandinavian Europe phrasebook • Scotland • Slovenia • Spain • Spanish phrasebook • St Petersburg • Switzerland • Trekking in Spain • Ukrainian phrasebook • Vienna • Walking in Britain • Walking in Italy • Walking in Ireland • Walking in Switzerland • Western Europe • Western Europe phrasebook
Travel Literature: The Olive Grove: Travels in Greece

INDIAN SUBCONTINENT Bangladesh • Bengali phrasebook • Bhutan • Delhi • Goa • Hindi/Urdu phrasebook • India • India & Bangladesh travel atlas • Indian Himalaya • Karakoram Highway • Nepal • Nepali phrasebook • Pakistan • Rajasthan • South India • Sri Lanka • Sri Lanka phrasebook • Trekking in the Indian Himalaya • Trekking in the Karakoram & Hindukush • Trekking in the Nepal Himalaya